THE COMPANION GUIDE TO
Venice

THE COMPANION GUIDES

GENERAL EDITOR: VINCENT CRONIN

*It is the aim of these guides to provide a Companion
in the person of the author, who knows intimately
the places and people of whom he writes, and is able to
communicate this knowledge and affection to his readers.
It is hoped that the text and pictures will aid them
in their preparations and in their travels, and will
help them remember on their return.*

LONDON · THE SHAKESPEARE COUNTRY · OUTER LONDON · EAST ANGLIA
NORTHUMBRIA · THE WEST HIGHLANDS OF SCOTLAND
THE SOUTH OF FRANCE · THE ILE DE FRANCE · NORMANDY · THE LOIRE
SOUTH WEST FRANCE
FLORENCE · VENICE · ROME
MAINLAND GREECE · THE GREEK ISLANDS · YUGOSLAVIA · TURKEY
NEW YORK

In Preparation
OXFORD AND CAMBRIDGE · PARIS

THE COMPANION GUIDE TO

Venice

HUGH HONOUR

A SPECTRUM BOOK

PRENTICE-HALL, INC..
Englewood Cliffs, N.J. 07632

COLLINS
St. James's Place, London

Library of Congress Cataloging in Publication Data
Honour, Hugh.
  The companion guide to Venice.

  Rev. ed. of: Fodor's Venice. 1971.
  "A Spectrum Book."
  Bibliography: p.
  Includes index.
  1. Venice (Italy)—Description—1981-
  —Guide-books. I. Title.
DG672.H6 1983   914.5'3104928   82-20511
ISBN 0-13-154666-X
ISBN 0-13-154658-9 (pbk.)

ISBN 0-13-154666-X

ISBN 0-13-154658-9 {PBK.}

First published in 1965
Second edition 1977
© Hugh Honour 1965
ISBN 0 00 216802 2
Maps by K. C. Jordan
Made and printed in Great Britain by
William Collins Sons & Co. Ltd, Glasgow

U.S. Edition © 1983 by Prentice-Hall, Inc.,
Englewood Cliffs, N.J. 07632

A SPECTRUM BOOK

Printed in the United States of America

10 9 8 7 6 5 4 3 2 1

Prentice-Hall International, Inc., *London*
Prentice-Hall of Australia Pty. Limited, *Sydney*
Prentice-Hall of Canada, Inc., *Toronto*
Prentice-Hall of India Private Limited, *New Delhi*
Prentice-Hall of Japan, Inc., *Tokyo*
Prentice-Hall of Southeast Asia Pte. Ltd., *Singapore*
Whitehall books Limited, Wellington, *New Zealand*
Editora Prentice-Hall Do Brasil Ltda., *Rio de Janeiro*

Contents

Introduction   *page* 9
1 In the Piazza   17
2 San Marco: Venice and Byzantium   28
3 The Doges' Palace: the Structure of the Republic   41
4 The Scuole: Titian and Tintoretto   53
5 The Renaissance Dawn: Bellini, Carpaccio and Cima 67
6 The Lombardi and Renaissance Sculpture   81
7 Books, Marbles, Paintings and Costumes   96
8 A Palladian Morning   107
9 The Accademia: Giorgione, Veronese and others   119
10 The Mercerie and Mannerism   131
11 Dorsoduro: Venetian Baroque   143
12 The Settecento: Tiepolo and Guardi   154
13 A House of Gold and a Church of Damask   166
14 Churches and Theatres: Music and Fantasy   177
15 Cannaregio   190
16 Markets and Modern Art   202
17 In a Gondola: the Grand Canal   213
18 A Journey on the Lagoon   225
19 Terra Firma   240
20 Epilogue: The Way to the Station   256

Appendices
I   Places of interest not mentioned in the text   263
II   Hotels   265
III Some restaurants   271
IV   Some books about Venice   272
V   Shops   274
     Index   276

Illustrations

San Marco   (*Edwin Smith*)   *facing page* 32

The south façade of San Marco   (*Edwin Smith*)   33

View of San Giorgio Maggiore from the Piazzetta   48
(*Edwin Smith*)

The Piazzetta   (*J. Allan Cash*)   48

Carving on the Doges' Palace   (*Leonard von Matt*)   49

The marble staircase in the courtyard of the Doges' Palace
(*J. E. Malcolm*)   84

The Great Council Chamber of the Doges' Palace
(*Edwin Smith*)   85

Santa Maria dei Miracoli   (*The Mansell Collection*)   92

San Giorgio Maggiore   (*Leonard von Matt*)   93

A Byzantine relief in the Cathedral at Torcello
(*Edwin Smith*)   112

A Gothic capital in the Doges' Palace   (*Edwin Smith*)   112

A well-head in the Palazzo Centani   (*Edwin Smith*)   112

" The spy " by Francesco Pianta   (*André Ostier*)   112

The Grand Canal and Santa Maria della Salute
(*Edwin Smith*)   113

The Ca' d'Oro   (*Edwin Smith*)   128

Santa Maria dell'Orto   (*Edwin Smith*)   129

Decoration of the gondola   (*Edwin Smith*)   208

A small canal, from the Ponte dell'Angelo   (*Edwin Smith*)   209

Burano   (*Stephen Harrison*)   224

The cathedral of Torcello   (*The Mansell Collection*)   224

Early morning on the Piazzetta   (*Edwin Smith*)   225

The Lagoon   (*Edwin Smith*)   225

Introduction

This book is written for the visitor to Venice rather than the arm-chair traveller. Each chapter from II to XVII is devoted to a building or group of buildings which may conveniently be visited in a single morning or afternoon. Chapters XVIII and XIX describe tours which need an entire day: at the end of them there are suggestions for other excursions on the lagoon and terra firma. I have planned the book as far as possible to provide a history of the Venetian state and an account of Venetian civilisation, linked to the monuments of the city. Thus, chapters I, II, III and IV are concerned mainly with history and Venetian institutions; chapters V to XII follow the development of the visual arts in Venice; the rest deal with various aspects of Venetian arts, and life. (Those who wish to follow the history of Venetian art in a more nearly chronological sequence are advised to take the walk described in chapter IV after that of chapter VII.) But Venice is a higgledy-piggledy place where objects of all periods are jumbled together in the most attractive confusion. One may set out to look at baroque buildings but one is soon distracted by a Gothic palace, a Renaissance painting or a neo-classical statue. I have seldom been able to resist the temptation to mention outstanding works which fall outside the period of my chapters.

All guide-books are bound to be selective—not even the invaluable Lorenzetti is comprehensive—and the present volume is no exception. The works of art mentioned here are but a tiny fraction of those which are worth the attention of visitors. I make no apologies for the personal nature of my selection. Sculpture and architecture are given rather more space than usual in Venetian guide-books. I have emphasised the early Renaissance for to my mind the best paintings, carvings and buildings created in Venice between about 1450 and 1510 have a poetic quality which makes this one of the golden moments in the history of European art.

9

Introduction

I have, however, tried to single out a few of the best works of art produced in every period from the eleventh to the present century.

In the descriptions of **churches** I have used the words left and right to refer to the left and right of someone looking towards the high altar, and the points of the compass in their liturgical sense, based on the assumption (usually wrong) that the high altar is at the East end. Churches usually open fairly early in the morning and are closed at midday; only the largest are open again from about three o'clock until six or seven. San Marco, however, remains open all day. The opening times for museums printed in the text are those in force in high summer. In the winter, museums close much earlier but usually remain open through the midday siesta. As opening times vary considerably according to the season it is worth obtaining a current list of times from the office of the Enti Provinciale per il Turismo in the Piazza San Marco (71c).

Explanations of Venetian words (*campo, calle,* etc.) and the dates of artists will be found in the index.

Each walk described in the book is designed to begin and end either in the Piazza San Marco or at a motor-boat station. There are three motor-boat routes. The *Canal Grande Accelerato* goes from the Piazzale Roma to the railway station, down the Grand Canal, along the Riva to the Giardini Pubblici and finally to the Lido (and vice versa) stopping at every landing stage on the way. The faster *Canal Grande Diretto* boats go from the Rialto to the railway station, Piazzale Roma, round by the back route to San Samuele, the Accademia, San Marco, the Giardini Pubblici and the Lido. The *Circolare* goes from San Marco to the Monumento on the Riva degli Schiavoni, San Giorgio Maggiore, Le Zittelle, Il Redentore and S. Eufemia on the Giudecca, the Gesuati and S. Biagio on the Zattere, Sacca Fissola, Piazzale Roma, the railway station, Fondamenta Nuove, San Michele, Murano and then back again. Fares are modest—probably cheaper than for the corresponding distance by London bus. During most of the day the boats leave their termini at fifteen-minute intervals—at busy times they are rather more frequent and at night very much less frequent. There are also *vaporetti* which ply between the Riva degli Schiavoni and the Lido, the Riva degli Schiavoni and Chioggia and the Fondamenta Nuove and Murano, Burano and Torcello (see back endpaper).

Introduction

I have often been asked when is the best **time of year** to visit
Venice. September is, or was, the fashionable month when the
international smart set foregather in their palaces on the Grand
Canal and when the film festival is held on the Lido. But I prefer
early spring and late autumn. Summer has obvious advantages too
—fine weather, long days which make it possible to visit churches
and museums in the late afternoon, bathing on the Lido, excursions
on the lagoon and such tourist attractions as concerts, operas and
regattas. The only serious drawback to a visit between early June
and late September is the crowd of other visitors who fill the place
to capacity. You avoid crowds entirely in the winter and early
spring. Venice then appears at her most beautiful especially when
the clear sunshine gives a more than usually brittle and crustacean
appearance to her towers and pinnacles, or when the sun begins
to penetrate an early morning mist and everything appears as
through the pink gauze curtain of a transformation scene in an
old-fashioned pantomime. Prolonged spells of bad weather in
early spring are no more frequent than the bouts of hot sticky
overcast weather in summer when the scirocco blows up from the
south. All the hotels and *pensioni* are well heated in winter and they
welcome visitors with greater eagerness than in the summer—indeed,
sometimes they are prepared to make reductions in their terms for
a stay of a fortnight or more. But, of course, the days are short,
sight-seeing in churches is out of the question after noon, and
apart from the operas at the Fenice, from early January until
March, there is little in the way of entertainment. Venice can
also be very cold: I have seen canals frozen across and when
I visited Torcello one January day the motor-boat had to plough
through thin ice. If I were to be limited to a single annual visit to
Venice, I should choose to make it in October, November, April
or early May, thus avoiding the summer crowds and the winter
weather, though unfortunately missing the pleasures of bathing,
concerts, operas and regattas.

Nowadays the best way to reach Venice is by air. Flights are
frequent both in summer and winter and many cheaper charter
flights are also available. *Alitalia* runs a service by way of Milan.
There are also flights—either direct or by way of Milan—from all
European capitals. One of the several advantages of approaching
Venice by air is that the plane usually circles high over the lagoon
before landing, and you can therefore see the whole lay-out of the

Introduction

city at a glance. The airfield is on the mainland, at the edge of the lagoon, and B.E.A. transport passengers by motor-boat to the LIDO and the Piazza San Marco: other lines take them more quickly but less romantically by bus to the Piazzale Roma at the head of the Grand Canal. Train services to Venice are fairly good. There are through coaches from Calais and Paris, though those who wish to travel in the comfort of a *wagon lit* must change trains in Paris and Milan. Those who go to Venice by road can leave their cars in one of the two vast garages at Piazzale Roma—though at the height of the season, from early July to mid-September, these tend to fill up and only the larger hotels seem able to reserve places in them. However, should the garages be full, you can leave your car in one of the large car-parks (as most of these are unattended at night you should remove all tempting objects such as cameras). There are plenty of porters at Piazzale Roma who will carry your baggage to the gondola or motor-boat station on the Grand Canal.

Hotels and pensioni are very thick on the ground in Venice. For a list of some of them see page 265. Ranging from the very luxurious and expensive to the rather uncomfortable and re-markably cheap, they cater for all degrees of taste. Prices vary from $175 (£100) per day for a double room and bath and meals (but not including a 15% service charge, wines and heating or air conditioning) to about $20 (£11) a night for a very simple room in a *pensione*. I cannot claim personal knowledge of all these hotels but there are a few which I can recommend from my own experience or from reports of close friends. In the De Luxe category the Gritti Palace is the most expensive by a short head and probably the most sybaritically comfortable. The Danieli is slightly less costly, but also very comfortable and has the added charm of association with the most distinguished list of visitors in the city, or perhaps of any hotel in Europe. Cipriani is famous for its food: it is very up to date and, a rare distinction, very quiet. It is on the Giudecca island and can be reached by the hotel motor-boat which hurries to and fro between it and the Piazza San Marco, day and night. In the winter it closes down. Among the first class hotels both the Monaco and the Regina are excellent and command wonderful views of the Grand Canal; the Gabrielli Sandwirth, rather farther away from the Piazza San Marco, is an attractive building and has the advantage of a quiet garden. In the second class the Savoia and Jolanda is well sited on the Riva degli Schiavoni and close to the Piazza San Marco: it is unpretentiously comfortable. Also on the Riva degli Schiavoni is the Metropole, which has no restaurant and therefore makes no fuss about visitors taking full pension terms though insists that they pay for breakfast. All' Angelo is probably the most convenient of the hotels in the third category and is attached to an excellent restaurant. Several of the *pensioni* can be recommended, notably the Accademia, which has a garden with a view down a *rio* to the Grand Canal, the Calcina and Seguso both on the Zattere looking across to the Giudecca, and the Alberotti which has unusually good food. The main disadvantage of the *pensioni* is that they are seldom prepared to accept visitors other than *en pension* and their food is usually very unimaginative. (You can, of course, take half pension terms which leaves you free for one meal a day.) Indeed the proprietors of most *pensioni* seem to cherish a nineteenth-century belief that nothing more exotic than *taglierini* in broth, a Milanese cutlet and rather soft sweet apples can appeal to the foreign palate. It is possible to stay in these places for weeks without being served a single one of the characteristic Venetian dishes and without savouring a suspicion of garlic.

Restaurants and **trattorie** (the name given to the simpler eating places though it may sometimes be applied to the very best) are still more numerous than hotels and the list on page 271 is a selective one. Here again, all tastes are catered for at a wide range of prices. Antico Martini near the Fenice theatre has an excellent international cuisine which makes it popular among Venetian residents, especially expatriates, though visitors tend to find it rather un-Venetian. The nearby Taverna "La Fenice" which is more moderately priced is much more characteristically Venetian in its decor and cooking. Al Graspo de Ua (near Campo San Bartolomeo) and Da Nane Mora-Malibran behind the church of San Giovanni Grisostomo (less expensive still) provide excellent local dishes though for the tourist rather than the Venetian-born. A favourite haunt of Venetian business men, and thus the place where the true quality of Venetian cooking can be judged, is the Madonna—near the Rialto bridge on the Frari side—where food is the only thing that counts and the decor is distinctly functional. Among the numerous smaller and cheaper restaurants, where the bill is seldom as much as $5 (£3) a head, Malamocco—just

Introduction

behind the Riva degli Schiavoni—and the Città di Milano—near the church of San Giuliano—are both to be recommended. Those in search of local colour, good inexpensive Venetian food and pleasant surroundings, will enjoy the Locanda Montin which has rooms hung with modern pictures and a large shady garden. If you are in a hurry or want only a light lunch there are several excellent *rosticcerie* snack bars—one of the best is in the Calle della Mandola—where for a remarkably low price you can have a plate of *lasagne* or *baccalá*, excellent cold roast beef and Russian salad, or fried shell-fish. Much patronised by the younger Venetians, the *rosticcerie* are very crowded at midday. But at nearly every café you can have a snack lunch of toasted cheese and ham sandwiches which are excellent and very cheap.

Unfortunately all recommendations for restaurants tend to be out of date before they are written down. One of the greatest pleasures of travel is, however, to find eating places for oneself. It should be mentioned that the usually good rule that all restaurants displaying multi-lingual menus are to be avoided does not apply in Venice. I sometimes suspect that the amusing mistranslations on these bills of fare—glutinous paste for *gnocchi* and mixed boils for *bollito misto*—are cunningly devised for the enjoyment of the more sophisticated visitors.

Venetian cooking has been much maligned. It relies very largely on Adriatic fish none of which can compare with a Scotch salmon, a Dover sole or a Turbot. Nevertheless, sampiero (John Dory) is excellent. I always find a *fritto misto* (mixed fry) of shrimps, scampi, small octopus, soft shelled crabs and sardines, a good and satisfying dish. Those who like eels—serpents as Oscar Wilde called them—praise *anguilla alla veneziana*, eel cooked in a sauce of lemon and tunny. True Venetians rave about *baccalà* which can be appetising despite its unpromising ingredients—dried cod, milk, onion, parsley and anchovies cooked together and stirred to a thick cream. Several small shell-fish are delicious when combined with spaghetti or rice—*spaghetti alle vongole* and *risotto con cozze* both make good first courses. *Zuppa di pesce*, the equivalent of *bouilla-baisse*, containing a wide variety of fish and molluscs is also good, though very satisfying and best treated as a main course. There are many Venetian dishes which do not depend on fish. *Risi e bisi*, a risotto made with peas and ham, is an old favourite with the populace and one of the best simple dishes. The staple item in the diet of the poor Venetian is *polenta*, a golden yellow but rather heavy doughy cake made from Indian corn flour and usually eaten with a little fish or liver. To my taste it is edible only when cut into slices and fried. In the better restaurants *polenta* is the usual companion of quails and other small roast birds. *Fegato alla veneziana*—liver fried with onions—is another favourite Venetian dish. Among cheeses, the rather dry Asiago is good. Creamy *mascarpone* curd is one of the most delicious of all Italian foods—it can be eaten either as cream cheese or mixed with ground coffee and sugar, or beaten up with eggs and candied fruits to make a pudding—but unfortunately it is very rarely found on restaurant menus.

Restaurants in Venice also serve the usual Italian dishes—the myriad varieties of *pasta*—*spaghetti* (round), *tagliatelli* (flat and usually freshly made), *lasagne* (large flat sheets cooked with a great deal of meat sauce and cheese to make a type of pie), *cannoli* (sheets wrapped round a mixture of cheese and minced meat)—excellent vegetable soup (*zuppa di verdura*), chicken breasts (*petti di pollo*) and of course veal (*vitello*) cooked in several different ways—*arrosto* (roast), *alla griglia* (grilled) *alla Marsala* (in Marsala) or made into a *saltimbocca* which consists of a fillet of veal glued to a slice of ham and a sage leaf with cheese.

In all but the most expensive restaurants, wines are divided with an admirable contempt for oenophil snobbery into white (*bianco*) and red (*rosso*). There is no nonsense here, or anywhere else in Italy, about drinking red wine with some dishes and white wine with others: you drink whatever you like with whatever you like. Most of the wines served in Venice come either from the district around Verona or from Conegliano. Of named wines the fairly dry Tokai from Friuli, the dry white Soave di Verona and the red Merlot are probably the best. Conegliano produces a good moderately dry sparkling white wine called *prosecco*—which can taste like champagne after the first bottle, if drunk in agreeable company. It is as well to beware of wines that go under the name of Chianti; they may come from any part of Italy and rarely bear any resemblance to the excellent red wine of the Chianti region. (Every bottle of true Chianti bears a special label on the neck with a number and a black cockerel.) The number of different vermouths drunk as aperitifs is enormous—my own favourite is *Punt e Mes*—but none is distinctly Venetian. Among the liqueurs the only one of Venetian origin is Grappa, a rather fiery type of *marc*. Many others are available, including Italian versions of Chartreuse, Curaçao, Cognac and so on, but none so good to my palate as the orange-flavoured Aurum, though rather sticky and very sweet. Coffee is rightly regarded as an essential of life by most Venetians. There is hardly a shopping street or *Campo* in the whole city without its café. Prices in all the cafés are rigorously controlled and naturally they are much higher in the Piazza San Marco than elsewhere. It is worth remembering that in all cafés imported drinks are very much more expensive than Italian ones.

CHAPTER 1

In the Piazza

There are few pleasanter ways of passing a summer's evening than sitting over a cup of coffee, and perhaps a glass of Aurum, in the **Piazza San Marco.** It is especially agreeable on those nights when the Venetian city band thunders away at some throbbingly romantic piece—an overture by Rossini or Verdi or any old favourite which calls for the traditional display of gestures from the conductor, gentle fingertip movements to the wood-wind, imperious waves at the percussion, and thrashings with the baton to bring in the brass for a particularly fruity *tutti.* As the conductor goes through all the histrionic gestures of passion, ecstasy, remorse and despair, the performers sit around him with the bored looks of world-weary croupiers. And all the while the younger inhabitants of one of the best-dressed cities in Europe parade around the square, chattering, flirting, quarrelling and staring at their numerous strangely attired visitors with that same unwinking gaze that Venetians have turned on their guests for the past five centuries. The façade of San Marco closes the scene in a glitter of golden mosaic and a bubbling of cupolas, while the great thick red campanile stretches up into the warm mothy darkness of the summer sky.

But the Piazza is beautiful at all times of day or night and all seasons of the year. It is one of the few delicate works of architecture that can absorb a bustling vulgar crowd without loss of dignity; one of the only great city squares which retains a feeling of animation when there are few people in it. I have never seen it quite empty, I must confess, for even in the early hours of a winter's morning the arcades shelter a few whispering, purposeful, loiterers. Sunshine makes the whole place glisten with gaiety, but sun is not as essential here as in most southern cities. A gauze curtain of mist gives greater grandeur to the buildings, especially if it enfolds

17

the top of the campanile. A blanket of snow, blotting out the strange lines on the floor and exaggerating every projection on the buildings, lends a bizarre enchantment. The Piazza looks beautiful even in rain or when floods convert the centre into a huge reflecting mirror. If there is a best time to see the Piazza San Marco it is immediately after your first arrival in Venice, whatever the hour and whatever the season.

Whether you sit outside Quadri's or Florian's—where Wagner sat complaining that no one applauded his music or where Proust corrected his translation of Ruskin—it is more than probable that the people at the next table will not be Venetian. That is not to suggest that Venetians spurn these excellent cafés; but in all the more expensive resorts they are outnumbered by foreigners. For Venice has long been and still remains an international holiday city, and this is one of its many peculiarities. The traveller with historical imagination in Paris is for ever meeting the ghosts of great Frenchmen—if not Parisians—writers, generals, kings, revolutionaries: in Florence he encounters Boccaccio, Dante, Macchiavelli and the Medici. But in Venice foreigners have always formed such an important part of the scene that he jostles the shades of far more visitors than of Doges and Venetian men of letters. You walk into the Piazzetta and find Ruskin busy with his water-colours, sketching the capitals of the arcade. Or you may find Nietzsche contemplating the pigeons which form the subject of one of his most beautiful poems. At the top of the campanile stands Goethe enthusing over his first view of the sea. You turn on to the Riva degli Schiavoni and catch Proust setting off from the Danieli in a gondola for a moonlight trip with Reynaldo Hahn who sings to him—a Venetian barcarolle? Certainly not: Gounod's setting of de Musset's
> Dans Venice le rouge,
> Pas un bateau qui bouge. . . .
From a building farther up the Riva, the bulky form of Henry James, spy-glass in hand, peers down at one. Turn the other way to the Bucintoro rowing club, in the hope of finding a spot exclusively Venetian, and there is Baron Corvo critically watching you through his pince-nez. Escape to San Lazzaro—and you find Byron helping with the translation of an Armenian grammar. And the Italians you encounter are less likely to be Venetians than visitors from Florence, or Milan or Rome—Dante surveying the

18

Arsenal, Petrarch sitting beside the Doge in the Doges' Palace, Aretino scribbling his venomous lampoons up by the Rialto, Galileo demonstrating his telescope on the Campanile, Manzoni pondering the *Promessi Sposi* in Campo San Maurizio.

Nevertheless, the city's famous and unique charm has sometimes failed to work. Montaigne found it " other than he imagined and not quite so wonderful." In the eighteenth century a large number of Grand Tourists voiced their displeasure. Horace Walpole, for one, remembered only the " pestilential air " of " stinking ditches." " For God's sake let's see to arrange affairs and get out of this vile prison," were James Adam's words on arrival in 1760. Five years later, Edward Gibbon, his mind already occupied with the *Decline and Fall*, found little that was good in the heir to a quarter of the Roman Empire. " The spectacle of Venice afforded some hours of astonishment and some days of disgust," he wrote. " Old and in general ill-built houses, ruined pictures, and stinking ditches dignified with the pompous denomination of canals; a fine bridge spoilt by two rows of houses on it, and a large square decorated with the worst architecture I ever yet saw." That same year James Boswell found that the novelty of " so singular a city " wore off after a week and he soon " wearied of travelling continually by water, shut up in those lugubrious gondolas." In fact, he would have accounted his visit a waste of time had he not been able to flirt with the Signora Michieli, enjoy the favours of some whores—" strange gay ideas I had of Venetian courtesans turned my head "—and show off in the Palazzo Ducale by reciting Otway:

> Curs'd be your Senate, cursed your constitution,
> The curse of growing factions and division. . . .

But with the cult of the picturesque, Venice returned to general favour. Even so, many voices dissented from the chorus of praise. " I don't care a bit for it and never wish to see it again," wrote Edward Lear of Venice in 1858; though he later changed his mind and declared " this city of palaces, pigeons, poodles and pumpkins (I am sorry to say also of innumerable pimps—to keep up the alliteration) is a wonder and a pleasure." " An abhorrent, green, slippery city," D. H. Lawrence called it—and many others have probably felt the same without saying so. Few cities in the world have aroused such extremes of adoration and dislike.

The truth is that there is something curiously melancholy and

19

sensual in the air of Venice which irritates the full-blooded and unromantic. The whole city has the atmosphere of a deserted ballroom on the morning after a ball. Every era has supposed that " Venice once was gay, the pleasant seat of all festivity," but of course those days of carefree gaiety are as remote and chimerical as the golden age. Even in the last hectic carnival years of the Republic's life, when the death of a Doge was concealed for a fortnight lest it should interfere with the tourist season, the jollifications were a little hollow. You have only to look closely at the dominoed figures jigging in Francesco Guardi's pictures to feel that they are executing a dance of death: you have only to peer through the eye-holes of a *bautta* or carnival mask to see that it conceals a skull. But those who have found an echo of their own mood in this melancholy, those who have been able to savour and, like Proust and Thomas Mann, relish an atmosphere of transience and decay have fallen in love with Venice. As Henry James, with his usual percipience, wrote: " almost every one interesting, appealing, melancholy, memorable, odd, seems at one time or another, after many days and much life, to have gravitated to Venice by a happy instinct, settling in it and treating it, cherishing it, as a sort of repository of consolations; all of which to-day, for the conscious mind, is mixed with its air and constitutes its unwritten history. The deposed, the defeated, the disenchanted, or even only the bored, have seemed to find there something that no other place could give."

This melancholy sensual strain is evident in most of the greatest Venetian paintings—the sad-eyed, apprehensive, Madonnas of Giovanni Bellini, the wistful hedonists of Giorgione, the introspective young men portrayed by Lotto, Titian's velvet-clad Saints, Tintoretto's mystics. Even the silken gods of Veronese and Tiepolo seem sometimes to remind us that " dust hath blinded Helen's eye, Queens have died young and fair." Partly, this is an effect of Venetian light which makes the most substantial building seem transient, as in a view by Francesco Guardi where churches and palaces are revealed as shimmering phantoms of light. Pietro Aretino noticed this one day from his window on the Grand Canal. " The air was such as an artist would like to depict who grieved that he was not Titian. The stonework of the houses, though solid, seemed artificial, the atmosphere varied from clear to leaden. The clouds above the roofs merged into a distance of smoky grey, the nearest

In the Piazza

blazing like suns, more distant ones glowing as molten lead dissolving at last into horizontal streaks, now greenish blue, now bluish green, cutting the palaces as they cut them in the landscapes of Vecelli. And as I watched the scene I exclaimed more than once, ' O Titian, where art thou, and why not here to realise the scene.' "

From Bellini and Carpaccio to Tiepolo, Canaletto and Guardi, the peculiar qualities of Venetian light have formed the essential subject matter of many a Venetian masterpiece. And not pictures only; many buildings seem to have been designed to catch and reflect the subtlety of this extraordinary light. With an appreciation of light went a love of colour, expressed in the lavish use of marble and mosaic on buildings, in rich costumes for the dignitaries of State, and still richer silks, satins, brocades and damasks for the Saints in altarpieces. Happily this feeling for colour and finery still survives in Venice. The younger people dress with an even more daring elegance than those of other Italian cities, and as they are very fashion-conscious, their clothes seem to last for no more than one brief season. The frowzy beatnik is unknown in their society and they tend to look askance at the English literary gent plodding from gallery to gallery and church to church in tweeds no longer quite new and shoes a trifle dusty. No matter how poor, they usually spend the greater part of their income on clothes. Colour plays a great part not only in the dresses of the girls but also in the pullovers, shirts and trousers of the boys, and a single combination of shades seldom remains popular for more than six months. Among the poor the home comes second to dress, but the apartments of the middle and upper classes reveal a passion for rich, glossy and juicily coloured materials which often appear garish to northern eyes. You can buy in the Piazza San Marco to-day cut velvets and brocades similar to those popular from the sixteenth to the eighteenth century—and they are as expensive now as ever they were. This passion for opulent colour went, and still goes, hand in hand with a taste for oriental carpets and porcelain and other objects which introduce a whiff of exotic fantasy.

A liking for bizarre fantasy is another trait in the Venetian character which is strongly manifested in the arts of the city. One recognises it in the backgrounds of paintings, in little bronzes of satyrs, in the preposterous forms of eighteenth century furniture and, most conspicuously, in the many strange carved heads attached

21

to buildings. Wherever you walk, wherever you go by gondola, these heads stare down at you, some quite small, but the majority more than life size—Polyphemus heads, truculent giants with their tongues wagging, grotesquely benign wizened heads, ferocious Amazons, heads with great tusks and eyes bulging like some Beckfordian caliph, heads winking lewdly in enjoyment of a scabrous joke. There are grotesque heads in other cities but nowhere are they so numerous or carved with such a range of bizarre fantasy as in Venice.

In contrast with this taste for grotesque fantasy, Venetian artists have shown a fascinated interest in the everyday life of their city. This aspect of their art is announced by the carvings of Trades on the main door of San Marco. It re-emerges in paintings of all periods from the fifteenth century onwards. In Carpaccio, Venice produced the first European painter of *genre*. And one finds a taste for *genre* often in the most surprising places—a little homely incident in the background to an opulent Titian, a detail of everyday life such as a woman doing her laundering which anchors one of Tintoretto's great cosmic dramas to the visible world, a couple making love in the corner of one of Tiepolo's great allegorical ceilings. Such scenes are partly the outcome of that most endearing of Italian passions—curiosity, personified in the faces of the young people staring at us as they walk round the Piazza. But in Venice it is more: it is the result of a desire to celebrate every aspect of a city which the Venetians, with some reason, consider the most beautiful in the world.

Nearly every great Venetian work of art is in some way a celebration of the beauty, the power or the magnificence of Venice. Her painters never wearied of representing the changing patterns of Venetian light, the landscape of the Venetian terra firma, the magnificence of Venetian ceremonies, the form of the ideally beautiful Venetian woman, if not the actual aspect of the city itself. Similarly, Venetian literature is one long, and to those from outside somewhat tedious, eulogy of Venice. Containing no novels, no philosophy of importance, it abounds in histories of the Serene Republic. The comedies of Goldoni and Pietro Chiari are Venetian *genre* pieces—Pietro Longhis in prose—Gozzi's *Fiabbe* are dramatizations of Venetian fairy tales. The popular songs in which the Venetian poetic genius most notably expressed itself usually celebrate the beauty of Venice or the Lagoon:

In the Piazza

Oh what a feast, how spectacular,
How beautiful the lagoon looks
When everything is silent
When the moon is high up in the sky.

Significantly enough such songs are anonymous. The Serenissima demanded such self-effacing devotion from its citizens that anonymity became a virtue. Anything approaching a cult of personality was discouraged. The Doge was an anonymous figure-head prevented by his coronation oath from meddling in politics. Government was conducted by a committee, or rather a frequently changing series of committees. Generals or Admirals who enjoyed too great a success were liable to find themselves in prison lest they achieve personal power. Every Venetian was expected to put the State before all else.

As one reads Venetian history, the term " team spirit " hovers at the back of one's mind, with memories of an English public school. For every detail of life, and even dress, was regulated in a very scholastic fashion by one sumptuary edict after another. Procurators (monitors) may wear red damask togas with stoles over their left shoulders: other Senators (prefects) may wear similar robes without a stole: members of the great council (sixth form) may wear not more than so many ducats worth of jewellery: the populace (fags) shall not dare to wear gold about their persons. Admirals (first colours) may erect obelisks on the roofs of their palaces. Pitched battles, horribly reminiscent of house matches, were organised between the two sections of the *popolo* to allow them to let off steam. Exeats were given only on special occasions and were regarded as a privilege. Many countries were permanently out of bounds. And it was at all times forbidden for anyone to have social contacts with visitors to Venice.

Such regimentation supported, and was supported by, the Venetian passion for anonymity, or submission of the personality to the State. And this anonymity bedevils all studies of Venetian history, whether social or artistic. Venice produced no Vasari with a sharp ear for gossip and a keen pen to record personalities. Of Giovanni Bellini, Cima, Carpaccio, Giorgione, of the Lombardi, Rizzo and Vittoria, of Veronese, Palladio, Longhena, Piazzetta, Canaletto, Tiepolo, Guardi, all of them famous in their lifetime, surprisingly little is known. They are very nearly as anonymous as the artists who created the mosaics in San Marco or the stone

23

masons who raised its fabric. It is significant that a long seventeenth-century poem by Marco Boschini, *La carta del navegar pitoresco*
which proclaims itself a eulogy of Venetian painting is far less
concerned with artists than their works and is mainly a celebration
of Venice as adorned by painters and architects. " Sta città,"
he writes:

> xè vaga, singular, unica al mondo,
> san xè l'agiere, el sito xè giocondo.

Only two Venetian artists stand out as personalities—Titian who
worked so much for foreign patrons and Tintoretto whose strongly
individualistic paintings fill out the scanty contemporary reports
of him as a man. For the rest, it was enough that they were
Venetians, that they embodied the corporate personality of the
Venetian school as a Doge embodied that of the State.

This is brought out very clearly in the Piazza San Marco. The
names of the architects of most of the buildings are recorded. But
of all these men only one lives as a human personality, and he
was a foreigner, Jacopo Sansovino who came from Florence and
whose life was written by Vasari. And his main building here,
the Libreria in the Piazzetta, is the only one which rates individuality above the traditions of the Venetian school. For the Piazza
was not intended to display the individual genius of artists. It was
intended to express the magnificence of the capital of the Venetian
Empire. In marble and brick and mosaic, it records the growth
of that Empire from the early days of the confederation of lagoon
islands to the final fall of the Republic in 1797.

As invasion after invasion of barbarians—Visigoths, Huns,
Ostrogoths, Lombards—swept down through the mountains to
attack the decaying Roman Empire in the fifth and sixth centuries,
a number of families from the Venetian plain took refuge among
the muddy islands of the lagoon. By the end of the seventh century
these communities had united themselves under a popularly
elected leader or Doge. At this time the largest of the several
townships was Malamocco on the Lido. But Malamocco proved
too vulnerable to attack, both from land and sea, so the adminis-
tration was moved to the central group of islands divided by a
deep channel from which it derived the name Rivo Alto or Rialto
—the islands we now call Venice.

Venice stands roughly in the centre of the crescent-shaped
lagoon the convex side of which borders the land while the concave

side faces the sea. The lagoon seems to have been created by three rivers, the Sile, the Piave and the Brenta rushing down from the Dolomites and bearing a quantity of silt which piled up where their waters met the force of the Adriatic, thus gradually forming the long line of the Lido. Further deposits of mud formed islands within the lagoon, some so low that they are submerged at high tide, others firm and high enough to permit the erection of buildings. Colonies of fishermen established themselves on the firmer islands at a very early period. Later it was discovered that the larger islands, or rather clusters of islands, notably Venice, Torcello, Murano and Burano, had a solid layer of heavy clay beneath the mud and that tall buildings could be erected on piles driven down to this substratum. Early in the ninth century a fortress for the Doge and government of the lagoon was built where the Doges' Palace now stands and the urban development of Venice began. *Campi*—or fields—were eventually made into paved squares and linked by pathways which, in time, were similarly paved. The narrow channels separating the innumerable little islands were dredged to make them into permanently open waterways, kept clean by the ebbing and flowing of the Adriatic tide. At this period considerable quantities of river water remained land-locked and stagnant in the lagoon, making it malarial. But in the course of centuries the Venetians diverted the rivers through wide canals which enter the sea at points outside the lagoon. Thus the lagoon was converted into a lake of sea water kept in motion by the tides—just strong enough to carry away refuse. This natural sanitation made the city one of the healthiest in Europe, while the treacherous mud banks of the lagoon protected it from attack by land or sea.

Venice was built on a compromise between land and sea. Her early development was made possible by the conflict between the Eastern Empire and the barbarians who ruled in the West. Officially, the early Doges held their titles by mandate of the Byzantine Emperors—but the coin used in the Republic was that of the German emperors. Cunningly, the tiny state played off the two empires against each other. As we shall see, the church of San Marco was built as an act of defiance to Byzantium and as a proclamation of independence. Though predominantly Byzantine in style, it is, none the less, a symbol of Venice's release from suzerainity to the Empire of the East and her final conquest of

25

Byzantium in the thirteenth century. Its most prominent decorations were looted from Constantinople. The two great oriental granite columns of the Piazzetta, which were set up in the twelfth century, also come from the Eastern Mediterranean. One bears a Hellenistic statue transformed into the figure of the Greek St. Theodore, the first patron of Venice. The other bears a fourth-century chimaera from the Levant transformed into the lion of St. Mark whom the Venetians chose as their protector in succession to St. Theodore and under whose banner they were destined to expand their Empire throughout the Eastern Mediterranean.

The Doges' Palace took its present form in the fifteenth century when the commercial and political power of Venice was at its greatest. This was the golden age of Venetian opulence when the tall **campanile**, its gilded angel glittering in the sun, served as a landmark to fleets of galleys bringing the riches of the Orient to Europe—silks, spices, jewels, slaves, relics, manuscripts, antique carvings. The campanile was begun in the ninth century and reached its present height in the sixteenth; it toppled down in 1902 but was rebuilt as an exact replica.

On the north side of the Piazza stands the **clock tower,** astride the entrance to the Mercerie. It was built in the 1490s and the two bronze figures who hammer the hours on the bell date from the same period. The clock is adorned with a piece of mechanism which is the sole survivor of the many pomps which celebrated the feast of the Ascension when the Doge performed the annual marriage ceremony with the sea. As every hour strikes during Ascension week, an angel with a trumpet emerges from the little door to the left of the statue of the Virgin and conducts the three Wise Men past her with wooden gestures of respect. Next to the clock tower stands the long building of the **Procuratie Vecchie** —originally constructed for the Procurators of San Marco, the highest Venetian dignitaries after the Doge. Though built in the early sixteenth century it retains many elements from the design of its Byzantine-style predecessor, notably the arcaded front which dissolves the fabric into an insubstantial flicker of light and shade.

The south side of the Piazza is lined by the **Procuratie Nuove,** a more pompously classical range begun in 1582 by Palladio's pupil Scamozzi in emulation of Sansovino's library which it joins at the angle of the Piazzetta. Nearly a century separates the two Procuratie. The first was begun before the jealous

European powers joined together to humble Venice in the war of the League of Cambrai. The second was begun when the political power and commercial prosperity of Venice were on the decline, partly on account of the opening of the sea route with India. And one can feel in its more elaborate decoration a somewhat self-conscious gesture, a wishful act of faith in the continuing power of the Republic.

The two Procuratie are joined by a wing built in 1807 to replace a church pulled down at Napoleon's command after the final demise of the Republic. Napoleon trifled with Venice in the most brutal fashion, selling her to Austria in 1797 and then winning her back as part of the kingdom of Italy in 1805. In 1815 there were no dynastic heirs to represent Venice at the Congress of Vienna. As the very name of a Republic was anathema in Vienna the Venetian states were given to Austria. And apart from the few months of Daniele Manin's heroic but futile revolution in 1848–9, Venice remained Austrian until 1866. During these years Venice's hostility to her ancient enemies and new overlords was pacifically expressed in the Piazza. Venetians frequented Florian's and boycotted Quadri's café which was patronised by the Austrians. When the Austrian band played in the centre, no Venetian ever applauded. Finally, through the good offices of Napoleon's nephew, Venice was added to the kingdom of United Italy—her other traditional enemy—and the Italian tricolour was raised on the three great flag-poles which stand in magnificent renaissance bronze bases in front of San Marco—those flag-poles which had originally borne the red and gold silk banners of the Serene Republic.

Venice lost her autonomy more than a century and a half ago. Yet the city maintains an individuality which is something more than the mere freak of situation. To this day Italians visit Venice as if it were a foreign city. Every street, every canal, proclaims that it was not merely the capital of an Italian state, but the centre of a mighty empire, the hub of a great civilisation. And the modern inhabitant is conscious of his heritage. One of them once remarked to me as we walked across the Piazza: " For us Venetians, the niggers begin at Mestre."

CHAPTER 2

San Marco: Venice and Byzantium

A first view of **San Marco** from the western end of the Piazza is one of the great experiences of a lifetime. It has an ethearial quality which only Ruskin has been able to describe: " a multitude of pillars and white domes, clustered into a long low pyramid of coloured light; a treasure heap, it seems, partly of gold, and partly of opal and mother of pearl, hollowed beneath into five great vaulted porches, ceiled with fair mosaic, and beset with sculpture of alabaster, clear as amber and delicate as ivory." Along the roof line " as if in ecstasy, the crests of the arches break into a marble foam, and toss themselves far into the blue sky in flashes and wreaths of sculptured spray, as if the breakers on the Lido shore had been frost bound before they fell, and the sea nymphs had inlaid them with coral and amethyst." A thousand indifferent paintings and a million garish picture postcards have failed to vulgarise or hackney the beauty of this extraordinary façade. Invariably it surprises the senses with delight. Standing in front of it, one finds that all cheapjack comparisons lose what little relevance they might otherwise have. It does not resemble an Arab encampment as some smart Alec recently remarked; still less does it look, as Mark Twain thought, " like a vast and warty bug taking a meditative walk." San Marco, like Venice, can be compared only with itself.

Purists may criticise the confusion of its architectural styles and forms. Yet no one can deny that it is among the most beautiful and moving buildings in the world. The work of many generations of artists harmonised together by the caresses of eight centuries, it has a style and unity of its own. For unlike most other buildings which are patchworks of the ages, San Marco had a constant unity of purpose: the glorification of the Venetian State. It is at once
28

the symbol of Venice's wealth and a pictorial narrative of her rise to Power. The dedication, the plan, the form, the decoration— everything in and about the church expresses some aspect of the history of Venice. So it is to the symbolism of San Marco rather than its more obvious aesthetic merits that I wish to draw your attention.

First of all, it is important to remember that San Marco did not become the Cathedral church of Venice until 1807. (The Patriarchal palace on the left dates mainly from the 1830s.) San Marco was built as the Doges' chapel—as a dynastic church and national shrine, to counter-balance the Cathedral at Castello, the easternmost point of Venice. Roughly the functions of San Marco and San Pietro in Castello may be compared with those of Westminster Abbey and St. Paul's Cathedral. The Doges took their coronation oaths in San Marco, and the first of them were buried here. Without ecclesiastical interference, the Doge nominated and invested the primarius of the church—the dean or chief priest entitled to use on occasion the mitre, ring and staff of a prelate (the office was limited to members of indigenous noble families). Among his titles the Doge bore that of " patronus et gubernator " of San Marco, and among his duties was the custody of the relics.

It is now rather difficult to appreciate the importance attached to relics in the Middle Ages. In addition to their mystical properties, they were symbols of the wealth and power of the State. A city without relics was like a man without a shadow. Venetians realised that if they were to have an internationally important church they would need relics of greater significance than any possessed by the nearby patriarchal churches of Grado and Aquileia under whose ecclesiastical jurisdiction the city fell. The most desirable were, of course, the relics of St. Mark who was believed to have written his Gospel in Rome for the " Italians " and who was also supposed to have been the Apostolic missionary to the north Adriatic and thus the true founder of the Venetian patriarchate. Men appear to have been dispatched to Alexandria with the express purpose of seizing the relics of St. Mark. The story goes that they smuggled them out by covering them with slices of pork which was abomination to the Moslems. But whatever the disguise, there can be little doubt that these relics reached Venice in 828 or 829. Almost immediately a church was built for them next to the Doges' Palace. The Venetians changed their allegiance from

29

SAN MARCO

1. Double ambo. constructed in 14th century out of earlier materials
2. Iconostasis surmounted by 14th century statues
3. Reliquary ambo, constructed in 14th century out of earlier materials
4. Bronze reliefs of the miracles and martyrdom of St. Mark by Sansovino
5. Altar of St. Paul, 15th century
6. *Madonna Nicopeia*, 13th century Byzantine icon
7. Chapel of St. Isidore (1354-5)
8. Chapel of the Madonna dei Mascoli (1430)
9. Relief of Madonna dello Scioppo, early 14th century
10. Capitello del Crocifisso, 13th century
11. Porphyry holy water basin on 2nd century BC base
12. Altar of San Giacomo (1462-71)
13. Sacrament altar (1617). Pavement 12th-13th century
14. Iconostasis supporting late 14th century statues
15. Chapel of San Clemente
16. High Altar
17. Pala d'Oro
18. Sacristy door by Sansovino (1546)
19. Treasury
20. Baptistery
21. Zen chapel with statue of Virgin and Child by Antonio Lombardo

- a. 12th century mosaics
- b. 13th century mosaics
- c. 14th century mosaics
- d. 15th century mosaics
- e. 16th century mosaics
- f. 17th century mosaics
- h. 19th century mosaics

their Greek patron St. Theodore to St. Mark, thus proclaiming their independence of Byzantium. St. Theodore was not again accepted as a patron of Venice until the late thirteenth century when all danger of Byzantine ambitions was past.

The first church of San Marco was begun in 830 on the cruciform plan normal for Apostles' churches and not on the basilican plan usual in Venice (ironically enough it is now called the Basilica). The model was provided by the church of the Holy Apostles in Constantinople, another Apostolic shrine and dynastic church. Apart from the core of some walls and a few panels of carved stone, nothing survives from this first San Marco, which was burnt down in 976. A second church was built as a replica of the first but this was pulled down to make way for the present one which was erected between 1063 and 1094 to the design of a Greek architect. The great innovation of this building was brick vaulting—instead of a wooden roof—which made the ceiling mosaics possible. After the fabric was completed the work of decorating the exterior and interior began; and this was carried on until the sixteenth century in spurts of activity, most notably in the thirteenth century when the church began to assume the appearance it has to-day.

The dates are very important. San Marco was begun during the ninth century when Venice was still officially a province of the Eastern Empire, though clearly emerging as an independent state. Unable to exercise its suzerainty by force, Byzantium was content to keep or even buy the friendship of the new power, while Venice was anxious to preserve the appearance of Byzantine rule as a protection from Imperial German ambitions. Thus the church was built in a Byzantine manner to enshrine relics which announced Venice's independence. Soon afterwards, Venice felt herself strong enough to break away from Byzantium. But the third church was built during a period of rapprochement, under three Doges all of whom were pro-Byzantine and one of whom was married to the sister of the Emperor Michael VII Dukas. This period of friendship lasted until the end of the reign of Doge Ordelaffo Falier under whom a large part of the Pala d'Oro (see p. 38) was commissioned in Constantinople. After the shameful sack of Constantinople in 1204 by the Crusaders the tables were turned between Venice and Byzantium. The Doge acquired the resounding title: *Dominator quartae et dimidiae partis totius Romanius* (ruler of a quarter and a half a quarter of the Roman Empire) and

31

for the next fifty years Venice was the power behind the Empire of the Latins in the East. It was during this period that the exterior of San Marco was transformed with incrustations of marble panels and carvings looted from Constantinople.

Venice took her role as heir to a part of the Roman Empire very seriously. And this accounts for the method of decorating the exterior of San Marco—and much else besides—in Veneto-Byzantine architecture. Many of the elements in the decorative scheme are Byzantine—notably the use of sculpture as surface ornament and not, as was normal elsewhere in Europe, to express the structure. But no parallel to the abundance of columns and marble cladding is to be found on any other Byzantine building of this period. Archaeologists have discovered behind these decorations the mid-twelfth-century brick façade which, somewhat surprisingly, was decorated not with round headed but with pointed arches and arcading. Thus, when the rest of Europe was developing the Gothic style, Venice was turning back to the ancient world for inspiration. Apparently this lavish use of marble was a conscious attempt to revive the splendours of ancient Rome—though the architect looked back no farther than to the Early Christian period. It was, however, by such a return to a form of classicism —also reflected in domestic architecture where the two-story portico became popular—that Venice triumphantly proclaimed her succession to the Roman Empire, if to no more than a "quarter and a half a quarter" of it.

Use of loot from Constantinople also declared the victory. The four wonderful bronze horses, made in Imperial Rome and later sent to Constantinople, were set above the central door like the quadriga on a triumphal arch. The south façade, by the entrance to the Doges' Palace and that which official visitors arriving from the water would see first, was entirely devoted to a display of spoils taken in the wars against Byzantium and against Genoa, Venice's main competitor in the eastern Mediterranean. Here the fourth-century porphyry tetrarchs—two pairs of embracing figures representing Diocletian and his Imperial colleagues—the porphyry head on the balustrade (third century Alexandrian), the paterae of marble and onyx, the columns and the capitals are all from Byzantium. Genoese trophies, taken from Acre in 1256, include the two large free-standing columns with Saracenic carving and the stumpy porphyry *pietra del bando*, the symbol of Genoese

32

San Marco, the masterpiece of Venetian-Byzantine architecture, encrusted with rare marbles and glittering golden mosaics which range in date from the 12th to the 18th century

San Marco, the south façade. Loot from Constantinople is embedded in
the wall like a marble patchwork hanging

jurisdiction and the platform from which public notices were read. The north façade is also encrusted with loot, though this appears to have been taken after the sack of Constantinople and was arranged decoratively rather than as a trophy of martial power. Some of the low reliefs are interesting. Above the most westerly arch there is a panel carved with twelve sheep on either side of a throne bearing a cross—a symbol of Christ and the Apostles, carved in Constantinople in the seventh century and a rare example of Byzantine sculpture from before the iconoclastic period.

On the main façade the carvings are arranged in a clear icono-graphic programme to stress the church's function as a national shrine. The basic construction is that of a vast triumphal arch with five openings. In the spandrels between the arches there are six relief carvings. That on the far left represents Hercules carrying the Erymanthean boar, a Roman work of the third century, that on the far right is a Venetian imitation of it carved one thousand years later. Hercules was supposed to have been the original tribal hero of the Veneti from whom the Venetians claimed descent, he had an allegorical role as the Saviour conquering evil, he was also recognized as the type of hero protector. The next two reliefs, reading inwards—Venetian carvings after Byzantine prototypes—represent the Virgin and the Archangel of the Annunciation both of whom were regarded as protectors of the ruler of the state. The two central reliefs represent Saints who were warriors and thus the protectors of warriors, St. Demetrius and St. George—the first a late twelfth-century Byzantine carving and the second a Venetian imitation of it.

With the carvings on the main porch we move from a Veneto-Byzantine to a predominantly Venetian world. They were executed between 1225 and 1260 and appear to be the first products of a truly Venetian style of sculpture, though based on a synthesis of other styles—Byzantine, Oriental and Romanesque. In form the porch is an adaptation of a Romanesque programme—such as one finds in many French and German churches—but with columns instead of statues and a mosaic instead of a relief carving. Each of the three arches is carved on the soffit and face, providing six bands of relief. In subject matter, the series, which should be read from the innermost outwards, represents a progression from the general to the particular, from the abstract to the concrete. The innermost arch has figures enacting fables on the soffit and fighting figures, symbolising the unruly world, on the face. On the second arch there are allegories of the months on the soffit and personifications of virtues on the face. The third, which is the most interesting, has lively figures of Venetian trades on the soffit—shipbuilders, carpenters, coopers, fishermen and so on—and Christ and the Prophets on the face which forms a frontispiece to the whole composition.

The central lunette is filled with a mosaic of the Last Judgement, a sad nineteenth-century substitute for the original one. The other lunette mosaics date from the seventeenth and eighteenth centuries, with the exception of that over the north door which is thirteenth century and represents *The Translation of the Body of St. Mark,* including the earliest known picture of the church. Above this series of portals runs the gallery on which the bronze horses stand. Four lunettes are filled with seventeenth-century mosaics of the main feasts of the Church. All five arches are crowned with a froth of late fourteenth and early fifteenth-century carving and are divided from each other by tall Gothic baldachins sheltering statues of Saints.

The central doorway leads into the **atrium** or porch which embraces the west and north sides of the church. It is floored with a geometrical carpet of rare marbles which include, just in front of the central door, a little lozenge of porphyry traditionally marking the place where the Venetians forced the Emperor Frederick Barbarossa to render homage to Pope Alexander III. Niches in the walls hold sarcophagi in which early Doges lie buried —in front of some there are grilles worked in the Moorish taste. Of the three doorways leading into the church that on the right has particularly fine doors of bronze made in Constantinople in the eleventh century and sent to Venice as a gift from the Emperor Alexios I Comnenos. The mosaics overhead, all thirteenth-century work and among the finest in Venice, represent scenes from the Old Testament. They are probably by Venetian craftsmen though based on a Byzantine pattern book. Particularly attractive is the cupola which begins the series with the Creation and story of Adam and Eve (the picture of them fidgeting uncomfortably in their first clothes is irresistible.) The great niched central doorway opening into the church and the mosaic figures of Saints on either side are the most notable survivors of the eleventh-century decorations of San Marco.

The **interior** is perhaps the most sombrely impressive in all Christendom. Encrusted from floor to roof with precious materials, it has a sultry opulence, dark and mysteriously vibrant with the swart glimmer of gold and ruby. It naturally appears at its best on high days when the vestments of the priests add a last touch of shimmering colour and when the candles flicker helplessly in the reek of incense-breathing smoke.

A relatively straightforward Greek cross plan has been given a sense of mystery by the colonnades dividing the central area from the darker side aisles. With its cupolas and mosaics, its iconostasis and ambos, it appears at first sight characteristically Byzantine. Up to a point this is true. A twelfth-century Byzantine treatise by Nicholas Mesarites singles out for praise as the cynosure of ecclesiastical architecture the church of the Holy Apostles which provided the model for San Marco. " It does not please the senses more than it impresses the mind," he wrote. " The lines bring delight to the senses, they make their impress on the mind. . . . It fills the sight with beauty of colour and the golden glimmer of mosaics, it strikes the mind by its surpassing size, its skilled construction." In the use of significant geometrical figures—the square, the circle and the cross—and the mystic relationship between the proportions, it answers the Byzantine passion for symbolism and the Byzantine belief in the laws of harmony and sanctity of mathematics, " the highest of the sciences." Nevertheless, it is essentially a Byzantine church with Italian decorations and nothing like it was ever built in the eastern Empire. The original effect was quite different and much more outspokenly Byzantine. There were many more windows and there were galleries above the aisles so that light flooded into the whole central area making a much stronger contrast with the surrounding shade. With their passion for surface decoration, the Venetians walled up many windows to make room for additional mosaics. This made the area under the galleries so dangerously dark that their floors had to be removed, leaving only the strange cat-walks you see to-day.

San Marco naturally owes much of its opulent effect to the **mosaics,** covering an area of about one acre and executed between the twelfth and eighteenth centuries. Their glitter is carefully contrived—for the individual tesserae are placed at slightly different angles to the bed so that they catch the light in different ways. By such devices did Byzantine-inspired craftsmen

35

seek to delight the senses. But the iconographical programme of the scenes depicted was intended to make a no less strong appeal to the mind. Whereas the mosaics in the atrium were devoted to Old Testament subjects—the world before redemption—those inside appropriately celebrate the triumph of the Church. As is normal in Byzantine iconography, Christ Pantocrator is enthroned in the apse. Beneath Him stand four protectors of Venice: Saints Nicholas, Peter, Mark and Ermagora. The cupola above the high altar is devoted to the Prophets—the heralds of Christianity. The central cupola has the Ascension in the middle and figures of virtues below. That above the nave, where the congregation would stand, represents Pentecost and the Apostles preaching the Gospel to the nations. On the wall above the doorway, Christ seated between the Virgin and St. Mark looks towards the high altar. Higher up there are scenes from the Apocalypse, and the arch connecting the body of the church with the façade, across the atrium, bears a representation of the Last Judgement, a subject which appears also on the central lunette of the façade. Minor mosaics follow out this general scheme: the Acts of the Apostles appear on either side of the Pentecost cupola. The central cupola is surrounded by scenes from the life of Christ. St. Mark, as patron of the church, has the two arches on either side of the chancel. The cupolas in the transepts fall outside the general scheme and their programme is more difficult to interpret. Both are surrounded by scenes from the life of Christ. The south cupola has figures of Saints Nicholas, Clement, Blaise, Leonard, and in the squinches, Erasmus, Euphemia, Dorothy and Tecla, all of them martyrs. The north cupola has scenes from the life of St. John the Evangelist supported by the Doctors of the Western Church in the squinches. Probably the two series were intended to represent, respectively, action and meditation in the service of the church.

The annotated plan on page 30 gives the approximate dates of the mosaics and also refers to some of the outstanding paintings and sculptures of which no more than a few can be singled out here. The **iconostasis** or screen dividing the nave from the chancel bears a silver crucifix, signed by Jacopo di Marco Bennato, between marble statues of the Virgin and Apostles carved in 1394 by the brothers Jacobello and Pierpaolo delle Masegne in a naturalistic Gothic manner revealing the final departure of Venetian artists from Byzantine conventions. Looking through the screen you can see on either hand two little galleries decorated with very beautiful high renaissance reliefs by Jacopo Sansovino. At either end of the iconostasis stand two ambos, both of them constructed in the fourteenth century out of earlier materials including Byzantine carved panels. That on the left is in the form of a double-decker pulpit, in which the Epistle was read from the lower tier and the Gospel from the upper. The right-hand ambo was used for the display of relics on high days. And it was here that newly elected Doges showed themselves to the people. In the left transept the altar is devoted to the Madonna Nicopeia (bringer of victory)—an icon painted in the tenth century for a monastery in Constantinople and set in a frame decorated with very fine enamel plaques.

Two chapels lead out of the left transept. The larger is dedicated to St. Isidore (7) who evangelised the island of Chios and, after enduring several tortures, was beheaded there in 250. His remains were brought, with other loot, from Chios to Venice in 1125 but hidden until about 1350 when Doge Andrea Dandolo had this chapel redecorated to enshrine them. The story of St. Isidore's life and the transport of his relics is illustrated in the mosaics. Two scenes—his torture and martyrdom—are repeated in low relief on the tomb, with a greater vivacity which announces the advent of Gothic sculpture in Venice. The other chapel, della Madonna dei Mascoli (8), (so called because it belonged to a confraternity of laymen—*mascoli* is Venetian for males—and not, as the old verger's story runs, because women came here to pray for male children). has an altarpiece with the Virgin and Child between St. Mark and St. James, carved in the late 1420s—a Gothic work, though its firmly individualistic statues hint at the first stirrings of the renaissance. In the fifteenth-century mosaic scenes from the life of the Virgin, the renaissance feeling is still stronger, especially in the architectural backgrounds. The cartoons for these mosaics have often been attributed to the originator of the Renaissance in the Veneto—Andrea Mantegna.

At the angle of the nave with the north transept stands (9) the Madonna del Scioppo (so called because of the gun placed beside it as an *ex voto*), an early fourteenth-century relief still following Byzantine forms, but carved with a greater tenderness and a greater awareness of the third dimension which shows a tentative move towards the Gothic style. This transition from Byzantine to Gothic

37

may be studied more clearly in the **Baptistery** (20). In the central cupola Byzantium prevails and the classical origins of Byzantine art are explicit in the nude angels surrounding Christ no less than in the larger figures with their regular features and decisive gestures. But in the lunette showing the martyrdom of the Baptist, Salome makes her appearance as a fashionably dressed lady of the 1350s, like a living actress on a stage of puppets. She reminds one that in Venice the short-lived Gothic style formed an essential bridge between the classicism of Byzantium and the humanist classicism of the Renaissance. Also in the Baptistery is the tomb of Doge Andrea Dandolo, the friend of Petrarch and the man who commissioned these mosaics as well as the decorations in the chapel of San Isidoro. His humanist leanings are perhaps reflected in the new realism which makes an appearance in both places.

The Baptistery altar—now crowned by a statue of St. Pius X who was Patriarch of Venice before he became Pope in 1903—is made of a slab of granite brought back from Tyre in the thirteenth century. Tradition has it that Christ rested on this stone. The font has a fine bronze cover designed by Sansovino and executed by his pupils.

From the chapel of San Clemente (15) with its wonderful blue and white and gold twelfth-century mosaic, you can enter the area behind the high altar to see the **Pala d'Oro** (open weekdays from 10–5.30, holidays 2–4.30). This gold altarpiece, one of the great treasures of San Marco, has a complicated history. The first Pala d'Oro was made in Constantinople in 976. Further enamelled gold panels to enlarge it were commissioned in Constantinople between 1102 and 1117, towards the end of the great period of Veneto-Byzantine alliance. In the thirteenth century it was enlarged again, probably to incorporate enamels looted from Constantinople as well as some panels painted in Venice. Finally it was rearranged and placed in its present Gothic frame in 1345. Thus there is a wide diversity of date and style between the various parts. But one needs no knowledge of dating to admire the elegance and glitter of this extraordinary work. The finest panels—like that of St. Michael or that of the Empress Irene near the centre of the lowest tier—are among the outstanding achievements of Byzantine civilization during its most sophisticated period.

The baldachin above the high altar is supported by four intricately carved columns which are another product of the thirteenth century "Renaissance." The concave bronze sacristy door (18) in the apse shows a very different type of classicism. Modelled by Sansovino in 1546, it is a masterpiece of high Renaissance sculpture and its two large reliefs of the *Entombment* and *Resurrection* have the classical poise and finality of paintings by Titian. The sculptor and painter were in fact friends, and their portraits, together with that of Aretino, are among the six which peer out from the door (Aretino top right, Titian opposite and Sansovino below him). It is tempting to suggest that these portraits were incorporated in the door to record the help Titian and Aretino afforded Sansovino when he was imprisoned in 1545 (see p. 96).

The ticket for the Pala d'Oro also gives admission to the *tesoro* —the **treasury**, entered through a Moorish horseshoe arch in the south transept. There are objects of many periods among this glittering hoard of gold, silver, onyx, rock crystal and enamelled glass, those of the Byzantine being the most interesting. A dark red glass bowl decorated in enamel with nude figures and classical busts is a fine example of the eleventh-century Byzantine classical "Renaissance." The so-called crown of Leo VI, decorated with enamel discs of Saints and an Emperor, was made in Constantinople between 886 and 912. It was probably the rim of some chalice like those nearby made of onyx and adorned with enamel plaques in the second half of the tenth century. An enamelled reliquary, with the Crucifixion in the centre, and an icon of the Archangel Gabriel (on the wall by the door) were made at about the same time and they similarly show the increasing tendency to depersonalise the human face and form into a pattern of glowing colour. Slightly later in date is an alabaster paten with jewels *en cabochon* set round the edge and an enamelled plaque of Christ in the centre. Here it is worth noting the mathematical symbolism of the six circles within a circle—for in Byzantium six was considered the perfect number. (As Methodios noted, " divided by 3 it becomes 2, divided by 2 it becomes 3, divided by 6 it becomes 1: and 2 plus 3 plus 1 equals 6.) All those works reveal the Byzantine preoccupation with symbolism as well as with richness, colour and texture. And they provide a key to the understanding of Byzantine art. For it is important to remember that in Byzantium, as in China, there was no dividing line between the major and minor arts. It would not be going too far to say that all Byzantine arts, including architecture, aspired to the jewel-like

The Companion Guide to Venice

delicacy and richness of an enamelled reliquary. In the Treasury there is a twelfth-century reliquary of gold and silver in the form of a church—it should be regarded as an ideal of what a church should look like rather than the model of a building. Had Byzantine architects been able to build with gold and silver and precious stones they would undoubtedly have done so.

A narrow doorway by the main entrance to the church opens on to the winding staircase which leads up to the **museo** (in theory open from 9.30–6)—a well-arranged collection of fragments of fresco and mosaics, textiles and carved standards. It is worth visiting for its own sake and still more because it gives access to the loggia for a closer look at the horses, and the catwalks traversing the nave and transepts of the church, for a closer look at the mosaics and a general view of the undulating pattern of marbles which carpets the floor.

CHAPTER 3

The Doges' Palace: The Structure of the Republic

San Marco illustrates Venice's relations with Byzantium and her growth from an insignificant city state to a great imperial power. The Doges' Palace illustrates the political structure of the Serene Republic and its development from a form of Roman democracy to oligarchy. It is to this aspect rather than to the aesthetic qualities of the painted and sculptured decorations which dignify the various rooms that I shall devote most of this chapter. For as San Marco is more than the Ducal chapel, so the palace is more than the residence of the Doges. Comprising council chambers, courts, a torture chamber and prisons besides the private apartments of the head of state, one might liken it to a combination of the palaces of St. James's and Westminster with the law courts thrown in for good measure.

The Doges' Palace is the work of several centuries. After many rebuildings it began to take its present form early in the fourteenth century. Work began at the angle between the Molo and the canal dividing the palace from the prisons. In the mid-sixteenth century a large part of the fabric was destroyed by fire but the more conservative councillors saw to it that the palace was rebuilt in its former shape rather than as a grandiose Renaissance structure according to the plans which Palladio and others had been prompt to offer.

The form of the building is unusual, with two loggias, one of simple Gothic arches, the other of very rich and lacy arcading, supporting a mass of masonry above. By all the laws of architecture such an arrangement ought to look uncomfortable if not downright ugly. But Venice tended to make rather than to follow architectural rules and, in fact, the effect of the building is remarkably successful. For the pink and white facing of the upper walls, worked in a kind

41

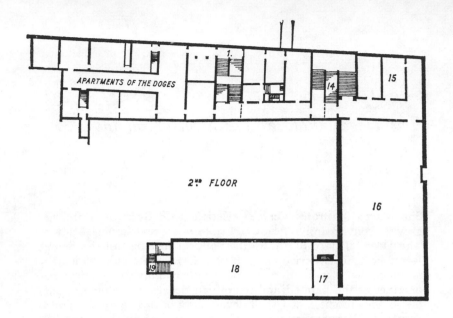

APARTMENTS OF THE DOGES

2ᴺᴰ FLOOR

THE DOGES' PALACE

1. Scala d'Oro
2. Atrio quadrato
3. Sala delle Quattro Porte
4. Anticollegio
5. Sala del Collegio
6. Sala del Senato
7. Ante-chapel
8. Chapel
9. Consilgio dei Dieci
10. Sala della Bussola

11. Capi del Consiglio dei Dieci
12. Inquisitori
13. Armoury of the Council of Ten
14. Scala dei Censori
15. Sala del Guariento
16. Sala del Maggior Consiglio
17. Sala Quarantia Civil Nuova
18. Sala dello Scrutinio
19. Staircase down to first floor

3ᴿᴰ FLOOR

of damask pattern, gives a buoyant lightness to this area. And one thinks of the delicate arcading at the bottom less as a support for the masonry than as a richly tasselled fringe, drawing down the upper part of the wall to hold it taut. The general effect is of a table covered by a rich cloth which so catches the eye that the existence of a solid framework beneath is taken for granted.

In the lower arcade, called the *broglio*—where merchants and politicans would walk and gossip and, from the name of the place, involve themselves in an occasional imbroglio—the capitals are carved with heads and allegorical figures, dating from the late fourteenth and early fifteenth centuries (though many have been restored and some replaced by modern copies). At the three angles there are larger carvings above the capitals—the Drunkenness of Noah (by the Ponte della Paglia), Adam and Eve (between the Piazzetta and Molo) and the Judgement of Solomon (by San Marco). The first two are by Venetian Gothic sculptors, the third which is slightly later (1424–38) shows Tuscan influence and may be by some Florentine like Niccolò di Pietro Lamberti. The somewhat strange choice of subject matter for the two looking on to the Molo can be explained only by the fact that both represent the weakness of mortal man.

The palace is divided from San Marco by the **Porta della Carta** which forms the main entrance to the courtyard. One of the richest examples of Venetian Gothic architecture and sculpture, this splendidly florid gateway was executed between 1438 and 1442 by Bartolomeo and Giovanni Bon. The figure of the Doge is however a modern replacement of the original which was smashed in 1797.

Inside the courtyard, homogeneity gives way to a medley of styles united only by a desire for impressive magnificence. Renaissance classicism predominates over the Gothic. A vast and imposing staircase, guarded by colossal statues of Mars and Neptune—by Sansovino who finished them in 1567—leads up to the first floor loggia. This staircase is not for us, however. We ascend that in the south-east corner by the ticket office (open from 9.30–4). The way in which the public is directed round the palace varies from time to time: the plan opposite will help you to identify the rooms if you cannot follow the itinerary suggested in the following paragraphs.

A group of three rooms on the first floor, called the Avogaria,

43

was originally the office of the three Avogadori de Comun, lawyers who kept the Libro d'Oro in which the names of noble families were registered and were also responsible for the prosecution of certain legal cases. Their rooms are hung with paintings, mainly of the seventeenth century.

You now climb up to the second floor by the famous **Scala d'Oro,** one of the most impressive staircases to be found anywhere. It took its present form in the mid-sixteenth century when it was decorated with gilt stucco reliefs by Alessandro Vittoria and painted panels by Battista Franco. Turning to the right, you enter the **apartments of the Doge**—first the room where he would assemble with the Procurators and others to process out on ceremonial occasions, then the large ante-chamber, its walls painted in the mid-eighteenth century with maps to show, rather optimistically, the extent of the Venetian dominions and, on that facing you, the voyages made by Marco Polo and other notable Venetian travellers. There follows a succession of rooms, some with massive, handsomely carved sixteenth-century chimney-pieces. A few works of sculpture have been assembled here, notably Antonio Rizzo's " Adam and Eve " which used to stand in the *cortile* where they have been replaced by bronze copies. Carved in the 1480s, they are among the major masterpieces of Venetian sculpture and seem to reveal a debt to the paintings of Giovanni Bellini. They are modelled with a much greater regard for the structure of the naked body and are less under the influence of antique marbles than most Renaissance nude statues. According to Coryate's *Crudities,* the Duke of Mantua vainly attempted to buy the Eve for her weight in gold. Beyond the grand reception rooms lie a series of much simpler apartments now used for a small collection of pictures which includes some macabre fantasies by Hieronymus Bosch and his followers.

In these rooms the Doges passed their nights, and much of their days, from the time of their election until death. Magnificently robed, splendidly lodged, attended by serried ranks of obsequious servants, yet impotent, anonymous, unloved, the Doge was a prisoner of the state. The Venetians evolved the first system of constitutional monarchy and they spared no pains to make sure that the head of state was kept firmly within his constitutional limits. After 1250, the oath he took at his coronation bound him to execute the orders of the Great Council, or any other council it might elect. He normally presided over council meetings but could do no more than put his seal to their decisions. The Great Council, on the other hand, could meet without him and act on its own. He was not permitted to trade, either in person or by proxy, he was not allowed to accept gifts or acts of homage that were not clearly intended for the state as a whole. No member of his family might hold office under the government and his sons were exempt from election to the executive councils. Confined by all these restrictions, it is hardly surprising that the Doges were rather a dull lot, no more interesting as personalities than George I and George II. With the exception of Enrico Dandolo who, though blind, led the Venetian forces to the sack of Constantinople in 1204, the only two who stand out in history are Marino Falier and Francesco Foscari. Falier was beheaded for a treasonable attempt to alter the constitution. Foscari was forced to see his son banished for treason and then deposed. With these examples before them, the later Doges fulfilled their decorative roles in the complaisant and anonymous manner the Serenissima demanded. Coryate was told that the two columns from Acre, outside the Porta della Carta (see p. 32) were placed there to form a gallows for any Doge who misbehaved—and although he was misinformed the story accurately reflects the Venetian attitude to their head of state.

The next flight of the Scala d'Oro leads up to the top floor and most of the council chambers. The first room (2) has a ceiling by Tintoretto and assistants, and leads into the Sala delle Quattro Porte (3), one of the most impressive in the palace with an exuberantly rich stucco ceiling surrounding paintings by Tintoretto. Next door, in the **Anti-Collegio** (4) there are four more Tintorettos, including one of his greatest, *Bacchus and Ariadne Crowned by Venus*, Paolo Veronese's masterly *Rape of Europa*, and Jacopo Bassano's *Return of Jacob with his Family*. The four Tintorettos were painted as an allegory of concord with, of course, additional propagandist significance—for instance, Venus (love) unites Bacchus (the Adriatic) with Ariadne (Venice) over whose head she places the starry crown of supremacy. It forms a fitting introduction to the **Sala del Collegio** (5) with a ceiling painted by Veronese in his most elegantly opulent manner and, behind the thrones, his vast canvas showing the Admiral of the Venetian fleet giving thanks to God for the victory of Lepanto. In this room the Doge surrounded by the College—the twenty-five members of the executive cabinet elected from the Great Council—met to discuss matters of state. And here they received ambassadors of foreign powers who were no doubt reduced to a suitably abject physical and mental condition after the long climb up four flights of stairs and the progress through so much gilded, stuccoed and frescoed magnificence. It was a characteristically Venetian stroke of genius to make their illustrious visitors undergo such an ordeal. One can almost hear the puffing and blowing of some pompous emissary only too delighted to fall on his knees before the rulers of the Serenissima.

The Sala del Collegio leads into the larger **Sala del Senato,** the seat of the Senate or upper house of the Venetian parliament and its legislative body. Here the Doge and members of the College together with some two hundred elected senators met for debates. So far as the decoration is concerned, this room has a splendidly gilded effect but the standard of paintings—mostly by artists of the generation younger than Tintoretto—has begun to fall off. Leading out of the Senate, behind the Ducal rostrum, there is an ante-chapel and a chapel, both with pretty eighteenth-century ceilings and the latter with a handsome *Virgin and Child* by Sansovino.

If you leave the Senate by the door at the other end, you will pass back through the Sala delle Quattro Porte to the **Sala del Consiglio dei Dieci** (9). This room originally had one of the best ceilings in the palace, dominated by Veronese's central panel which is now in the Louvre. However, Veronese is still represented by the oblong panel with *Juno Offering the Ducal Crown to Venice* another example of mythology conscripted into Venetian service) and a smaller oval of a turbanned Oriental with a girl. This was the room in which the notorious Council of Ten met and deliberated. Called into being as an emergency act in the fourteenth century, this body gradually came to occupy one of the most important roles in the machinery of government. Its members held a position below the Collegio and roughly parallel with the Senate whose functions they quietly usurped. For while the ordinary business of State was debated in the Senate, all extraordinary, and thus highly important, matters were discussed by the Ten whose meetings were held in secret and consequently feared. In the next room, the **Sala della Bussola** (10), those

summoned by the Ten waited to be examined. In a corner there
is a famous Bocca de Leone—one of the boxes into which secret
denunciations were dropped. Much romantic nonsense has been
written about such letters and it is worth recording that all anonymous denunciations which did not cite at least two witnesses were
burnt unless the Ten and the Ducal Councillors by a five-sixths
majority declared that the accusations contained matters affecting
the State.

The next room (11) belonged to the three magistrates elected
from the Council of Ten to read letters and call assemblies. Leading
out of it is the more sombre room of the Inquisitors of State—a body
consisting of two members from the Ten and one ducal councillor
who investigated cases of suspected treason. From here a staircase
leads to the conveniently close torture chamber and another to the
Piombi, the prisons under the leads. A third staircase which we,
more happily, may take, leads into the **armoury** (13).

Among an abundance of halberds, pikes, swords, cuirasses,
helmets and elaborate and primitive firing pieces in this armoury, a
few objects are outstanding. There is a mounted figure in sixteenth-
century armour (popularly but mistakenly associated with the
Condottiere Gattamalata), a child's suit of armour pathetically
found after the battle of Marignano in 1515, and a suit presented
to the Republic by Henry IV of France in 1603. One or two notable
works of sculpture are also shown here—fine bronze busts of
Sebastiano Venier and Agostino Barbaro by Tiziano Aspetti and
a fantastic baroque bust of Francesco Morosini by Filippo Parodi.

The **Scala dei Censori** leads down to the second floor. Here
a small room (15) is devoted to some rather pale fragments of
fresco—all that remains of the *Paradise* or *Coronation of the Virgin*
which the Paduan artist, Guariento, painted in 1365 for the Sala
del Maggior Consiglio which was burnt out by the great fire of 1577.

In the **Sala del Maggior Consiglio** (16)—perhaps the most
pompously imposing room in all Europe—you can see the picture
which Tintoretto painted in place of Guariento's. Though largely
the work of assistants, it is a painting of great splendour and a
masterpiece of dynamic composition. As in Guariento's fresco,
the subject matter, following the 30th canto of Dante's *Paradiso*, is
based on the order of the Litany with angels and saints ranged in
their proper rank—Christ and His Mother in the centre at the top,
then the archangels and angels, then notable Old Testament

figures, the Evangelists (St. Mark prominent among them) and Fathers of the Church, while the rest is given up to the saints. Paintings which Gentile da Fabriano, Pisanello, Bellini, Carpaccio, Titian and others, including Tintoretto and Veronese, had executed for the other walls and ceiling were replaced after the fire by works by the best painters available in the last quarter of the sixteenth century. But, unfortunately, with the notable exceptions of Tintoretto and Veronese, who painted the best panels on the ceiling, they were not a very gifted group. Some of the paintings on the walls barely surpass a modest level of decorative competence. As one might expect, all the scenes except the *Paradiso*—and perhaps that also, for Venice placed herself under the special protection of the Virgin—reflect the glory of Venice and illustrate scenes from her real and mythical history: land battles, sea fights, triumphs, diplomatic victories and various apotheoses of the Venetian state. The frieze is decorated with portraits (mostly imaginary) of all the first seventy-six Doges with the conspicuous exception of Marino Falier whose place is filled by a black curtain inscribed: *Hic est locus Marini Falethri decapitati pro criminibus*—a salutary warning to his successors on the Ducal throne.

The Sala del Maggior Consiglio was the seat of the lower house of the Venetian parliament. In the earliest days, Venice was a true democracy and all important decisions, like the election of Doges, were taken at tumultuous meetings of the whole body of citizens. With the growth of the population such meetings grew riotous and an elective system was introduced whereby every sector of the confederation annually chose delegates for the assembly. But even these democratic parliaments had many disadvantages in a period of political instability which was the direct result of increasing prosperity. By the early thirteenth century a new aristocracy had arisen, composed of families enriched by colonial and commercial expansion in the Eastern Mediterranean. Every election became a contest between these new men and the old aristocracy descended from the original leaders of the Venetian confederation. When the office of Doge fell vacant in 1289 the citizens elected by popular clamour an aged representative of the old aristocracy, Jacopo Tiepolo, who declined the honour and retired to terra firma. Seizing their opportunity, the new men elected Pietro Gradenigo, a young and ruthless member of their own party. And in 1297 Gradenigo moved the famous Serrata del

The Piazzetta. *Above*, in the early morning, looking across to the island of San Giorgio Maggiore. *Below*, the columns of St. Mark and St. Theodore, with the Doges' Palace on the left, bask in the mid-day sun

The Drunkenness of Noah, an early 15th century carving on the Doges'
Palace by the Ponte della Paglia

Maggior Consiglio—an act which abolished popular elections and restricted the membership of the great council to those who could prove that a paternal ancestor had sat in it. Besides excluding the populace from the government, the act tended to favour the politically active new men at the expense of the old aristocracy, many of whose members had never stood for election to the Council. In 1300 there was a popular revolt but its leaders were enticed into the Doges' Palace never to emerge alive. Ten years later the conservatives, headed by Bajamonte Tiepolo, staged a rebellion, but their forces were routed. Henceforth, Venice was peacefully divided between the nobles who by right of birth alone had seats in the Great Council and the populace who could never hope to obtain them. (Not until the seventeenth century could patents of nobility be purchased.)

This move from democracy to oligarchy—in many ways reminiscent of the Augustan Revolution in Rome—proved a blessing to the " eldest child of Liberty." The outcome of increased prosperity in the thirteenth century, it made possible the further expansion of the fourteenth and fifteenth centuries. By eliminating the demagogue from the political scene, it preserved the State against the demagogue's half-brother, the tyrant. It placed the government in the hands of a large body of men whose commercial prosperity and mutual jealousy prevented any one family from acquiring supreme influence or power. So efficacious was the system created by the Serrata del Maggior Consiglio that it survived unchanged for half a millenium.

The function of the Maggior Consiglio during these centuries was a purely elective one. It met in the great hall to elect members of Senate and other government offices (there was an election of some kind at least once a week). It also elected the first of the series of committees which elected the Doge. Every nobleman over the age of twenty-five had a seat in it, provided that he had not committed the unpardonable indiscretion of marrying a commoner which excluded him and all his heirs.

The Sala del Maggior Consiglio was not, however, reserved exclusively for parliamentary affairs. On occasion it was used as a banqueting hall. Henry III was entertained here in 1574 when 3000 guests were invited and the sideboards were loaded with silver and gold worth 200,000 crowns. At another sixteenth-century banquet the guests were delighted to discover that all the

49

objects on the tables—loaves, plates, knives, forks, glasses, table-cloths, napkins and statuettes designed by Sansovino—were made of sugar.

It was in this same room, on Friday, 12th May, 1797, that the final act in the history of the Serene Republic was played out as the last Doge, Ludovico Manin, announced his acceptance of Napoleon's ultimatum. The great hall seemed filled with indistinc. shudders and whispers, wrote Ippolito Nievo describing the eventt " In that dim, withdrawn spot silence and sadness reigned. The Doge rose to his feet, pale, trembling, before the sovereign council of which he was the representative, and to whom he dared to propose an act of cowardice without parallel." After reading the propositions of the French he " shamelessly proposed the abolition of the old form of government and the establishment of a democracy. For half such a crime Marino Falier had died on the scaffold. Ludovico Manin proceeded with his stutterings to dishonour himself, the Great Council, and his country; and not a hand was raised to pluck from him the ducal mantle and break his head upon the pavement on which the ministers of kings and the legates of Popes had knelt. . . . Suddenly, a few musket volleys were heard: the Doge stopped in consternation and made as if to descend the steps of the throne." A crowd of frightened Patricians gathered round him crying " to the ballot." "Outside the people howled with fury; within all was confusion and terror. With cries, jostling, haste and fear " the assembly abdicated its rights and established a provisional government to anticipate Napoleon's demands. " The Doge rushed to his apartments, plucking off the insignia of his office as he went, ordering that the ducal hangings should be stripped from the walls." Corrupt, impotent, ruined, Venice had long outlived her days of wealth and glory. Yet her passing demanded a tribute of regret, nobly paid in Wordsworth's famous sonnet:

Men are we, and must grieve when even the Shade
Of that which once was great is pass'd away.

Leading out of the Sala del Maggior Consiglio is the Sala della Quarantia Civil Nuova, the court of civil appeal for Venetians of the terra firma. In the next room, the **Sala dello Scrutinio** (18), the various commissions for the election of a Doge met, debated and voted. The process was one of Chinese complexity, involving no fewer than nine ballotings to elect the committee of forty-one who elected the Doge. Apart from a Tintoretto on the wall towards the courtyard, the paintings were executed by minor artists of the sixteenth century, including Palma Giovane who was responsible for the long *Last Judgement*—a painfully inadequate imitation of Tintoretto. Running around the ceiling there is a frieze of portraits of the last forty-two Doges, the first seven by Tintoretto and the rest done from the life by later painters. At the end of the room a triumphal archway celebrates the victories of Francesco Morosini in the Peleponnesus, the last important victories achieved by the Venetian State.

In the dim annals of the Venetian Doges, Morosini shines out as a personality on account of his career before his election. He became Captain General of the army in 1658 when Venice had already been for thirteen years involved in the war of Candia—a vain attempt to preserve Crete from the Turks. After a further eleven years of fighting, which occasioned a ruinous drain on the Republic's resources, Morosini capitulated and obtained remarkably favourable terms from the Turks who were no less weary of the war than he. On his return to Venice he was, naturally, put on trial for cowardice and inefficiency but contrived to acquit himself well. In 1684 when Venice joined the Holy League against Turkey—whose armies had reached the very gates of Vienna—he was once again Captain General. Leading a campaign in Greece he won back the whole of the Morea. But his victory was accompanied with one of the saddest losses in European history, for while he was besieging Athens a Venetian cannon ball struck the Turkish powder magazine on the Acropolis and set off the explosion which wrought such havoc to the Parthenon. However, he returned triumphantly to Venice bearing with him two large marble lions which had guarded the Sacred Way and Piraeus harbour (see p. 77). In 1688 he was elected Doge but five years later he was once again called to command the Venetian army which was suffering reverses in Greece for want of a capable general. He was thus the first Doge to leave Venice since Enrico Dandolo. But after an initial victory he fell ill and died. Although he became a popular symbol of Venetian power, his were Pyrrhic victories which proved disastrous to the exchequer and contributed to the final ruin of the Republic.

A staircase (19) leads from the Sala del Scrutinio to the Loggia on the floor below. As you walk round you pass, on the south side,

the Sala del Piovego (no admission) where the Doges lay in state.
Newly elected Doges were brought here at the end of the ceremonies
of their coronation and were addressed in the following brutal
words: " Your Serenity has come here in the pride of life to take
possession of the palace; but I warn you that when dead, your
eyes, brains and bowels will be removed. You will be brought to
this very spot, and here you will lie for three days before they
bury you." It was the last clause in the sentence of life imprisonment.

But to turn from metaphorical to real **prisons.** Notice boards
point the way to the Prigioni—and no visit to the Palazzo Ducale
is complete without a glimpse into them. The entrance is by way
of the seventeenth-century Bridge of Sighs. The days of political
unrest were long past before this famous bridge was built and only
one political prisoner ever passed across it—for this reason the
romantic W. D. Howells called it a " pathetic swindle." The
prisons themselves are as dark and dismal as any of their period.
Dickens gloated over them in an ecstasy of horror and with much
lip-smacking claimed: " I set my foot upon the spot where, at the
same dread hour (midnight) the shriven prisoner was strangled;
and struck my hand upon the guilty door—low-browed and
stealthy—through which the lumpish sack was carried out in a
boat and rowed away and dropped where it was death to cast a
net." These lower prisons, called the *pozzi*, were in fact reserved
for petty thieves and other ruffians; and although they cannot
have been comfortable they were no less hygienic than those in
nineteenth-century England. In 1746 a Greek priest left them at
the age of eighty after forty years confinement and he was said to
be in perfect health. The *piombi*, the prisons under the leads of the
Doges' Palace, were, as Balzac pointed out, no worse than many
a garret in Paris. Casanova, who made a daring escape from
them, records that he passed a relatively happy confinement,
diverting himself with the records of a scabrous lawsuit among the
archives in an adjoining room. When, in the first flush of democracy in 1797, the revolutionaries burst open the prisons they were
disappointed to find none of their languishing fellow travellers—
the *pozzi* were empty and the *piombi* contained only four common
criminals.

CHAPTER 4

The Scuole: Titian and Tintoretto

Scuola di San Giovanni Evangelista—Santa Maria dei Frari—Scuola di San Rocco—San Rocco—Scuola dei Calegheri—Palazzo Centani (Casa Goldoni)

By all the laws of political science, the quickest way to bring about a revolution is by excluding a prosperous middle class from all say in government. Yet in Venice a muzzled and politically impotent middle class seems to have lived fairly happily for nearly five hundred years under an all powerful oligarchy. One of the explanations for this strange state of affairs is to be found in the *scuole* which provided a substitute for political activity. These lay confraternities are of considerable interest both for this reason and because their wealth enabled them to play an important part in the patronage of Venetian artists.

The Venetian *scuole*—the word cannot be translated as schools without leading to misconceptions—were associations of laymen similar to the Livery companies of the City of London and combined with the charitable aims of the Freemasons and the devotional practices of religious fellowships. Their members practised a common craft (cobblers, barbers, painters and so on), had a common national ancestry (the Slavs, Greeks and Albanians), were united in a particular form of charitable service (the members of one *scuola* visited prisoners and paid for the last rites to those who were executed), or professed devotion to a particular religious cult. Members bound themselves to certain religious duties and to the assistance of their fellows, especially in sickness. They elected their own officers. And they paid an annual subscription which financed the organisation and usually left a balance which was spent on the decoration of their premises. The magnificence of their buildings, many of which are decorated by the greatest of

53

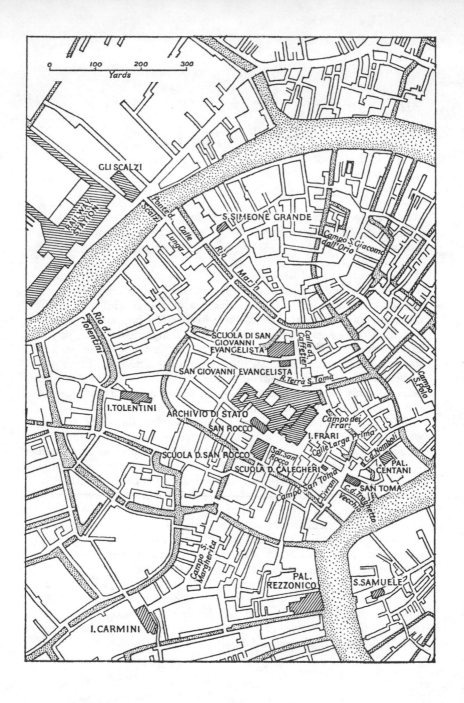

The Scuole

Venetian artists, reveal the wealth of these institutions, especially the religious ones, and suggest the passionate devotion of their members. Napoleon closed them all, but two were resurrected and still survive as charitable associations—the Scuola Grande di San Rocco and the Scuola di San Giorgio degli Schiavoni.

One of the earliest and most interesting of the *scuole* is that of **San Giovanni Evangelista.** It was founded in the thirteenth century as a confraternity of flagellants who walked in religious processions whipping their bared backs with scourges and sprinkling the pavements with blood. Its buildings are a five-minutes' walk from the railway station. (Cross the Scalzi Bridge, take the Calle Lunga, cross the bridge over the Rio Marin, turn right, cross the Rio again by the next bridge and follow it as far as the Calle del Caffetier off which the courtyard of the *scuola* opens.)

The courtyard of the Scuola di San Giovanni Evangelista is a little masterpiece of Venetian Renaissance architecture—an exquisite composition of grey and white marble, stone, brick and stucco, and as Ruskin remarked " the most characteristic example in Venice of the architecture that Carpaccio, Cima and John Bellini loved." Yet this apparently harmonious courtyard is in fact the work of several different periods and architects. The façade of the *scuola*, with its tall ogee windows dates from the 1450s and incorporates two little reliefs carved, as the inscription reveals, in 1349: a Virgin and Child and a little group of members of the confraternity kneeling before their patron saint. The elegant renaissance screen, dominated by St. John's eagle, the colonnade of Corinthian pilasters and the frieze crisply carved with foliage, were added in the early 1480s, possibly to the design of Pietro Lombardo. And the main door to the *scuola*, with kneeling figures carved on the lintel, was erected in 1512.

Inside the *scuola* there is a large cavernous hall littered with fragments of carving on the ground floor (ring the bell for admission: open every morning from Monday to Friday except holidays). The upper floor is reached by a double staircase of serene and exquisite beauty, lit by handsome round-headed windows, domed and vaulted with ribs of grey marble blossoming into roses. Built to the design of Mauro Coducci in the last years of the fifteenth century, it is marked by that spacious lightness which is one of the finest characteristics of Venetian Renaissance architecture. The large upper room, redecorated by Giorgio Massari in 1727, is as rich and fussy

55

as the staircase is simple and elegant—with a patterned marble floor and large paintings on the walls and ceiling (the most notable are two L-shaped visions of the Apocalypse by Domenico Tiepolo in the corners far from the altar). The oratory, or room of the Cross, leading out of the *Salone*, was made to house a relic of the True Cross and decorated with a fascinating series of paintings now, alas, in the Accademia where they lose much of their significance (see p. 127). The relic remains in a fine Gothic reliquary behind the doors over the altar. On the ceiling there is a painting by Francesco Maggiotto framed with a ripple of white and gold stucco curlicues.

From the Scuola di San Giovanni Evangelista, the Calle del Caffettier leads to the Rio Terrà San Tomà (the term *rio terrà* refers to a canal filled in to make a street). Here a solemn and very solid early nineteenth-century building houses the Archivio di Stato—the great collection of Venetian state papers of outstanding interest to historians for the numerous reports which the eagle-eyed ambassadors of the Serenissima wrote of the political life and intrigues of the capitals they visited.

If you turn left in front of the Archivio di Stato and then cross the Ponte San Stin you will see the soaring Gothic façade of Santa Maria Gloriosa dei Frari, usually known as **I Frari.** The fabric was begun in 1340, the façade finished in the 1440s and the interior in 1469. Built for the Franciscan friars (or *frari*), it is similar to many churches constructed for this order elsewhere in Italy, with the addition of a very few characteristically Venetian trimmings, like the little stone canopies perched on the gable of the main façade. The materials are as simple and as practical as a friar's russet habit—reddish brown brick with a very sparing use of terracotta and white stone. The interior (door by the campanile on the north side: admission 200 lire) is similarly plain and adapted to the Franciscan ideal of poverty, designed to provide a handsome but economical auditorium for sermons, and altars for the Mass. No attempt was made to embellish the elegant pattern of the vaulting ribs or to disguise the transverse beams. Indeed, decorations were everywhere kept to the barest minimum even on the capitals of the sturdy columns. Despite the addition of numerous paintings and sepulchral monuments in later periods, the church retains a dignified air of Apostolic austerity.

The church is rich in sculpture of all styles from the Gothic to

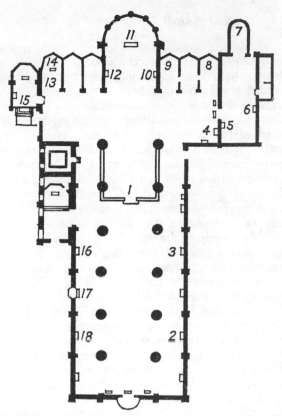

S. MARIA DEI FRARI

1. The Friars' Choir—screen and statues by Pietro Lombardo and assistants: carved wood stalls by Marco Cozzi (1468)
2. Monument to Titian (1852) by the Zandomeneghi brothers
3. Statue of St. Jerome by Alessandro Vittoria
4. Tomb of the Blessed Pacifico (c. 1440)
5. Reliquary of the Holy Blood, attributed to Pietro Lombardo
6. Reliquary alter by Cabianca with carved wood statues by A. Brustolon (1711)
7. Altarpiece by Giovanni Bellini
8. Polyptych by Bartolomeo Vivarini (1482)
9. Statue of St. John by Donatello (1451)
10. Monument to Doge Francesco Foscari by Antonio Bregno
11. *The Assumption* by Titian (1518)
12. Monument to Doge Niccolò Tron by Antonio Rizzo
13. Memorial to the musician Claudio Monteverdi
14. Altarpiece by Alvise Vivarini and Marco Basaiti (1503)
15. Statue of St. John by Sansovino (c. 1550)
16. Virgin and Child with members of the Pesaro family by Titian (1526)
17. Monument to Doge Giovanni Pesaro by M. Barthel (1669)
18. Monument to Antonio Canova (1827)

the neo-classical. In the south transept there is the flamboyant Gothic tomb (4) of the Blessed Pacifico, in marble and terracotta which must have looked still richer in its original brightly painted and gilded state. Nearby there is the earliest of the equestrian monuments in the city, commemorating a *condottiere*, Paolo Savelli, who fell while leading the Venetian army against the Carraresi of Padua in 1405. The Renaissance is introduced by Donatello's painted wood statue of St. John the Baptist in the Florentine chapel (9)—a noble figure, carved with a naturalism and humane pathos which must have astonished, if it did not shock, the Gothic sculptors working in Venice when it arrived here from Padua in 1451. The contrast in technique and artistic quality between this statue and the two Saints on either side provides a striking illustration of the way in which Donatello leaped ahead of his contemporaries. Antonio Bregno's vast and rather confused Foscari monument, to the right of the high altar, is still Gothic in form though it was carved in the 1450s and incorporates such Renaissance elements as two figures in ancient Roman armour. Facing it, Antonio Rizzo's monument to Niccolò Tron, of some two decades later, reveals a more completely assimilated Renaissance style in its architecture, ornamentation and, especially, its allegorical figures in tight-fitting drapery, page boys, and reliefs of *putti*. Yet Rizzo's assistants who carved the figures on the upper tier were clearly used to working in the Gothic style. The classical poise and repose of the Renaissance is better represented by another statue of St. John the Baptist carved in the 1550s by another Florentine, Jacopo Sansovino (15). In the nave there is an outstandingly fine statue of St. Jerome by Alessandro Vittoria, a work of great spiritual beauty. Originally it was the centrepiece of a very elaborate stuccoed altar of which no more than the statues of two saints and two sibyls now survive. The baroque style makes its bow with the monument to Doge Giovanni Pesaro (died 1659) by a German sculptor Melchiorre Barthel (17). A weighty fantasy of blackamoors, skeletons and skulls, it is one of the many examples of the Venetian taste for the bizarre. There is another splendidly pompous baroque monument above the west door, commemorating Senator Girolamo Garzoni who stands heavily periwigged listening to the confidences of an angel fluttering beside his head.

The two most prominent monuments in the church are those to

Canova and Titian, facing each other across the nave. That to Canova (18) was carved by his pupils and is similar in design, but alas not in execution, to a model he had made for a monument to Titian and later used for his monument to Maria Christine in Vienna. But this vast pile of Carrara marble enshrines no more than the heart of the great sculptor whose body was buried in his native village of Possagno (see p. 251). The Titian monument (2) was carved by two of Canova's protégés between 1838 and 1852 after neo-classical inspiration had gone rather stale.

The church contains three masterpieces of painting: one by Bellini and two by Titian. **Giovanni Bellini's triptych** on the sacristy altar (7) represents the Virgin and Child with Saints Nicholas, Peter, Benedict and Paul and is still set in its original frame which continues the architecture of the picture. It is a heavenly vision of serene joy, suffused by the tranquil spirit of the prayer inscribed in gold mosaic above the Virgin's head. Painted in 1488, it represents the perfection of the tradition in which Titian, then a boy in Cadore, was to be trained and from which he was to break away.

Static, calm and ineloquent, the Bellini perfectly expresses the mood of *quattrocento* painting in Venice. Titian's great **Assumption** on the high altar (11), painted exactly thirty years later, in 1518, is dynamic, turbulent and rhetorical, setting the tone for the further development of art in Venice and, indeed, all Europe. A seventeenth-century writer, Ridolfi, relates that Titian's work on this painting was frequently interrupted by the friars who expressed dissatisfaction and proffered advice. Hearing this, the Emperor's envoy offered a large sum for the picture, but the friars prudently refused to surrender it, " recognizing finally that art was not their profession, and that the use of the breviary did not convey a knowledge of painting." Whether it is true or not, the story illustrates what must have been the attitude of many Venetians to this revolutionary work, the first in which Titian displayed the full range of his genius.

Looking at the picture to-day, one is struck first by its opulence of colour—reds as rich and glowing as oriental rubies, yellows of heavy beaten gold, blues of lapis lazuli. Then the figure of the Virgin commands the eye. As Berenson remarked, she " soars heavenward, not helpless in the arms of angels, but borne up by the fullness of life within her, and by the feeling that the universe

59

is naturally her own, and that nothing can check her course. The angels seem to be there only to sing the victory of a human being over his environment. They are embodied joys, acting on our nerves like the rapturous outburst of the orchestra at the end of *Parsifal.*" This almost miraculous effect is achieved partly by the astonishing realism of the shadow which the figure of the Virgin casts on the Apostles, throwing the face of one into complete darkness. And it is partly due to the intricacy of the composition which is based on the dynamic line curving upward from the bare leg of an Apostle on the right, through his upstretched arm, and then through the body of the Virgin to the face of God the Father. Other figures, like the cherub whose foot almost touches an Apostle's head, accentuate this thrusting movement which gives the picture its power.

The other painting by Titian, the **Madonna of Ca' Pesaro** (16) was finished in 1526. Its colour is no less brilliant, its composition no less revolutionary. Defying the old rule that the most important figure in an altarpiece should be given the central place, Titian created an illusion of greater depth by placing the Virgin and Child boldly off centre, in an elevated position dominating the scene. The composition is based on a reversed S curving up from the group of kneeling figures on the right, by way of those on the left, through the heads of St. Peter and the Virgin to end in the pair of cherubs holding a cross and standing on a cloud which drifts in front of the columns—a typically Venetian touch of *trompe l'oeil* wit.

This is not in any sense a mystical picture. It celebrates the glory of the House of Pesaro whose gilded banner is flaunted on the left. The artist's belief in the importance of the individual is apparent in the finely observed portraits of the Pesaro family, one of whose younger members stares out at us with the disarming curiosity of a child turning round to watch a late arrival in church. Like so many of Titian's mature works, the whole picture is a glorification of the visible and tangible world. St. Peter is clearly about to admit the Pesaro to the only heaven they would deign to inhabit, where silks are glossier, brocades richer and velvets more caressingly soft. The mood is similar to that of one of the many sonnets in which Gaspara Stampa poured out her passion for the young Conte di Collalto, some two decades after the picture was painted.

Io non v'invidio punto, angeli santi,
le vostre tante glorie e tanti beni,
e que' disir di ciò che braman pieni,
stando voi sempre a l'alto Sire avanti;
perchè i delitti miei son tali e tanti,
che non posson capire in cor terreni,
mentr'ho davanti i lumi almi e sereni,
di cui conven che sempre scriva e canti.

E come in ciel gran refrigerio e vita
dal volto Suo solete voi fruire,
tal io qua giù da la beltà infinita.
In questo sol vincete il mio gioire,
che la vostra è eterna e stabilita,
e la mia gloria può tosto finire.

(I don't envy you at all, holy angels, your many glories and blessings and your fulfilled desires, who stand ever before Our Lord; because my joys are such that they cannot be comprehended by earthly hearts while I have before me those divine calm eyes of which I must always write and sing. As you in heaven draw refreshment and light from His Countenance, so do I below from his infinite beauty. Your joys surpass mine only because they are eternal and mine can quickly end.)

Titian, the first fashionable portrait painter in history, the friend of Aretino, the creator of so many seductive Venuses and libidinous fauns, shared with his patrons a strong and well-cultivated taste for the pleasures of the flesh. An accomplished yet quite unservile courtier, he seems to have been born to depict the pleasures and worldly aspirations of the courts of the High Renaissance. But his letters also show him as financially grasping and arrogant, especially to fellow painters whom he regarded as his inferiors. Tradition has it that out of jealousy he expelled Tintoretto from his studio after a single day, and it is tempting to suggest that he did indeed foresee how the younger man would bring his own technical achievements to their logical conclusion—and in a spirit antithetical to his own.

The works of Tintoretto can best be seen in the **Scuola di San Rocco** which stands on the other side of the little Campo at the east end of the Frari church. This imposing structure of white marble, encrusted with discs of porphyry, squares of green marble, and various carved details like the little nightmare monsters at the feet of the columns, was built to the design of Bartolomeo Bon and Antonio Abbondi between 1515 and 1560. Despite a lavish use of classical detail, this building must have shocked classicists of Palladio's generation by its wilful asymmetry no less than its cavalier treatment of the Orders. And even the modern observer feels the dissonance between the lower and the upper stories, no less than between the round-headed windows and their pedimented frames, which belong respectively to the early and middle phases of Venetian Renaissance architecture—the result of a foolhardy attempt to keep up with stylistic changes over a period of half a century. You enter the *scuola* through the far door (now only open in the mornings from 10 till 1). It is now as well to go straight up Abbondi's noble staircase, walk through the Sala Grande to the Sala dell' Albergo where the first paintings Tintoretto executed for the Confraternity may be seen.

Jacopo Robusti, the son of a dyer and called for that reason **Tintoretto,** was born in 1518, the year in which Titian's *Assumption* was completed. Whereas Titian had known the great days of the power, wealth and glory of the Serenissima, had shared its optimism and exulted in its opulent splendour, Tintoretto was born into a Venice already saddened, impoverished and humbled by the League of Cambrai. The former was the child of the humanist Renaissance, the latter grew up in the counter-reformation atmosphere of religious revival. But it was not merely a difference in age that separated the two artists. They represent the twin strains in the Venetian character. Titian answered its craving for sensuous richness: Tintoretto its taste for mystical fantasy. In character as well as in his art, Titian was self-controlled, almost calculating and would correspond at length with his Royal and Imperial patrons about the payment he was to receive for a picture. Tintoretto, who worked mainly for the churches and *scuole* of Venice, was fervently devout, volatile and unworldly. Unlike Titian who travelled widely and frequented the courts of kings, Tintoretto was a stay-at-home, a paterfamilias devoted to his wife and children. He appears to have left Venice on only one occasion, to deliver a series of pictures to Mantua, and then he insisted on taking his wife with him. It is said that he was an accomplished musician but otherwise he was interested in little save his religion and his art; and so great was his urge to paint, especially for religious bodies, that he frequently offered his services free. Never before can a single city have contained two artists so great, so different and so complementary. They have created a lasting division between lovers of Venetian painting. Great collectors have usually admired the worldly Titian above all artists. Ruskin infinitely preferred Tintoretto, and so, incidentally, did Ruskin's other idol, Turner. Recently Jean-Paul Sartre has also championed Tintoretto. But both can be admired if the disparity of their aims is recognised.

A colourful, revealing, and probably true, story relates how Tintoretto began to paint this great series of pictures for the Scuola di San Rocco. In 1564 the Confraternity invited various artists to submit designs for the central ceiling panel of the *Glorification of St. Roch* in the Sala dell' Albergo. While Veronese, Salviati and Zuccari were painstakingly drawing their compositions, Tintoretto with characteristic impetuosity painted the whole panel and surreptitiously had it installed and veiled. On the day of the judgement the other artists produced their drawings while Tintoretto, much to their wrath, pulled a string to reveal his own work glowing in the middle of the ceiling and offered it as a gift to the Confraternity. Although accused of cheating, he won the day and, to the great good fortune of posterity, was commissioned to execute the entire series of ceiling and wall paintings for the *scuola*. In 1567 he completed the paintings in the **Sala dell' Albergo** (where the Chapter met). They represent *Christ Before Pilate*, *Christ Bearing the Cross*, the *Ecce Homo*, and, most profoundly moving of all, the vast *Crucifixion*, a work of such nobility and pathos that it silenced even the eloquent Ruskin: " I must leave this picture to work its will on the spectator, for it is beyond all analysis and above all praise."

Tintoretto executed the ceiling and wall paintings in the large upper hall between 1575 and 1581, adding the now rather dark altarpiece of *The Vision of St. Roch* in 1588. In the eighteenth century the small rectangular panels in the ceiling were repainted and ruined. The ceiling paintings depict episodes from the Old Testament while those on the walls are devoted to the New. And, as one might expect, the two groups are linked by an iconographical programme. For example, *The Fall of Man* is connected with the wall paintings of *The Nativity* and *The Temptation of Christ*. The series also emphasises the charitable aims of the *scuola*—giving drink to the thirsty, tending the sick, feeding the hungry. The largest ceiling panels, *Moses Drawing Water from the Rock*, *The Brazen Serpent* and *The Miracle of Manna* are echoed on the walls by *The Baptism*, *Raising of Lazarus* and, jointly *Feeding the Five Thousand* and *Last Supper*.

The paintings themselves are distinguished by the visionary qualities of *The Crucifixion*: the same mystical aura surrounds the central figures while the others are rendered with the same keenly observed naturalism. And Tintoretto's personal mannerisms are still more conspicuous—his delight in foreshortening, his artificial use of light to emphasise action or suggest spiritual content rather than to reproduce a natural effect, his *penchant* for oblique composition, his preoccupation with the movement of the human body, running, swooping and soaring, and his use of subdued, subaqueous and sometimes weirdly unrealistic colour.

There are several other notable works of art on the upper floor of the *scuola*. A portrait by Tintoretto hangs beside the door to the Sala dell' Albergo, often called a self-portrait but unlike the authentic one in the Louvre. In the Sala dell' Albergo there is a painting of *Christ Carrying the Cross*, possibly one of the last works of Giorgione. Four paintings are displayed on easels in front of the altar in the Sala Grande: a lovely *Annunciation* by Titian, a *Visitation* by Tintoretto and two youthful works by G. B. Tiepolo, *Abraham and the Angels* and *Hagar and the Angels*.

Under the Tintorettos on the walls there is a series of carvings of strange armless figures and an alarmingly deceptive *trompe l'oeil* bookcase, which would be much more arresting if they were seen in less overpowering company. They are the work of Francesco Pianta, a highly talented if somewhat perversely bizarre sculptor active in Venice between 1630 and 1690. These curious, exquisitely carved figures, hung about with bric-à-brac—shoes, weapons, masks, chains, bottles, baskets—seem at first to be no more than the fantasies of a disordered baroque mind. But Pianta took good care to proclaim their emblematical significance on an inscribed scroll held by the figure of Mercury beside the main door. The ruffian in a slouch hat and cloak drawn up to his eyes is a spy representing Curiosity; the figure balancing him represents Frenzy; the bald-headed man with a monstrous foot in front of him is—surprisingly enough—Cicero defending the art of sculpture; the caricature of a man with brushes is Tintoretto symbolising

64

painting; and so on, all round the enormous room with fantastic nightmare ingenuity.

On the **staircase** which leads down to the ground floor there are two canvases commemorating the plague which afflicted Venice in 1630—one by Antonio Zanchi and the other, on the right, by Pietro Negri. Both are competent performances, but they pale into insignificance beside the works of Tintoretto to which—like the majority of Venetian *seicento* paintings—they owe almost too much.

In the **ground floor** room there are eight more paintings by Tintoretto, executed between 1583 and 1587, and all fine examples of his still more ethereal late style. They represent *The Annunciation*, with the Archangel followed by a flight of cherubin bursting into the Virgin's room—while St. Joseph works away outside with one of those perilous contraptions of wood, string and steel which Italian carpenters still use as saws, even to this day; *The Adoration of the Magi* with a phantom cavalcade in the background; *The Flight into Egypt* set in one of the most beautiful, lush, luminous landscapes ever painted; *The Presentation in the Temple*; *The Massacre of the Innocents*, a violent confusion of foreshortened figures; the *Assumption* and two long canvases which depict *St. Mary Magdalene* and *St. Mary of Egypt* meditating in moonlit landscapes of unearthly calm. The last two paintings, executed when Tintoretto was nearly seventy, are suffused by that elegiac mood of tranquillity after the storm which marks the work of many artists who lived into benign old age.

The **church of San Rocco** is separated from the *scuola* by a little *campo*. It has a fine façade built in the 1760s and liberally decorated with statuary by the Austrian G. M. Morlaiter. Inside, flanking the main door, stand marble figures of David and St. Cecilia by Giovanni Marchiori (1743), perhaps the most elegantly refined works of Venetian rococo sculpture. Above the first altar on the left there are paintings of St. Martin and St. Christopher by that strangely neurotic artist Giovanni Antonio Sacchiense called Pordenone. And there are several more paintings by Tintoretto which might command greater attention if they did not come as something of an anticlimax after the great series in the *scuola*. The two most interesting are those of *St. Roch Ministering to the Plague Stricken* and *St. Roch in Prison* (1567) where the powerful treatment of the nudes reminds one that Tintoretto originally painted his great *Crucifixion* with naked figures to which he later added draperies.

The two *scuole* already described were both devotional and charitable confraternities. Nearby stood the much simpler **Scuola dei Calegheri** where the cobblers had their headquarters. It is in the Campo San Tomà, reached down the Calle Larga Prima from the south-west corner of the Frari. Although converted into an upholsterer's shop—which specialises in the more brightly coloured modern fabrics—the exterior of the building survives intact. There is a bleached relief of the Virgin protecting members of the guild in the centre of the façade and, above the door, an attractive relief by Pietro Lombardo of St. Mark healing the cobbler Annanius who was subsequently baptised, made Bishop of Alexandria, canonised and adopted as the patron of shoe makers. On the lintel are three low reliefs of shoes.

In the Campo San Tomà a signpost points the way to the nearby boat station on the Grand Canal. But before leaving this district it is worth making a brief visit to the **Palazzo Centani** which is two minutes' walk along the Calle dei Nomboli from the bridge on the north side of the dreary church of San Tomà. (From the bridge you can see to the left the water entrance of Palazzo Bosso, a thirteenth-century archway finely carved with foliage and animals in the Veneto-Byzantine style.) Palazzo Centani is of interest as the only relatively small fifteenth-century Venetian house open to the public—it has a strikingly picturesque courtyard with a well-head and a handsome stone staircase leading up to the *piano nobile* which was redecorated in the eighteenth century. Here Carlo Goldoni was born in 1707, and in his memory a little museum of the Venetian theatre has been established inside with prints of theatres and scenery, and portraits of actors and playwrights (open 9.30 to 4 and on holidays from 9.30 to 12.30). The most prolific of Italian dramatists, Goldoni wrote no fewer than 136 comedies some of which, like *La Locandiera*, are works of genius while the vast majority differ from one another only in their settings, names and more or less complicated twists of their plots. Some regard him as the greatest Italian playwright. But he has a formidable rival in his more poetic and more genuinely original Venetian contemporary, Carlo Gozzi, whose weird fantasies are among the most appealing Italian literary works of the eighteenth century. For, like Titian and Tintoretto or, to descend a little from the sublime, Canaletto and Guardi, the two dramatists represent once again the two strains in the Venetian character.

66

CHAPTER 5

The Renaissance Dawn: Bellini, Carpaccio and Cima

San Zaccaria—Scuola di San Niccolò dei Greci (Byzantine Museum)—Scuola di San Giorgio degli Schiavoni—San Antonin—San Giovanni in Bragora—Arsenale—Riva degli Schiavoni—Santa Maria della Pietà

The Renaissance reached Venice relatively late. Long after Masaccio had frescoed the Brancacci chapel in Florence, Venetian artists continued to produce altarpieces in a florid Gothic style while some, still more old-fashioned, pursued an almost Byzantine manner of icon painting. Ogee arches continued to raise their nodding heads over Venetian windows long after friezes and pediments had spread their chastening regimen throughout Tuscany. This tardiness in accepting the new classicism has been ascribed to a strain of conservatism in the Venetian character and the geographical position of Venice itself. But the isolation of Venice was broken by several Tuscan artists—notably Castagno and Donatello. And in other periods the Venetians were anything but artistically conservative—both Titian and Tintoretto made a leap towards the baroque in the mid-sixteenth century. A more satisfactory explanation is to be found in the perennial Venetian desire for rich and elaborate surface ornamentation and in a somewhat blasé acceptance of classical antiquities which were much more conspicuous here than in Florence. All the great classicizing artists who worked in Venice—the Lombardi, Palladio, Sansovino, San Michele—came from the terra firma.

The ideal place in which to observe the emergence of the Venetian Renaissance style in architecture and painting is in the church of **San Zaccaria.** You can reach it from the Piazza by going along the Riva degli Schiavoni, over the Ponte del Vin and turning left up the second *calle* which opens under the Sottonportico San Zaccarai.

67

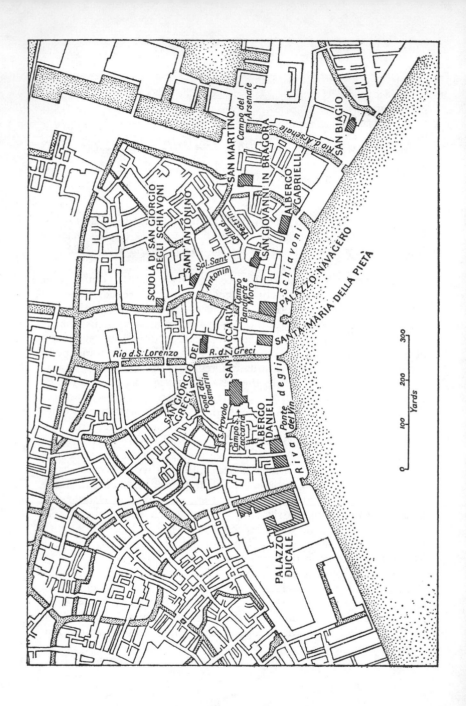

SAN BIAGIO

Campo del Arsenale

Rio d. Arsenale

SAN MARTINO

SAN GIOVANNI IN BRAGORA

ALBERGO GABRIELLI

SAN GIOVANNI IN BRAGORA

SCUOLA DI SAN GIORGIO DEGLI SCHIAVONI

SANT'ANTONIN

Sal. Sant Antonin

Calle d.

Pestrin

PALAZZO NAVAGERO

Schiavoni

SANTA MARIA DELLA PIETÀ

Campo Bandiera e Moro

SAN ZACCARIA

Rio d. S. Lorenzo

SAN GIORGIO DEI GRECI

R. d. Greci

Fond. dei Osmarin

S. Provolo

Campo S. Zaccaria

ALBERGO DANIELI

Ponte del Vin

Riva degli Schiavoni

PALAZZO DUCALE

0   100   200   300

Yards

It is a very tall church, much too tall for its width by the canons of classical architecture, and its Gothic skeleton is barely disguised by an incrustation of Renaissance motifs. Begun by Antonio Gambello in the 1440s, it was completed in the last two decades of the century by Mauro Coducci who designed three tiers of round-headed windows and shell-capped niches crowned by a curious semi-circular pediment. It is easy to see how this façade must have appealed to the Venetians, for while it was up to date in classical detail it yet retained the opulent elaboration of the flamboyant Gothic style. But whereas the façade is the result of a successful compromise, the interior suggests a state of hostility. The proportions of this lofty church, and its plan—with a screen round the high altar, an ambulatory and apsidal chapels—are Gothic. But most of the decorations are outspokenly Renaissance. Behind the elegant Gothic screen surrounding the high altar there is open warfare where octagonal Gothic piers suddenly develop into Corinthian half-columns.

The most interesting part of the church is the **Cappella di San Tarasio,** reached through the nuns' choir to the south of the ambulatory (ask sacristan). It was built in the fifteenth century on the site of the twelfth-century church of which traces survive in the mosaic floor around the altar. An inscription reveals that the paintings in the groined Gothic vault were executed in 1442 by *Andrea de Florentis et Franciscus de Faventia*—that is to say Andrea Castagno of Florence and Francesco da Faenza. They are the first swallows of Renaissance art in Venice. The short-lived Andrea Castagno (*c.* 1423–57) was probably the most gifted Florentine artist of the generation after Masaccio. And although they are his earliest known works, these statuesque figures already show the characteristics of his mature style. Each saint is an individual human personality—St. John the Evangelist stands with an absorbed look sharpening a quill which he appears to have plucked from the disgruntled eagle at his feet, St. Luke scratches his ear, like any Renaissance writer searching for the *mot juste* to complete an epigram. No Gothic artist could have depicted saints in this intimate manner, or painted the classically inspired frieze of *putti* on the soffit of the main arch. Vigorously dancing and kicking as they revel in the freedom of nakedness, these *putti* are in more senses than one children of the Renaissance.

On the main altar and the two side walls of the chapel there are polyptychs, painted after Castagno executed the frescoes in the apse and yet as outspokenly Gothic as his works are Renaissance. With the exception of the three central panels in the main altarpiece, they were all executed by Giovanni d'Alemagna and Antonio Vivarini between 1443 and 1444. Gaily painted in bright heraldic colours and set in their original fretted, crocketed and pinnacled frames (carved by one Lodovico da Forli who proudly signed his name on them in a way no Renaissance framemaker would have dared), they are good examples of the Venetian late Gothic style. But in contrast to the scrawny saints glowering down from the ceiling, their figures are not merely expressionless but insipid, mere decorative symbols and elegant arabesques as attractive and as lifeless as dolls dressed in silks and brocades.

The Renaissance style in painting was finally brought to maturity in Venice by **Giovanni Bellini** who is represented in San Zaccaria by a magnificent altarpiece above the first altar on the north of the nave. It depicts the Virgin and Child with Saints Peter, Catherine, Lucy and Jerome who stand around her in attitudes of self-absorbed meditation while an angel plays on a viol what can only be some very slow chaconne. This is one of the loveliest of the numerous angelic musicians who appear more frequently in paintings of the Venetian school than of any other. It is a relatively late picture, dating from 1505, and like so many works of art created in Venice in the decade before the war of the League of Cambrai it radiates a spirit of harmony and peace with the world —the peace of the lull before the storm in Venetian history and Venetian art.

Giovanni Bellini is one of the most vitally important personalities in the history of Venetian painting, but he is also one of the most elusive. The date of his birth is unrecorded but we do know that he came from a family of painters. The father, Jacopo, worked in the 1420s in Florence and Rome where he contracted the current mania for classical antiquities which he passed on to his elder son, Gentile. Giovanni's sister married the Paduan painter Andrea Mantegna who was similarly engrossed in the study of the Antique. From these three artists Giovanni was able to absorb the spirit of classical art without subscribing to its cult. Though often indebted to antiquity he appears to have been more interested in exploring the visible world around him than in studying Roman marbles. This attitude enabled him to translate the ideals of the Renaissance into a Venetian idiom; and the San Zaccaria altarpiece reveals the triumphant success of his translation. It is not merely that a Venetian hall-mark is impressed on certain details—the mosaics of the apse, the hanging lamp of Murano glass and the carving of the pilasters which might be by Pietro Lombardo. The whole work is conceived with a love for rich colour, with a sensitivity to the pellucid light of a Venetian dawn and with an appreciation of intricate decorative patterns which at all times characterised the finest works of the Venetian school. The painting goes far to explain why Andrea Castagno's severe saints exerted so little influence in Venice.

There are several other notable works of art in the church, though none as fine or as historically interesting as those already mentioned. Alessandro Vittoria lies buried here and his memorial, which he designed himself, stands at the entrance to the north side of the ambulatory. Also by Vittoria are the two little bronzes of Zaccharias and the Baptist in the holy water stoups and the large statue of Zaccharias over the central door on the main façade.

The convent of San Zaccaria was one of the rowdiest in early sixteenth-century Venice. The nuns openly entertained lovers, and they greeted the patriarchal officials sent to close their parlour with a barrage of sticks and stones. But affairs were probably no worse here than elsewhere: in the Convent of Santa Maria Celeste, in 1509, the nuns held a ball for young patricians and danced through the night to the music of trumpets and fifes: in 1502 the Prioress of Santa Maria Maggiore was discovered having a love affair with a priest and banished to Cyprus. Another priest, who was appointed confessor of the Convertite convent on the Giudecca, treated the four hundred nuns in his spiritual care as a very extensive seraglio, arranged naked bathing parties for the novices, bore off the fairest to his bed, sadistically torturing any who failed to surrender promptly to his will. Law reports tell many other stories of corruption in the convents—of nuns who wore their hair in ringlets, who dressed in silks and satins, who philandered with young men (called *moneghini*), who gave birth to considerable families. There were, no doubt, some convents where no such unseemly incidents disturbed a life of tranquil adoration: but the practice of sending young girls to nunneries against their will, to save the expense of dowries, tended to introduce the rebellious and the libidinous into the ranks of the devout and chaste—with results which were often disastrous for a whole community.

From the Campo San Zaccaria, the Salizzada San Provolo passes under a gateway bearing a fifteenth-century relief of the Virgin and Child. The *calle* on the right winds round to the Ponte dei Greci where you have a good view of the sixteenth-century church of **San Giorgio dei Greci** with its gently tilted campanile, the seventeenth-century Scuola di San Niccolò—headquarters of the Greek confraternity—and the rather simpler building which houses the Greek college, both by Longhena.

A colony of Greeks, adherents to the Orthodox creed, had been established in Venice for several centuries before 1539 when they contributed to build the church of San Giorgio where the creed is still chanted without the *Filioque* clause. Like the Jews, they preserved in Venice their own language as well as their own religion. And they supported a college where their children could be prepared for entrance to the University of Padua. The existence of this Greek colony was another of the factors which softened the impact of the classical Renaissance in Venice. For whereas Greek scholars were sought as rarities in other states, here in Venice men capable of settling *Hoti's* business and expounding the doctrine of the enclitic *De* were to be seen every day in the streets, just as classical statues were familiar to every artist. Even at Padua, barely twenty miles away, the force of the Renaissance was much stronger and an important school of Aristotelean scholars established itself at the university in the fifteenth century.

The Scuola di San Niccolò has been transformed into a well arranged little museum (open 9–12 and, except holidays, 3–6). It includes some eighty paintings in the Byzantine style, ranging in date from the fourteenth to the eighteenth century. All these works maintain the traditions of the icon established in the eighth century—they are painted in dark rich colours with a lavish use of gold, rigidly composed, and tend to represent figures with a symbolic rather than a realistic significance. A few of the seventeenth-century icons reflect traces of the momentous developments which had taken place in Western painting during the previous four hundred years, and they are perhaps the least artistically satisfying. The following are among the best paintings in the museum: (6) a fine fourteenth-century altar frontal; (63) a sixteenth-century Cretan *Dormition of the Virgin* (49) and (53)

Christ and St. John and *The Tree of Jesse*, rather large seventeenth-century paintings by Emanuele Zane, a Cretan who worked mainly in Venice. The museum also includes a group of rich embroidered vestments of the seventeenth and eighteenth centuries. Paintings similar to those in the museum are to be seen in the church of San Giorgio dei Greci.

If you now return to the Ponte dei Greci, cross the *rio*, turn right along the *fondamenta*, cross it again by the next bridge and walk straight ahead you will find on the far side of the next *rio* the **Scuola di San Giorgio degli Schiavoni**, a simple little building which contains one of the greatest treasures in Venice. This *scuola* was the headquarters of the Confraternity of Slavs—or Dalmatians —for the most part merchants engaged in trade with the Levant (10–12 and, except holidays, 3–5).

The ground floor room has a frieze of paintings by Vittore Carpaccio—the only one of his five cycles of paintings to survive in the *scuola* for which it was executed and to be seen more or less in the way he intended (they were moved from the upper to the lower room in the mid-sixteenth century). All but two of these pictures—which were executed between 1502 and 1508—depict stories of the three protectors of Dalmatia, St. George, St. Tryphon and St. Jerome. They represent, from left to right, *St. George Killing the Dragon, The Triumph of St. George, St. George Baptising the Heathen King and Queen*. The altar with a *Virgin and Child* by Vittore Carpaccio's less able son, Benedetto, breaks the series which continues with: *St. Tryphon Exorcising the Daughter of the Emperor Gordianus, The Agony in the Garden, The Calling of St. Matthew, St. Jerome Leading his Lion into a Monastery, The Funeral of St. Jerome* and *St. Augustine in His Study*. Carpaccio was such a prince of story tellers that none of these scenes needs explanation except the last. This illustrates a letter in which St. Augustine related that he was writing to ask the advice of St. Jerome on a theological point, unaware that he had died, when his cell was flooded with light and a voice from heaven reproved him for his presumption. A Venetian edition of this apocryphal letter had been published in 1485.

Carpaccio is a still more elusive figure than Giovanni Bellini. He is known to have been working in Venice between 1490 and 1523 but the dates of his birth and death are unrecorded. Only once does he come to life as a personality, in a letter he wrote in 1511

73

offering the Marquess of Mantua a picture and saying that the age could produce no work to compare with it for perfection and size. As a compensation, his artistic personality is as clear as the Venetian light which illuminates his pictures. Like Giovanni Bellini, to whom he was much indebted, he adapted the Renaissance style to the needs of Venice. He is, indeed, a still more exclusively Venetian painter and one wonders if he ever left the islands of the lagoon.

All the characteristics which mark the Venetian school are magnified in his work. Each picture shows a love of colour arranged in intricate patterns, and an appreciation for the surfaces of rich materials whether rare marbles or opulent silks and velvets. The taste for oriental exoticism appears in the fantastic tower behind the dragon in the first picture (the gateway to the left of it is derived from a print of Cairo) no less than by a band of Turkish musicians in that to the left of the altar. There is a touch of wit in the scene where St. Jerome's singularly tame lion flutters a group of Dominicans in a delicate pattern of black and white habits, and a touch of the macabre in the rotting corpses of *St. George and the Dragon*. Glimpses of beetling crags and mountain peaks still more fantastic than those of the Dolomites reveal the Venetian's urban appreciation of the distantly " picturesque " landscape. The scenes on either side of the altar reflect the Venetian passion for the pomp of state, and the figures on the loggias are such as could be found watching any religious or ducal procession—then as now it was the custom to hang carpets out of the windows on such occasions. St. Augustine's study is surely a *genre* scene, a view of some Venetian prior's chamber. Some scenes include views of Venice: *The Calling of St. Matthew* takes place in the Ghetto, the old Scuola di San Giorgio appears in the left background of *St. Jerome and the Lion*. While the fantastic marble-clad buildings seem to represent the aspirations of a Coducci or a Pietro Lombardo for the further adornment of Venice. And each picture shows a slightly different aspect of Venetian light, from the clear morning sunshine which floods St. Augustine's study, to the midday heat haze hanging over the funeral of St. Jerome, and the evening glow in which St. George fights the dragon.

Carpaccio has often been regarded as a naïve painter of the Venetian scene. It is true that a sense of childlike wonder inspires his works. But these very carefully composed pictures in which every line leads the eye through the intricate surface pattern of colour to point to the narrative content are the work of no ingenuous realist. Out of the everyday splendours of Venice he created a vision of a still richer and more fantastic world—a world where we may wander for hours, exploring its marble buildings, and mingling with its brightly clad crowd, brushing their damask sleeves and patting their lapdogs. His genius was such that he was able to impose his vision on posterity so completely that we still see Venice partly through his eyes.

From the Scuola di San Giorgio the Fondamenta dei Forlani leads to the **Campo Sant' Antonin** with a dull seventeenth-century church containing little of interest apart from a fantastic *Sacrifice of Noah* by Pietro della Vecchia (right of high altar). As the pig is the emblem of St. Anthony the Abbot, the monks of this church kept a notorious herd whose members were allowed to wander and rootle where they wished until they became such a nuisance that their liberties were brusquely curtailed by a pompous sumptuary edict of 1409. The Salizzada S. Antonin (the word *salizzada* signifies a paved street and records the time when most Venetian by-ways were simply earth tracks), bright with green-grocers and redolent with the smell of bakeries, opens into the wide and usually empty **Campo Bandiera e Moro.** Here the fifteenth-century Gothic Palazzo Gritti-Badoer (No. 3608) bears a handsome tenth-century relief of that favourite Byzantine bird, the peacock. (The numbering of Venetian houses is by the six *sestieri* or wards of the city, not by the street. In the Sestiere di San Marco, for example, the Doges' Palace is No. 1 and every building is numbered in ruthlessly logical sequence, round the Piazza and the *campi*, into the *campielli*, up and down the *calli* until no. 5562 is reached by the Rialto bridge.)

On the other side stands the church of **San Giovanni in Bragora** with a fifteenth-century Gothic façade as simple as it is pleasing.

With its squat columns and low Gothic arches, the interior of this church has a very cosy air. The present fabric dates from between 1475 and 1490 but the Renaissance has barely crept into the chancel. However, the paintings once again illustrate the growth of the early Renaissance style. In the chapel to the left of the high altar there is a triptych of the Virgin between St. John the Baptist and St. Andrew painted by Bartolomeo Vivarini in 1478. Against a gold ground, the figures stand in somewhat affected postures, their sharply crinkled draperies making a pattern of Gothic frets. On the wall between this chapel and the chancel hangs a *Resurrection* painted by Bartolomeo's nephew, Alvise Vivarini, two momentous decades later. Here Christ is depicted almost nude in a pose none the less naturalistic for being derived from a statue of Apollo (see p. 100). It is as outspokenly Renaissance as Bartolomeo's triptych is tenaciously Gothic. Balancing it, on the other side of the chancel, hangs a painting of *The Emperor Constantine and St. Helen* by **Giovanni Battista Cima** who included in the background a distant view of his native town of Conegliano. To be up to the moment he showed the Palazzo del Podestà damaged by a tower that fell in 1501. A still finer product of Cima's genius, a large *Baptism* painted between 1492 and 1495, hangs behind the high altar: it has the sparkling dewy freshness of a spring morning in the Dolomites.

Cima was the Carpaccio of the terra firma. Like Carpaccio, he fell under the influence of Giovanni Bellini whose grandeur has tended to overshadow his delicate ability. He was similarly interested in the quality of light and similarly attracted by graceful surface patterns of colour. While Carpaccio created a vision of an ideal Venice, Cima represented an ideal of the landscape of northern Venetia. In this *Baptism* the pensive figures have great spiritual beauty, but the eye is led past them into Cima's idyllic countryside, to watch the water-fowl splashing in the river, to join the ferryman as he rows across it, to follow the horseman riding towards the castle, while the ear is strained to catch what plaintive tune the shepherd may be piping as he watches his flock on the hill in this enchanted world of silence and slow time. For like Carpaccio's ideal city, his landscape is suffused by a quiet elegiac melancholy which echoes the profounder note struck in Giovanni Bellini's greatest paintings.

If you leave the *campo* by the *calle* nearest the church and then turn left along the Calle del Pestrin, passing the severely restored façade of San Martino, you will reach the main entrance to the **Arsenale**. This is one of the several words given to Europe by Venice—for all the arsenals are called after this one which derives its name from the Arabic *darsina'a*—a house of industry. From 1155 onwards all the galleys of the Republic were built in this vast dockyard which was the scene of constant bustling activity throughout the great ages of Venetian history. Dante was much impressed and described it in the *Inferno*, likening the pitch in which he placed barterers of public offices to that boiled in the arsenal for caulking the damaged hulls of Venetian ships.

The gateway was built in 1460 and is the earliest specimen of Renaissance architecture in Venice—a triumphal archway with a pediment supported by double columns, subsequently elaborated with earlier and later statues, including a warlike lion of St. Mark who has closed his book to conceal its pacific legend *Pax Tibi Marce*. In front, a pride of Greek lions stands guard. The two flanking the entrance were brought back from Athens by Francesco Morosini: that on the right from the Sacred Way, its fellow from Piraeus harbour. The back of the latter beast is carved with runes which refer, rather surprisingly, to the deeds of Haakon and Ulf, Harold the Tall, Asmund and Orn, Norsemen who appear to have been employed by the Byzantine Emperor as mercenaries in the eleventh century. The lion on the far right, which has a new head, came originally from Delos and dates from the sixth century B.C. In the middle of the little *campo* there is a seventeenth-century bronze socket for a flagpole.

The Fondamenta dell' Arsenale leads down to the **Riva degli Schiavoni,** following a *rio* which is spanned at the end by a modern bridge—curiously Fascist in style despite the architect's attempt to copy old examples. To your left the Riva sweeps up to the public gardens where every other year (the even numbers) the vast Biennale exhibition of modern art is held. In the other direction a great panorama is spread out before you—a seemingly continuous crescent of buildings, punctuated by the campanile and the cupolas of Santa Maria della Salute and terminating in the island of San Giorgio Maggiore. From this distance the buildings are but a fringe to the sky, and there is no better place to study the quality of Venetian light—" *la plus belles des lumières* " as Henri de Regnier remarked, in which one leads the life " *des ombres heureux.*" That the light of Venice differs from that of any other place there can be no doubt, but to discover precisely how it differs is a task that has baffled both writers and painters. (It is worth noting that whereas most of the best paintings of Rome are by foreigners to the city, only the Venetians have been able to capture the atmosphere of Venice: even Turner and Monet failed, hard though they tried.) It is not, save on fine winter days, a particularly clear light and never as sharp as that of Greece.

77

Usually it is slightly powdery and at evening it can take on a rare apricot tinge. One of its peculiarities is that the intensity seems to derive as much from the horizon as from the sun—the result no doubt of reflection from still waters. I, for one, am prepared to leave it at that and accept it as a mysterious enchantment, for mystery is the essence of poetry.

As you walk through the ever thickening crowd towards the Piazza, you pass several buildings of historical interest. The Albergo Gabrielli, a fourteenth-century Gothic palace heavily restored, was once the home of the philosopher Trifone Gabrielli, celebrated in his time as the " Venetian Socrates " though now barely remembered. Just before the next bridge stands the Palazzo Navagero, on the site of the house given by the Republic to Petrarch in return for his library which no one bothered about for more than a century and a half in materialistic, bibliophobic, Venice. He describes in one of his letters how he was sitting at his window here one day in June 1361 chatting to the Archbishop of Patras when suddenly he noticed a galley hastening to the shore. " As the swelling sails drew near, the joyful aspect of the sailors became visible, and a handful of young men crowned with green leaves, and with joyful countenances, standing at the prow, waving flags over their heads and saluting the victorious city as yet unaware of her own triumph." Venice had regained Crete.

Next door stood one of the most famous hostels for pilgrims who paused in Venice to venerate the relics of St. Mark before proceeding to the Holy Land. After the next bridge stands the church of **Santa Maria della Pietà.** It is worth going up the *calle* beside it to read a curious inscription beginning with the powerful words *Fulmine il Signore Iddio Maledetione e scomuniche* and warning unnatural parents of the eternal penalties of entrusting their legitimate or illegitimate children to the institution if they could afford to support them. This orphanage was very famous for the singing of its girls who performed under the direction of no less a master than Antonio Vivaldi from 1703 to 1745. Music had for long played a very important part in the life of Venice—far more than literature. The accounts of private concerts, serenades, and musical boating parties on the lagoon are innumerable, and the Venetian pictures which contain figures of musicians are legion. The Republic encouraged music by granting copyright patents to notable instrument makers and to printers. In the seventeenth century Claudio

Monteverdi and Giacomo Carissimi, two of the finest composers of the age, worked in Venice. The city attained European renown for its music in the eighteenth century, both on account of its many opera houses and for the conservatoires attached to the *Ospedali*—the Incurabili, Mendicanti, Ospedaletto and Pietà. The President de Brosses remarked that the girls in these institutions " *chantent comme des anges* " and declared " La Chiaretta " at the Pietà to be the best violinist in Italy, save perhaps for Anna Maria at the Ospedaletto. Rousseau, Goethe and the English musicologist, Dr. Burney, were among others who celebrated the music of Venice. The choir of San Marco is still one of the best in Italy. There are also numerous concerts and two operatic seasons which keep the tradition alive—though they are poorly attended by Venetians nowadays. Yet Venice still echoes with ancient harmonies. " When I search for a word to replace that of music," wrote Nietzsche, " I can think only of Venice."

The façade of Santa Maria della Pietà was designed by the eighteenth-century architect Giorgio Massari but not erected until 1906. Its interior, dating from between 1745 and 1760, is built on an almost oval plan which helps to soften the rigidity of the pilasters and cornice. One of the most satisfying buildings of its period in Venice, it owes much of its beauty, however, to G. B. Tiepolo's ceiling painting of the *Triumph of Faith* with a swirl of gaily dressed figures eddying out from the central fount of light. Another, smaller, painting by Tiepolo shines out of the ceiling above the high altar. Beside these vibrant and vivacious works, the altarpieces by minor masters of the *settecento* seem tame indeed. More impressive are the carved processional standards on either side of the altar rails, the work of some highly talented but forgotten eighteenth-century sculptor. The pulpit with its pigeon-toed scroll feet is a handsome piece of rococo furniture.

Farther down the Riva stands the very large equestrian monument to Victor Emmanuel II by Ettore Ferrari (1887)—the central figure has a certain panache though the allegories and reliefs are much less successful. Nearby, at No. 4161, Henry James stayed in 1881 while finishing *The Portrait of a Lady*. His apartment was on the fourth floor and enjoyed a permanently fascinating view which he would survey through his opera glass in the " fruitless fidget of composition," always wondering whether " out in the blue channel, the ship of some right suggestion, of some better phrase, of the next

79

happy twist of my subject, the next true touch for my canvas, mightn't come into sight." Nearer to the Piazza stands the Albergo Danieli, once the Palazzo Dandolo where the first opera was performed in Venice: Monteverdi's *Proserpina Rapita*. Since 1822 it has been an hotel and boasts the most distinguished list of visitors in all Venice, including George Sand, Alfred de Musset, Charles Dickens, Ruskin, Wagner and Proust.

CHAPTER 6

The Lombardi and Renaissance Sculpture

Santa Maria deï Miracoli—Scuola di San Marco—Colleoni Monument—
Santi Giovanni e Paolo—Ospedaletto—Santa Maria Formosa—Galleria
Querini-Stampalia

Seldom in the history of European art have painters, sculptors
and architects worked in such close harmony as in early Renaissance
Venice. They were bound together by a rare unity of purpose as
well as an intricate network of personal friendships. In this web
the Lombardo family occupies a position of capital importance, for
they invented the style of architecture and sculpture which is
depicted in so many paintings by Giovanni Bellini and his contemporaries. Pietro Solaro, called Lombardo, was born in Lombardy
(*c.* 1435), trained in Tuscany and worked for a while in Padua
where he came into contact with the humanist scholars of the
university for one of whom he carved a Florentine style monument.
In 1475 a writer declaimed: " O Padua thou art resplendent for
thy buildings and thy citizens, also for the work of the famous
sculptor Pietro Lombardo." But by this time he had already
forsaken Padua for Venice and begun to practise as an architect.
His first performance was the Chancel of San Giobbe, a work so
strongly Florentine that it looks like an unhappy exile. But
Pietro Lombardo soon acquired a Venetian accent and his later
buildings, with their abundance of marble panelling and crisply
carved decorative ornament, are brilliantly successful adaptations
of the Renaissance style to the needs and conditions of the lagoon.
What Giovanni Bellini had done for painting, he did for architecture, and his sons, Tullio and Antonio, who worked in close colla-
boration with him, achieved the same for the art of sculpture.
The great masterpiece of the Lombardi is the church of **Santa**

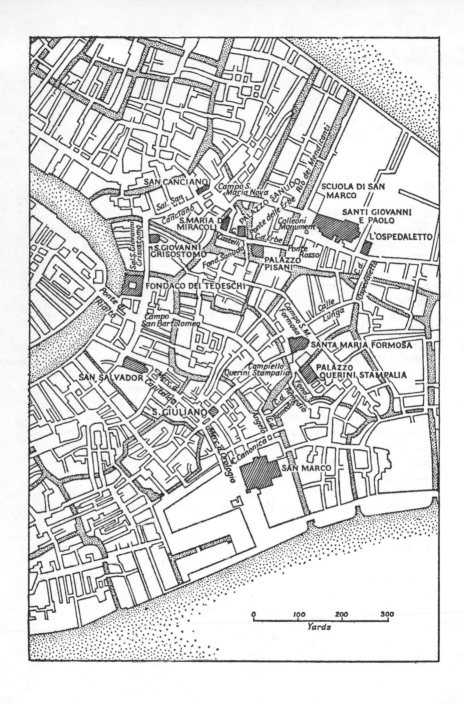

SAN CANCIANO

Campo S.
Maria Nova

SCUOLA DI SAN
MARCO

Sal. San
Canciano

PALAZZO SANUDO

Rio dei Mendicanti

S.MARIA DE
MIRACOLI

Ponte delle Erbe

Colleoni
Monument

SANTI GIOVANNI
E PAOLO

Castelli

C.d. Erbe

L'OSPEDALETTO

Sal S.Giovanni
Grisostomo

S.GIOVANNI
GRISOSTOMO

Fond. Sanudo

Ponte
Rosso

PALAZZO
PISANI

Ponte di
Rialto

FONDACO DEI TEDESCHI

Campo
San Bartolomeo

Campo S.M.
Formosa

Calle
Lunga

Calle
Querini

SANTA MARIA FORMOSA

SAN SALVADOR

Merceria
Capitello

Campiello
Querini Stampalia

PALAZZO
QUERINI STAMPALIA

Fond.

S. GIULIANO

Merceria
dell'Orologio

C.d.
Angelo

C.d.
Remedio

C. Canonica

SAN MARCO

0   100   200   300
Yards

Maria dei Miracoli—one of the most beautiful small buildings in the world. You can reach it from the Campo San Bartolomeo (on the San Marco side of the Rialto bridge) along the Salizzada San Giovanni Grisostomo, over the bridge of the same name, up the Salizzada San Canciano, to the right, and then to the right again through the Campo Santa Maria Nova where you finally escape from the buzz and bustle of the shopping streets. Here you obtain your first enthralling view of the east end of the church. Entirely coated with panels of white, grey and rich yellow marble, crowned by a buoyant dome which completes and complements the square casket-like structure, it looks at first sight almost too good to be true—not a real church but part of the background of a painting by Bellini or Carpaccio.

Santa Maria dei Miracoli was built between 1481 and 1489 to enshrine a miraculous image of the Virgin. On the exterior a nicely controlled balance of straight lines and curves produces an effect of harmonious tranquillity comparable only with that of a monastic choir singing the slow precise phrases of Gregorian chant. On closer inspection the ingenious complexity of the design becomes apparent. To make the church look larger than it really was Pietro Lombardo resorted to various optical illusions. Instead of placing the windows in the middle of the arcades, he pushed them to the sides to create the impression that they are inset behind the arches and thus give an appearance of depth to the flat surface. Similarly, by the use of rather more pilasters than would be normal on a building of this size he created a perspective effect which seems to extend the building considerably along the side of the canal. He also subtly enlivened the exterior by using slightly different colour schemes: the east end is in shades of blue-grey and white, while the north and south sides derive a rosy hue from panels of a reddish-yellow marble. On the entrance façade the decoration is appropriately more elaborate with panels of porphyry and verd antique marble. Of course, much of the effect of the building is due to the beauty of its materials which Lombardo wisely left to speak for themselves. There is very little sculptural ornament and that little exquisitely carved—the half-length Saint in the centre of the east end, the freshly cut panels of foliage which surround the doors and the little medallions on their jambs.

Inside, the walls of the church are coated with panels of grey

83

and coral marble which give it a cool, almost submarine appearance. As one's eyes become accustomed to the dim light, the dispassionate faces of saints and prophets materialise, staring down from the richly gilt ceiling. At the east end a steep flight of steps leads up the chancel cut off from the nave by an elegant balustrade with an ambo at either end. On the balustrade there are half-length figures of St. Francis, the Archangel Gabriel, the Virgin and St. Clare. The bases of the pilasters on either side of the chancel arch are intricately carved with sea monsters, *putti*, and faces peering out of leaves. Similar motifs—so like those applied to the architecture in Giovanni Bellini's later altarpieces—appear on the pilasters and walls. The altar is surrounded by a low, lacy marble screen which has the intricate quality of a Byzantine ivory carving. On the altar itself stands the miraculous image for which the church was built. Up above, in the squinches of the little cupola, there are low relief carvings of the Evangelists. Only one thing is missing in this perfect synthesis of early Renaissance art—the painting of the Annunciation, set in a room lined with marble like the church, which Giovanni Bellini executed for the doors of the organ, but which was barbarously removed in 1807, and is now in the Accademia.

From the little Campo dei Miracoli, the Calle Castelli leads to the Fondamenta Sanudo, with a pretty eighteenth-century statue of the Virgin on the wall at the corner. To the left stands Palazzo Sanudo (Palazzo Soranzo-van Axel-Barozzi to give it its modern name and record its subsequent owners), built in the 1470s but still Gothic, with ogee windows nodding over its windows and doors. The massive carved wooden doors are the only ones in Venice to survive intact from the fifteenth century. If you cross the bridge by another fifteenth-century Gothic building—Palazzo Pisani—the Calle delle Erbe will lead you past an undertaker's shop, displaying photographs of pompous funeral gondolas, to the Ponte Rosso. Here you get a distant view of the cypresses of San Michele along the line of the Rio dei Mendicanti which, as Corvo remarked, has " quite the most fancy stench in Venice at all seasons of the year and at all stages of the tide." To the right stands the **Scuola di San Marco,** now the civic hospital of Venice.

It is important to approach the *scoula* from this point to appreciate the *trompe l'oeil* effect of the façade, called by the Gothic

Opulence. The marble staircase leading from the courtyard of the Doges'
Palace to the council chambers and apartments of the Doge

The Great Council Chamber of the Doges' Palace with Tintoretto's vast "Coronation of the Virgin" covering the end wall

The Lombardi and Renaissance Sculpture

revival architect, G. E. Street, "a horrible sort of perspective, which is the lowest depth to which architecture has ever reached." Now that we are less concerned with the "lamp of truth" we may enjoy the picturesque grandeur and sophistication of this remarkable building. The lower part of the façade was designed and erected by Pietro Lombardo whose sons carved the large reliefs of St. Mark healing and baptising St. Annianus, the cobbler of Alexandria. The upper part of the building with its attenuated windows and bobbly semi-circular gables was designed by Lombardo's rival, Mauro Coducci.

In the Campo stands one of the finest statues in Venice: the equestrian **monument to Bartolomeo Colleoni.** Its story is slightly complicated. In 1475 the *condottiere*—general of mercenaries—Bartolomeo Colleoni, who had commanded the land forces of the Republic, died leaving the bulk of his fortune to Venice on the condition that an equestrian monument should be erected to his memory in the Piazza San Marco. Precedent forbade the erection of statues to individuals in so prominent a place, but as the Senate was reluctant to forgo the bequest they claimed that the terms of the will allowed them to raise the statue by the Scuola di San Marco. The Florentine sculptor Andrea Verrocchio was commissioned to execute the monument in 1479 and completed a full scale model by 1483 but died before it was cast in bronze. The casting was entrusted to Alessandro Leopardi who placed his signature prominently on the girth of the horse and also designed the plinth for the monument which was finally unveiled in 1496. It is probable that the bronze would have been more highly finished had Verrocchio lived to complete it.

"I do not believe that there is a more glorious work of sculpture existing in the world," wrote Ruskin of this monument. The horse has indeed a sense of lively, powerful movement hard to parallel in Western art. Colleoni frowns down with a fierce pride which seems to communicate his character across the centuries, and has tempted several writers to derive evidence for his life from the statue. In fact, he was a somewhat dim character, distinguished neither as a general nor as a personality, a condottiere like many others and much less interesting than Carmagnola whom the Senate had tortured and executed lest he should desert their banners to accept better pay from another state. Colleoni's sole distinction was that he kept to the letter of his commission to lead the Venetian

85

armies in return for a handsome salary. It is almost certain that Verrocchio never saw him—the Senate itself was much more interested in the rendering of the horse than the rider—and the portrait is an imaginary one, an evocation of what a fifteenth-century condottiere should ideally look like. It is a monument less to an individual than a whole class of men, the most mercenary captains of all time—proud, treacherous, money-grubbing, rapacious, chivalrous only to those who could reward chivalry with hard cash or to those of their own kind from whom similar treatment was expected by the code of thieves. Hence its fascination. This statue brings to life the distant world of fifteenth-century Italy in all its brilliance and brutality, providing a timely antidote to the impression of sweetness and light conveyed by the church of Santa Maria dei Miracoli.

The fact that Colleoni wanted to have himself recorded in an equestrian monument is the only interesting thing known about him, for he wished to be immortalised in the guise of a Roman hero. Verrocchio seized the opportunity to rival not merely Donatello, whose Gattamelata monument had been erected at Padua some twenty-five years previously, but also the unknown author of the famous antique bronze of Marcus Aurelius in Rome. And the Venetian Senate was happy to adorn the city with a statue worthy of the Roman Empire, thus provoking the censure of a Dominican who noted that they were " imitating the custom of heathen nations." The statue is one of the purest embodiments of the Renaissance desire to re-create the splendour of the classical world.

The church of **Santi Giovanni e Paolo**—known by the Venetians as San Zanipolo—is one of the largest in the city. A vast brick structure in the Venetian Gothic style, it was begun in the late thirteenth century but not finished and consecrated until 1430. The exterior is picturesque: the interior grandiose, with an impressively high nave and an apse lit by slender double-lancet windows. But it commands attention for its numerous works of sculpture and painting rather than for its architecture.

Among the many monuments the earliest of note is that to Doge Marco Cornaro (10): a group of figures from a much larger composition, carved by Nino Pisano in Pisa in the early 1360s, ranged above a stiff reclining effigy, evidently of Venetian workmanship. The central Virgin is perhaps the finest Gothic statue

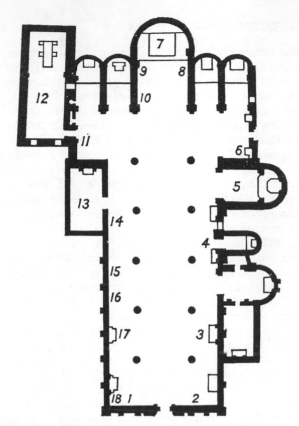

SS. GIOVANNI E PAOLO

1. Monument to Doge Giovanni Mocenigo by Tullio Lombardo (1500-10)
2. Monument to Doge Pietro Mocenigo by Pietro Lombardo (1476-81)
3. Polyptych by Giovanni Bellini (1460s)
4. Valier family monument designed by A. Tirali (1705-8)
5. Chapel of San Domenico
6. *St. Anthony Giving Alms* by Lorenzo Lotto (1542)
7. High altar, 17th century
8. Monument to Doge Leonardo Loredan by G. Grapiglia and Danese Cattaneo (1572)
9. Monument to Doge Andrea Vendramin by Tullio Lombardo (1492-5)
10. Monument to Doge Marco Cornaro by Nino Pisano (*c* 1360)
11. Monument to Doge Antonio Venier by Pierpaolo dalle Masegne (*c.* 1400)
12. Cappella del Rosario
13. Sacristy
14. Monument to Doge Pasquale Malipiero by Pietro Lombardo (1460s)
15. Monument to Doge Tommaso Mocenigo by Pietro di Niccolò Lamberti and Giovanni di Martino (*c.* 1425)
16. Monument to Doge Niccolò Marcello by Pietro Lombardo (*c.* 1475)
17. *St. Peter the Martyr* a 17th century copy of Titian's painting
18. Monument to Marchese Chastler by Luigi Zandomeneghi (1825)

in Venice, delicately graceful in her gently swaying movement. The tomb of Doge Antonio Venier (who died in 1400), by Pierpaolo dalle Masegne, reveals the not very distinguished quality of Venetian Gothic sculpture some forty years later (11). This monument is, indeed, of interest mainly for its peculiarly Venetian design which was used, with slight variations, by the Tuscan sculptors Pietro di Niccolò Lamberti and Giovanni di Martino for their monument to Doge Tommaso Mocenigo in about 1425 (15). A curious mélange of Tuscan and Venetian, Renaissance and Gothic motifs, including a figure of St. George derived from Donatello's famous statue in Florence, this tentative essay in a mongrel-Renaissance style set the pattern for Venetian monumental sculpture until the advent of the Lombardi.

The **Lombardi** are represented by five monuments ranging in date from the 1460s to 1510. The earliest is that by Pietro to Doge Pasquale Malipiero (14) which, apart from a Gothic canopy, is purely Renaissance in style, with delicately carved foliage and a lovely lunette of the Dead Christ supported by Angels. In the nearby Marcello monument (16), of about 1475, Pietro Lombardo abandoned the Gothic canopy in a work that is more uncompromisingly classical, though spoilt by the unhappy relationship of the oversize figures to the architectural framework. But in the monument to Doge Pietro Mocenigo (2), carved between 1476 and 1481, the Venetian Renaissance style in sculpture and architecture finally reaches its self-confident maturity. All elements copied from Tuscan monuments have vanished, the relationship of the statues to the architecture is nicely controlled, while the sturdy warriors supporting the sarcophagus and the Risen Christ on top have an heroic yet individual vitality. At the base there are two reliefs of the Labours of Hercules—characteristic examples of the desire to apply pagan mythology to Christian purposes—in which the hands of Tullio and Antonio Lombardo have been recognised. The last two Lombardo monuments in the church are mainly the work of Tullio, one to Doge Andrea Vendramin (9) the other to Doge Giovanni Mocenigo (1), dating from 1492–5 and 1500–10 respectively. Both reveal his desire to express a vision of the ancient world by working in a classical manner without resorting to the servile imitation of antique prototypes. The same attitude is evident in the prose of Pietro Bembo who sought to write in Ciceronian Tuscan rather than Ciceronian Latin and, together with many fellow humanists, elevated the vulgar tongue to the status of a classical language. Tullio Lombardo owned at least one antique statue and he drew inspiration from many others. But the solemn allegories on the Mocenigo monument, though clearly derived from Graeco-Roman marbles, are not based on any particular statues. On this same monument there are two very beautiful nudes in the relief of *St. Mark Baptising Annianus.* There were originally nude statues of Adam and Eve on the Vendramin monument but they were prudishly removed in the nineteenth century and statues by Lorenzo Bregno now stand in their place (the Adam is now in the Metropolitan Museum, New York).

In comparison with the springlike freshness of the works by the Lombardi such a monument as that to Doge Leonardo Loredan (8) completed in 1572 has a high summer luxuriance. It was designed by the architect Girolamo Grapiglia; the sculpture is by Danese Cattaneo, who was responsible for the fine bronze reliefs, and Girolamo Campagna who carved the central figure of the Doge. Summer moves into autumn and solemnity gives way to hollow pomp in the vast Valier monument (4) carved between 1705 and 1708 by a group of the leading sculptors in Venice (though some of the reliefs and individual figures, like that of Humility holding a lamb, have great charm). The elegance of the eighteenth century marks Giuseppe Mazza's series of refined bronze reliefs in the chapel of San Domenico (5), dating from about 1720, and the series of high reliefs by Giovanni and Antonio Bonazza, G. M. Morlaiter and others in the Cappella del Rosario (12). A graceful epilogue to the history of Venetian sculpture illustrated in this church is provided by Luigi Zandomeneghi's little romantic period monument to the Marchese Chastler (18).

Although the church is not as rich in paintings as in sculpture, it contains several of note. On one of the nave altars (3) there is a polyptych by Giovanni Bellini, a very early work, probably of the 1460s. Comparison between the angular semi-naked St. Sebastian and the carvings of Hercules on the nearby Mocenigo monument (2) suggests that at this stage of his career Bellini regarded the nude as a somewhat painful iconographical necessity rather than a joy in itself. He was later to derive inspiration from the Lombardi. Perhaps the finest painting in the church is Lorenzo Lotto's *St. Anthony Giving Alms* (6) in which the warm colour scheme seems to have been derived from the soft Turkish carpets which play a prominent part in the composition. The work dates from 1542. In the Cappella del Rosario (12) there are some luminous paintings by Paolo Veronese set in a modern ceiling. A seventeenth-century copy of Titian's *St. Peter Martyr* (17) is a sad record of what was once among the most celebrated pictures in Venice but was destroyed by fire in 1867. The chapel of San Domenico (5) has a ceiling by G. B. Piazzetta, lightly touched and delicately coloured.

If you leave the church by the south door and turn left you will come into a *calle* dominated by the façade of the **Ospedaletto** church, bulging with great muscle-bound telamones, lion masks and the heads of giants, one with his tongue stuck truculently out of the corner of his mouth. Built to the design of Baldassare Longhena between 1662 and 1674, it is a *tour de force* of grotesque architecture, a masterpiece of baroque extravagance and exaggeration on which all the carved details are much too large—and intentionally so. It is the manifestation of a desire to shock, to thrill and chill the spectator, and shares a strange surrealist quality with several other works of sculpture and architecture produced in seventeenth-century Venice. Many of the decorative elements are derived from antique sources, but nothing could be further removed from the serene and gentle classicism of the Lombardi. It typifies not merely the Venetian taste for the bizarre but also a seventeenth-century revolt against the classical canons. A similar spirit inspired much of the literature of the day—such a burlesque poem as Francesco Loredano's *Iliade giocosa,* many sonnets which reversed the traditional qualities of female beauty laid down by Petrarch and Tasso (blonde hair, blue eyes, white complexion), and an almost gleeful awareness of the skull beneath the skin, no less than a cult of " *orrida bellezza.*"

A little beyond the church, the Calle dell' Ospedaletto leads by way of the Calle Lunga to the **Campo Santa Maria Formosa** where, at the base of the campanile, you may see another of the grotesque heads which are such a prominent feature of the street architecture of Venice. This one provoked from Ruskin the following splendid invective: " A head—huge, inhuman and monstrous—leering in bestial degradation, too foul to be either pictured or described, or to be beheld for more than an instant; for in that head is embodied the type of the evil spirit to which Venice was abandoned in the fourth period of her decline; and it is as well that we should see and feel the full horror of it on this spot, and know what pestilence it was that came and breathed upon her beauty, until it melted away like the white cloud from the field of Santa Maria Formosa."

The last roll of Ruskin's thunder refers to the traditional foundation of the church by a Bishop to whom the Virgin appeared in a vision as a *formosa* matron commanding him to raise a church wherever a white cloud should rest. The word *formosa* is difficult to translate, meaning both beautiful and buxom. Perhaps the best definition of it is provided by Palma Vecchio's painting of St. Barbara, a personification of robust Venetian female beauty, over the altar in the south transept of the church. St. Barbara was the patron of the artillerymen who had the chapel of their *scuola* in this church, and it is hard to imagine a figure more suitable for military devotion. George Eliot was much struck by her—one may imagine Dorothea Casaubon to have looked somewhat similar—and wrote that she was " an almost unique presentation of a hero-woman, standing in calm preparation for martyrdom, without the slightest air of pietism, yet with the expression of a mind filled with serious conviction." The sentence could hardly be more characteristic of its writer and of England in the 186os, yet it does accurately describe this impressive figure.

There is one other painting of great interest in this church, the polyptych of the Madonna of Mercy by Bartolomeo Vivarini, signed and dated 1473. Documents reveal that the congregation subscribed to pay for this altarpiece and the figures huddled around the Virgin appear to be portraits of the parish priest, wearing his best cope, the curate and their little flock. Venetian types have changed little in the five intervening centuries. Any day you may see the old lady in the white head-dress shuffling through a Venetian market, or you may find yourself asking the white surpliced sacristan to turn on the lights.

Architecturally this interior is unique. Rebuilt by Mauro Coducci in 1492 on an earlier, probably eleventh century, plan it is a peculiarly attractive cross between the Veneto-Byzantine and the Venetian Renaissance styles, reminding one of what the latter owed to the former. With its screens of slender columns supporting the little cupolas and barrel vaults, the interior combines the elegance of early Renaissance ornament with the spatial effects of a Byzantine church.

A chapel in the church was originally the oratory of the Scuola dei Casselleri—makers of marriage coffers—who played the leading part in one of the more colourful Venetian legends. One day in 944 a number of girls were going to the Cathedral to be married when a party of Slavs arrived on the scene and carried them off, intending to ship them to Dalmatia. But the Casselleri gave chase and rescued the girls. As a reward they asked the Doge to visit them at their *scoula* on every anniversary of the event. " But what shall I do if it rains? " asked the Doge—" We shall give you a hat." " And what shall I do if I am thirsty? " " We shall give you wine." So every Candlemas day until 1797 the Doge, accompanied by the officials of state, went in procession to the church of Santa Maria Formosa where he was solemnly given a straw hat and a glass of wine. You can see one of the hats in the Museo Correr and a painting of the ceremony in the Galleria Querini-Stampalia.

The Campo Santa Maria Formosa is a very attractive square, bright with stalls of fruit and vegetables every morning and always animated. Though only a few minutes walk from the Piazza, it has the atmosphere of one of the remoter parts of the city where tourists rarely penetrate. Around it stand several notable palaces. No. 5246, Palazzo Vitturi, is encrusted with some fine fragments of Byzantine carving, including a cross much praised by Ruskin. No. 5250, Palazzo Malipiero-Trevisan, with marble discs on its walls, is a handsome sixteenth-century building, possibly by Sante Lombardo, the son of Tullio.

On the south side of the church a passage-way leads into the Campiello Querini-Stampalia named after the **Galleria and Bibloiteca Querini-Stampalia** housed in the early sixteenth-century Palazzo Querini on the far side of the little *rio*. The library, rich in Venetian books and prints, is on the first floor and the gallery on the floor above (open from 9–5; holidays 10–12). This palace and the contents of the gallery were left to the City of Venice in 1868 and the large *piano nobile* apartments still preserve the appearance of a patrician house in the early nineteenth century. One of the least frequented of Venetian museums, it is one of the pleasantest for the saunterer in search of the atmosphere of old Venice. Most of the pictures and other works of art are labelled and the following paragraphs are intended to draw attention to no more than a few of the best.

Santa Maria dei Miracoli. One of the great masterpieces of Italian renaissance architecture, but unmistakably Venetian

San Giorgio Maggiore. Palladian precision in the shimmering Venetian light

The Lombardi and Renaissance Sculpture

Leading out of the gaily painted and stuccoed entrance hall, there is a room devoted to sixty-nine paintings of Venetian life in the second half of the eighteenth century by Gabriele Bello. One depicts the carnival crowd in the Piazzetta, with tumblers and mountebanks, another the marriage of a noble couple in Santa Maria della Salute. Masked and dominoed figures are glimpsed in the Ridotto. There is a view of the Piazza on Ascension day with the temporary stalls in the centre. Others depict the pageantry of State—the election of a Doge, the visit of Doge and Senate to Santa Maria Formosa and so on. Despite, or perhaps because of, their childish incompetence, they present a vivid picture of Venetian life in the years of feverish gaiety just before the fall of the Republic.

On the other side of the entrance hall there are eighteen rooms each one of which contains something of interest, whether a painting or some handsome piece of Venetian furniture. In room III there are works by the best seventeenth-century Venetian portrait painter, Sebastiano Bombelli, including a full-length of the young sensuous mouthed Girolamo Querini swaggering in his red toga. Room VIII has attractive neo-classical décor which provides a suitable setting for a brilliantly fresh and lively terra cotta statuette by Antonio Canova—the sketch for the marble statue of Napoleon's mother (now at Chatsworth) or possibly that of his sister Elisa (now in Vienna).

Room IX is devoted to the best Renaissance paintings in the collection. There is a *Presentation in the Temple* by Giovanni Bellini, closely copied from a Mantegna with the addition of a couple of heads. (There is a photograph of the Mantegna behind the nearby curtain.) The *tondo* of the *Virgin and Child* is by the Florentine Lorenzo di Credi, the other *Virgin and Child* is attributed to Bellini. But the most arresting paintings in the room are the unfinished portraits of Francesco Querini and his wife, Paola Priuli, by Palma Vecchio, commissioned to mark their wedding shortly before Palma's death in 1528. The portrait of Paola Priuli is peculiarly fascinating on account of its lovely soft yellow and brown colour scheme, no less than the wistful expression of the sitter, gazing in shy curiosity across the centuries. I often wonder if this was the picture Browning had in mind when he wrote:

Was a lady such a lady,
Cheeks so round and lips so red,

93

Above the small neck buoyant, like a bell-flower on its bed,
O'er the breast's superb luxuriance where a man might rest his
head?

In the next room there is another work by Palma, an idyllic *Holy
Conversation* painted in his usual soft autumnal palette, though
finished after his death by a follower. This room is, however,
dominated by Vincenzo Catena's brilliant if unattractive *Judith*.
Catena, like Palma, followed in the wake of Giorgione, though here
he forsook his master's warm colours and misty touch for a hard
starchy colour scheme which gives the picture a somewhat surgical
atmosphere. The ceiling of this room is gaily painted by some
eighteenth-century artist, perhaps Sebastiano Ricci.

After a passage, the next two rooms are devoted to works by **Pietro
Longhi**—mainly *genre* scenes, though one of the most attractive
depicts members of the monastic orders. They show us a geography
lesson, the interior of the Ridotto, members of the Sagredo family
dressed in their party clothes and, to be grave, Venetians receiving
the Seven Sacraments, from Baptism to Extreme Unction. These
vivid glimpses into Venetian private life, painted in cool pastel
colours, have great charm. But do they merit the praise that has
often been lavished on them by Italian critics? One examines
them in vain for the wit of Domenico Tiepolo, for the exquisite
refinement of Chardin, for the vivacity and social criticism of
Hogarth. They are in fact little superior to Gabriele Bello's amusing
naïveties. Only one picture is of much higher quality—the group
of men shooting duck on the lagoon, and this may well be the work
of another artist.

The next rooms contain some characteristic examples of eighteenth-century Venetian furniture—coarsely made but designed
with a sense of fantasy and decorated with delicate little paintings.
In Room XVIII there are some very large and very pompous
portraits of eighteenth-century Querinis. One is the work of
G. B. Tiepolo. Facing it is the portrait of Daniele IV Dolfin by
Alessandro Longhi—Pietro's son—which is perhaps more lively,
animated by the subject's humorously twinkling, self-indulgent
face. Two notable seventeenth-century paintings are to be seen
in Room XIX—a *Virgin and Child* by Bernardo Strozzi, a Genoese
artist who worked in Venice, and a *Milo of Crotona* by Francesco
Maffei of Vicenza, an engaging painter who sometimes seems to
anticipate the elegance of the *settecento*.

The Lombardi and Renaissance Sculpture

The bridge in the corner of the Campiello Querini-Stampalia leads to the Fondamenta Remedio. The first right (Calle del Remedio), the first left (Calle del Angelo) and the second right (Calle Canonica) will lead you through narrow streets to the Piazza.

CHAPTER 7

Books, Marbles, Paintings and Costumes

Biblioteca Marciana—Museo Archeologico—Museo Correr

On the side of the Piazzetta facing the Doges' Palace stands the Libreria Sansoviniana which Palladio considered the richest and most ornate building erected since ancient times. It was designed by Jacopo Tatti, called **Sansovino,** begun in 1540 and finished after his death by Vincenzo Scamozzi. As he was a Florentine and provided a good subject for a biography by Vasari, Sansovino emerges as a much clearer personality than his Venetian contemporaries. He made his name as a sculptor and restorer of antique statues in the Rome of Julius II and Michelangelo. But in 1527, at the time of the sack of Rome, he fled to Venice, intending to go on to France. He was promptly asked to repair the main cupola of San Marco and effected this so well that he was appointed first architect and engineer of the Republic. In addition to the library and the *Loggietta* at the base of the campanile he built several palaces, the church of San Giuliano and that of S. Francesco della Vigna (completed by Palladio). But when the library was nearly completed in 1545 he met with a sudden reverse. The cupola of the building collapsed and Sansovino was clapped into prison as if he had been a *condottiere* who had lost a battle—and it took all the eloquence of Titian and Aretino to get him released. According to Vasari he was very handsome as a young man, with fair hair and a red beard and " many ladies of rank fell in love with him." Even in old age he remained something of a dandy. He was hot-tempered and Benvenuto Cellini—of all people—called him a braggart. Blessed with a remarkably sound constitution, he survived four strokes to die at the age of eighty-four in 1570. Vasari records also that in old age his summer diet consisted largely of fruit and vegetables and that he often ate " three cucumbers at

96

a time with half a lemon." One seeks in vain for similarly intimate glimpses of any Venetian-born artist.

Although an essential part of the Venetian scene, the *Libreria* is strikingly un-Venetian in style, making no reference to earlier buildings in the city and answering no Venetian demands save that for opulent richness of decoration. With its profusion of columns and statues and reliefs, it realises a vision of antique Roman splendour. And as such it was destined to influence later Venetian architects, especially in the seventeenth century. Sansovino's work as a sculptor may be seen in the handsome classicising bronze statues of Pallas, Apollo, Mercury and Peace on the *loggietta* at the base of the campanile (the building was, however, altered in later periods and crushed beneath the fall of the campanile which damaged most of the sculptures). Like the *Libreria* this building reveals Sansovino's desire to integrate sculpture and architecture in a way that had not previously been achieved in Venice except in the sepulchral monuments of the Lombardi.

The end of the *Libreria* towards the water originally housed the *zecca* or mint where *zecchini* or sequins were made—another word, like arsenal, given to Europe by Venice. But the **Biblioteca Marciana,** the main public library of the city, has long since overflowed into this part which now contains the catalogue and reading rooms. It is a large library, rich in Byzantine and medieval manuscripts and possessing press after dusty undisturbed press of beautifully printed incunabula. As in most Italian libraries, the catalogue is inscribed by hand in a style more flowery than legible. There is a large domed reading room which reaches fever temperature in summer and which in winter is one of the coldest spots south of Aberdeen—though the thoughtful authorities provide little wooden foot-rests to protect readers' toes from the full force of the icy draught exhaled by the floor.

Although the tables of the library are usually full—and those who use them cannot be accused of sheltering from heat or cold—Venice has never been a great literary city. She has played host to many writers of other nations but has produced few of more than local renown apart from the poetess Gaspara Stampa (author of a cycle of burning love sonnets), Fra Paolo Sarpi, Goldoni and Gozzi. One might add the name of Pietro Bembo to whom all historians of Italian literature pay lip-service, though few are so unkind as to quote *in extenso* from his works. He was a writer of brilliant ability: his Latin epitaph on Raphael is a little masterpiece of compression. But his most famous work, *Gli Asolani*, an involved and tedious discussion about the nature of love, though written in an exquisite prose with occasional snatches of metrically perfect verse, is far less frequently read than mentioned. (It was dedicated to Lucrezia Borgia.) His influence was baneful, for he was the first Venetian to write in Tuscan and establish it as the "literary" language of Venice. As the rhythms of the Tuscan and Venetian dialects are quite different—you have only to travel from Venice to Florence to discover this—Venetians had understandable difficulty in writing poetry in what was to them as foreign a language as Latin. As a result, the supposedly " great " poems are lifeless metrical exercises while the true Venetian poetic gift continued to find expression in ephemeral dialect songs. This is, I think, one of the reasons why Venice's great achievement in the visual arts and in music was not matched in her literature. Another is that the Venetian tends to be more sensual than cerebral and more practical than theoretical. Few Venetians have been great readers or bibliophiles. Petrarch gave his library to the Republic in 1366 but the precious volumes were put away and forgotten for more than 150 years by when the majority had disintegrated. Cardinal Bessarione made a further gift of a priceless collection of manuscripts in 1468 but fifty years passed before the Senate considered erecting a library to house it. Yet, in the history of printing, Venice occupies a place of capital importance. Block printing of missals, playing-cards and so on was practised here as early as 1441, and printing with movable types within the lifetime of Gutenberg. In 1457 Johannes de Spira set up a press in Venice: thirteen years later he was followed by a greater printer, Jensen. And, greatest of all printers of all ages, Aldus Manutius pulled the first crisply printed sheets from the famous Aldine press in 1492. Before the end of the century this press had published the first great picture book, that weird phantasmagoric, obscurantist erotic, mystagogic performance—one can call it neither treatise nor novel—*Hypterotamachia Poliphili*. In the sixteenth century the city became a hive of busy compositors. During the first two decades no fewer than sixty-five presses were active: three times as many as there were in Rome and six times as many as in Florence. (The telephone directory now lists thirty-six *tipografie* only one of which prints books.)

It was not, of course, to answer the demands of the Venetian reading public that printers settled in the city. In an age of political and religious dispute, of tract and counter-tract, they came to take advantage of the Republic's liberal attitude towards censorship and traditional hostility to the Vatican. The State began to profit from a brisk export trade in books which the Senate, characteristically, fostered not only by allowing the production of controversial works but by granting copyright privileges to notable printers and seeing that no bad editions of the classics should damage the city's reputation.

A fine array of Venetian books from editions of the classics printed by Johannes de Spira to the best Aldine productions is shown in the upper rooms of the **Biblioteca** (open 10–12). Other cases contain illuminated manuscripts—tenth-century Byzantine codices, Venetian Gothic Gospels, glowing with brilliant colour, the famous fifteenth-century Grimani breviary with its Flemish miniatures, chastely decorated and elegantly inscribed humanist manuscripts. The two richly decorated rooms provide a fit setting for these treasures. The ceiling of the first room, painted with *trompe l'oeil* architecture in the 1550s (an early instance of this practice), has in the centre an allegory of Wisdom by Titian. In the main room paintings of twelve Philosophers by Tintoretto, Andrea Schiavone, Paolo Veronese and others look down from simulated niches on the walls. The richly gilt ceiling is set with allegories painted by Veronese, Schiavone and others.

A doorway at the end of the loggia of the *Libreria*, near the campanile, leads into the **Museo Archeologico** (10–3; holidays 9–1; closed Mondays). It contains Greek, Graeco-Roman and Roman sculptures which are interesting for the influence they exerted on Venetian artists as well as on their own account. The most important part of the collection was assembled by two members of the Grimani family in the sixteenth century including works brought direct from the Greek islands and, probably, statues which had been in Venice since the fifteenth century. In the courtyard you are greeted by a colossal Roman statue, once supposed to represent Marcus Agrippa, which remained in the Grimani palace long after the other marbles had passed to the Republic. In the eighteenth century some foreigner—probably an English grand tourist—bought the statue from the Grimani. But just as it was about to be shipped a sergeant appeared on the scene and raising his hat to the statue said: "The Supreme Council of the Inquisitors, understanding that you, Sior Marco, are about to leave this city, have sent me to wish you *and* his excellency Grimani a pleasant journey." Preferring to stay in Venice, Grimani cancelled the deal.

A staircase leads up to the rooms of the museum on the *piano nobile*. The finest works by far, from an aesthetic as well as an archaelogical point of view, are the eleven headless statues of girls dressed in chitons, advancing with a stately stride from the walls of Room IV. These korai were carved in the late fifth century B.C. and were among the very few original Greek works of this period to be seen in western Europe until the late eighteenth century. But although they were brought to Venice in the sixteenth century, these beautifully carved figures which epitomise the sense of classical poise, exerted no influence whatever until the time of Canova. Renaissance artists in Venice, as in other Italian cities, drew inspiration from Hellenistic and Roman carvings like those shown in other rooms of the museum.

To walk through these rooms is to visit the "life" class of the Venetian school. One figure after another reveals the origin of poses adopted by painters and sculptors of the Renaissance. In Room V there is an Apollo, his right hip swung out, his left leg slightly advanced, standing in an attitude "borrowed" by Antonio Vivarini for a painting of Christ in San Giovanni in Bragora and adapted by others for representations of St. Sebastian. A passionate love scene between a satyr and a nymph on an altar in Room VI recurs frequently in Venetian art from Titian to Canova. In Room VIII there are statues of a falling warrior and a running Ulysses (an exquisite Hellenistic work) which helped artists to solve the problem of representing the nude body in action and reappear in the work of Bellini, Tullio Lombardo, Titian and Tintoretto. Nearby stands an unappealing statue of Leda and the Swan which makes a very surprising reappearance, without the swan, as an allegory of Faith in the San Marcuola *Institution of the Eucharist* by Tintoretto. This instance provides a good example of the way in which Venetians used antique statues. Whereas Florentine artists, in their devotion to the idea of antiquity, made their debt to ancient statues explicit, in the manner of a writer quoting from the classics, the Venetians plundered the ancients merely to acquire a stock of poses—without any learned overtones.

Books, Marbles, Paintings and Costumes

Yet it would be a mistake to regard this collection primarily as interesting source material for the Renaissance. Many of the carvings are as aesthetically satisfying as the fifteenth and sixteenth-century sculptures which nowadays receive so much more attention and applause. (There are incidentally a few Renaissance works in the museum—a candelabra base in Room XII copied from that in Room III, and two reliefs of centaurs by Tiziano Aspetti.) Rooms VIII, IX and X contain some vivid Republican and Imperial Roman busts. In Room VII there is a case of engraved gems—cameos and intaglios carved with miniscule perfection— which were so rightly admired by connoisseurs and artists in the Renaissance. A different world, but one in which intricate craftsmanship was no less deeply appreciated, is represented by two Byzantine ivories in a vitrine in Room XI. One represents St. John the Evangelist and St. Paul in long formalised garments—carved in Constantinople in the reign of Constantine VII Porphyrogenitus (912–959)—the other shows St. Theodore and St. George in military uniform, dates from a little later and is provincial work. Both serve as reminders of the classical elements which survived in the Byzantine style and were thus present in Venetian art long before the fifteenth-century Renaissance. Among many other objects of interest there is a little collection of Assyrian reliefs of the eighth and seventh centuries B.C. in Room XX—they were found at Nimrûd by Sir Austen Layard, for many years a Venetian resident, who left them to this museum.

The rooms of the Museo Archeologico are dovetailed into those of the Museo Correr which occupies most of the range of the Procuratie Nuove. But to pass from one to the other you must go downstairs and cross the Piazza. The entrance to the **Museo Correr** is under the arcade of the Napoleonic wing at the west end (open 9.30–4 except on holidays when it closes at 12.30). This fascinating civic museum is devoted partly to works of art and partly to relics of the Doges and of Venetian life generally. After inspecting the collection of maps in the first room (including that by Jacopo de' Barbari of 1497–1500 and the original wood block from which it was printed), it is advisable to walk straight through the rooms on the *piano nobile* and begin by visiting the **Quadreria** or picture gallery on the floor above. All the works here are well labelled so I shall confine my remarks to no more than a few of the most important.

The first two rooms are devoted to fourteenth-century paintings: little icons with saints in robes of jewel-like colour staring out impassively from their gold backgrounds. An example of Venetian Gothic painting is provided by Giambono's mid-fifteenth century *Virgin and Child* (1083) in Room VI. In the next room there is an exquisite little *Pietà* (9) painted in the 1460s by Cosmè Tura of Ferrara where a vital school of Renaissance painting flourished under the rule of the Este family. The Ferrarese school is also represented in Room VIII by Baldassare Estense's portrait of a man by a window which looks on to a shipyard (53).

Rooms X and XI are devoted mainly to Flemish paintings which remind one of the commercial and artistic ties between fifteen-century Venice and the Low Countries. In the history of technique, the Flemish painters made an important development in the use of oil colour which replaced tempera as the most popular medium for painting before the end of the fifteenth century. One of the first Italian artists to use oil paint was **Antonello da Messina** who is represented in Room XI by a *Dead Christ Supported by Angels* (42). Of Sicilian origin, Antonello received his training in Naples where he appears to have studied works by Jan van Eyck and Rogier van der Weyden, mastering their technique and learning much from their style. In 1475 he arrived in Venice and painted an altarpiece (the surviving panels are now in Vienna) which caused something of a stir and may have set the pattern for the great architectural altarpieces painted by Giovanni Bellini and others. Despite its very poor state of preservation, the *Dead Christ* —the only work by Antonello now in Venice—displays some of the qualities which must have impressed Venetian painters in the 1470s: the oil technique which permits great subtlety of tone, the effortless ability at foreshortening, the solid three-dimensional forms of the figures, and the exquisitely painted landscape stretching away to the horizon. Giovanni Bellini may well have had direct access to Flemish paintings in Venice but there can be little doubt that he and all Venetian painters up to the time of Lotto were strongly influenced by Antonello's brief visit to their city.

Works by the Bellini family and their followers are shown in Room XIII. Jacopo, the father, is represented by a little *Crucifixion* (29) of about 1450, a work in which Giovanni may also have colla-borated before he began to develop his mature style under the influence first of Mantegna and then of Antonello. The impact of Mantegna is clearly evident in the statuesque figures of Giovanni's *Transfiguration* (27), the firmly modelled little head of a Saint (10), by some artist in the Bellini circle, reveals the influence of Antonello. Another attractive anonymous picture (71) shows Doge Pietro Orseolo and his Dogaressa kneeling in a courtyard fashionably decorated with antique marbles.

In Room XV there is another major treasure of the Museum—Carpaccio's fascinating genre scene which, for a variety of reasons, Ruskin deemed the " best picture in the world " (46). Apparently a fragment cut from a larger composition, its significance is obscure. It has been named " The Two Courtesans ", largely because of the daringly décolleté dresses. But these were in fact quite normal for bourgeois women in the 1490s, and the very high shoes are of a type worn only by the respectably married—" those pattens must make it difficult for your wife to walk " remarked a traveller to a Venetian: " So much the better " was the reply. Blonde hair was very fashionable in Venice where women passed hours sitting on their roof-tops bleaching their hair in the sunshine, though shading their faces and shoulders by crownless straw hats, rather like those which London cart-horses used to wear.

Room XIX contains a notable collection of **maiolica**. This pottery, technically described as tin-glazed earthenware, derives its name from Majorca whence such wares were imported in the fifteenth century. The Italian production of maiolica began shortly before 1450, and during the next century the potteries of Faenza (the origin of the French term *faience*), various towns in Umbria, and Venice itself, made wares which could be equalled nowhere else in Europe either for texture or delicacy of ornament. Painted with religious or mythological scenes in a range of colours restricted by the oxides available—cobalt blue, antimony yellow, iron red, copper green and manganese purple—some of these plates rank among the minor masterpieces of the Renaissance and mannerist periods. The Correr collection includes examples from Faenza, Casteldurante, Urbino and Venice, notably a seventeen-piece table service painted in cool colours by one of the greatest maiolica artists, Niccolò Pellipario.

Passing through the fine eighteenth-century library—originally in the Palazzo Manin—you return to the staircase which goes down to the main floor. It also gives access to the **Museo del Risorgimento** where you may follow the history of Venice after the fall of the Republic. A succession of rooms are filled with paintings, drawings, prints and relics illustrating the brief period of democratic liberty from 1797–8 (there is a drawing by Giacomo Guardi of the Tree of Liberty in the Piazza), the following eight years of Austrian rule, the period from 1809 to 1814 when Venice formed part of the Napoleonic kingdom, and the long Austrian domination from 1814 to 1866. Several rooms are devoted to the memory of Daniele Manin who led the heroic but futile rebellion again the Austrians in 1848. The last room contains records of Venice in the First World War, when Austrian troops came within shell-shot of the city.

If you turn right at the bottom of the stairs you will find yourself in a room devoted to the history of the **Venetian navy,** with an engaging eighteenth-century model of a galley in the centre. The next six rooms contain objects from Palazzo Morosini, most of them connected with Doge Francesco Morosini, the last Venetian hero (see p. 51). An elaborate painted and gilt *prie-dieu*, his two standards—one displaying the Crucifixion—and the triple lantern, all adorned his *galera* or flag-ship. There are some Turkish banners which he captured. His dogal hat—*cornu*—is displayed in a vitrine. And a series of crude paintings records the main incidents in his career.

Two rooms are filled with halberds and other weapons no less lethal for being decorative. There follows a room which illustrates Venice's relations with the Far East. The next is devoted mainly to the **Bucintoro,** the elaborate vessel in which the Doge rode out to the Lido to perform the marriage with the sea every Ascension Day. The red and gold banner which fluttered from its mast is shown above the doorway. But all that survives of the vessel itself—the last was built in 1724 and destroyed at the fall of the Republic—is a group of carvings by Antonio Corradini. The little relief of St. Mark adorned the door through which the Doge threw the ring into the sea, saying: "We espouse thee, O Sea, in token of perpetual sovereignty." Though as early as the sixteenth century a French writer commented that Venice had been cuckolded by the Turk.

After a room which records the Venetian part in the victory of Lepanto, with Vittoria's terra-cotta bust of the admiral Francesco Duodo, there is a room devoted to coins. Here there are examples of **coins** issued by every Doge from Sebastiano Ziani (1172–8) to

Books, Marbles, Paintings and Costumes

Ludovico Manin. A case is devoted to medals peculiar to Venice called *oselle*. Until the sixteenth century the Doges bound themselves by their coronation oaths to give a New Year's present of five ducks to each patrician. But as the size of the patrician families increased it became more and more difficult to provide enough birds. In 1521 no fewer than 9000 were needed so the Doge obtained permission from the Senate to distribute silver medals in their stead, and these were called *oselle* (Venetian for birds). Great ingenuity was applied to the design of the reverses of the medals which were altered each year and usually referred to notable events.

The next room is given to portraits of the Doges, interesting mainly as records of costume. That of Paolo Renier by Ludovico Gallina hangs in a particularly elegant rococo frame. Two rooms are now devoted to the **costumes** of the officials of the Serenissima. The togas remind one that Venice preserved a relic of Ancient Rome in her official robes. Those of red silk with cut velvet stoles were worn by the Procurators of San Marco; those without stoles by the Senators. The dark blue robes belonged to the Savi—the heads of the various ministries. There is one Ducal robe in the room—of scarlet wool lined with red silk, worn only during the Good Friday ceremonies in San Marco. Paintings reveal other costumes like that of red and gold brocade worn by the Admiral of the Fleet.

In the library the walls are covered with seventeenth-century book cases made originally for the Theatine monastery. The vitrines contain an array of handsomely bound commissions given by the Doges to ambassadors, admirals and other high dignitaries when they took office. The two following rooms are devoted to the Doges and hung with paintings of their main ceremonial functions. In the glass case you can see a late fifteenth-century Ducal *cornu*, an eighteenth-century ballot box used for voting in the Palazzo Ducale, one of the straw baskets which were presented to the Doges on their annual visits to San Zaccaria and one of the straw hats which were given them when they went to Santa Maria Formosa (see p. 92). In the next room there are fragments of carving, including some early lions of St. Mark.

The last two rooms, decorated in neo-classical style with delicate little paintings by Giuseppe Borsato, bring us to the Napoleonic wing. They are charmingly furnished with early nineteenth-century chairs and tables. And they contain three of **Antonio Canova's** earliest statues. He carved those of Orpheus and Eurydice for his first patron, Senator Fallier, between 1773 and 1776 when they were exhibited in the Piazza on Ascension Day. These works reveal that, at the age of nineteen, he was already the most technically accomplished sculptor in Venice. Three years later he exhibited the gracefully naturalistic group of *Daedalus and Icarus*, by far the most outstanding work of sculpture carved in Venice since the sixteenth century. Plaudits and commissions rained down on him. But he very soon turned his back on his early successes and left Venice for Rome where, largely under the influence of a group of British artists, he abandoned his early style for Neo-classicism. Within ten years he had established himself as the leading sculptor in Italy and before the century was out he was widely regarded as the greatest that Europe had produced since Michelangelo. Popes, emperors and kings competed for his services and treated him with a deference accorded to no Venetian artist since Titian. But in his mature style there remains no more than the faintest hint of his Venetian training. For while he was the last of the great Venetians, he was the first of the international artists of the nineteenth century.

CHAPTER 8

A Palladian Morning

San Giorgio Maggiore—the Giudecca—Il Redentore

Whether seen from the Dogana, where the Grand Canal opens into the lagoon, or from between the columns of the Piazzetta, or from anywhere along the Riva, the island of **San Giorgio Maggiore** completes and holds in delicate equilibrium the shimmering elements of the Venetian scene. It has " a success beyond all reason," wrote Henry James. " It is a success of position, of colour, of the immense detached campanile tipped with a tall golden angel. I know not whether it is because San Giorgio is so grandly conspicuous, with a great deal of worn, faded-looking brickwork; but for many persons the whole place has a kind of suffusion of rosiness." The island is set at exactly the right distance from the Piazzetta and from the church of Santa Maria della Salute. And so perfect is the relationship of the buildings and their materials—red brick and white marble—one with another and with the patch of green behind them, that it is sometimes difficult to realise that this eminently picturesque group was not designed and placed by some architect and town planner of genius. As Marco Boschini wrote in the seventeenth century:

> St'isola veramente è un zogelo,
> Ligà da sto cristal che la circonda;
> dove flusso e reflusso bate l'onda.
> No' par che la sia fata co'l penelo?

(This island is truly a jewel, set in this crystal which surrounds it where ebbing and flowing the waves beat. Doesn't it look as if it were done with a paint brush?) Like practically everything else that is beautiful in Venice, the island owes much to the happy chance of its position—and, of course, to the good taste of successive

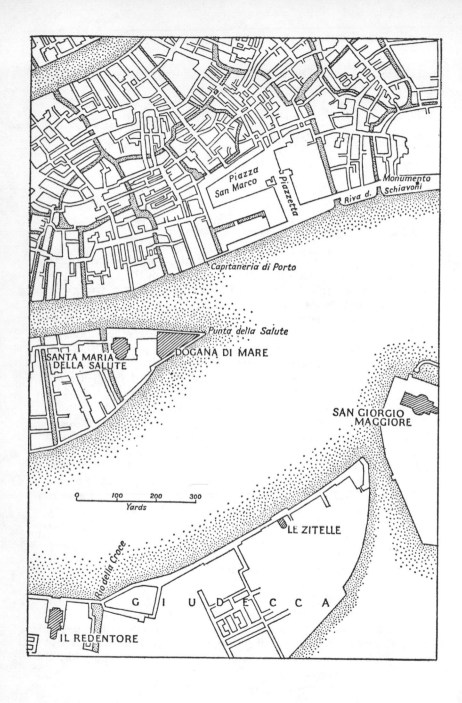

Piazza
San Marco

Piazzetta

Monumento

Riva d. Schiavoni

Capitaneria di Porto

Punta della Salute

SANTA MARIA
DELLA SALUTE

DOGANA DI MARE

SAN GIORGIO
MAGGIORE

0   100   200   300
Yards

Rio della Croce

LE ZITELLE

G I U D E C C A

IL REDENTORE

generations of Venetian architects who understood and took full advantage of their unique opportunities.

The first church was built on the island in about 790 and some two centuries later a Benedictine monastery rose beside it; but all these buildings were destroyed by an earthquake in 1223. The monastery was rebuilt and in 1443 the monks played host to the exiled Cosimo de' Medici who is said to have brought the famous Florentine architect, Michelozzo, with him. Michelozzo designed a new library for the monastery and although this vanished long ago his influence is apparent in the dormitory which he may also have begun (though it was completed much later, between 1494 and 1513 by the Lombard architect Giovanni Buora).

Buora's dormitory façade, faced with marble and crowned by three rounded gables, can be seen at the far left of the group of buildings on the island. The most conspicuous of the buildings is, of course, the church which is the work of Andrea Palladio. To the right you can see a range of red seventeenth-century buildings by Baldassare Longhena. The campanile which holds the whole composition together and anchors it to the lagoon, like a pin in the back of some exotic butterfly, is much later, as its neat neo-classical urns and columns reveal. It was rebuilt, to replace an earlier one which had toppled down, shortly before 1792. And the endearingly toy-like harbour with its twin lighthouses, which adds the finishing touch to the group, was built between 1808 and 1828.

San Giorgio Maggiore may be reached either by gondola or by the *motoscafo* which stops there in its run from the *Monumento* on the Riva degli Schiavoni to the Giudecca and Piazzale Roma. But before we reach the landing-stage in front of the church something should be said of the great genius to whom San Giorgio Maggiore owes so much of its beauty: **Andrea Palladio.**

He was born in or near Padua in 1508 and apprenticed to a stonemason in Vicenza in 1524. It is said that he had a gracious way with workmen, whom he kept happy, and a pleasing wit in conversation, which endeared him to his patrons. Palladio was not his surname but a nickname (derived from Pallas the Goddess of Wisdom) given him by his first patron and mentor Gian Giorgio Trissino who discovered his talents and persuaded him to become an architect. Humanist, poet and amateur architect, Trissino introduced the young Andrea to the world of classical thought and the ideals of classical architecture. A contemporary records that "when Trissino noticed that Palladio was a very spirited young man with an inclination to mathematics, he decided in order to cultivate his genius to explain Vitruvius to him and take him to Rome . . ." (the visit lasted from 1545 to 1547). This remark indicates the three main sources of Palladio's style: Vitruvius, the Roman architectural theorist of the first century B.C.; Rome, the site of the largest collection of classical buildings; and mathematics which governed not only the rules of sound construction but also the all-important question of proportions.

To Palladio and his contemporaries, as to Byzantine architects of the ninth century, the mystique of numbers had an appeal which is now difficult to appreciate. Believing that mathematics and music were intimately related, they thought that a study of this relationship would reveal laws to govern proportions in the visual arts. The ancients had discovered that if two strings are twanged under the same conditions the difference in pitch will be one octave if the shorter is half the length of the longer, a fifth if the shorter is two-thirds of the length of the longer, and a fourth if the relationship is 3:4. It was therefore supposed that a room in which the shorter wall was one-half, two-thirds or three-quarters of the length of the longer would be similarly harmonious in its proportions. Palladio and his contemporaries developed this idea to produce a far more complex series of ratios based on the major and minor third (4:5 and 5:6), the major and minor sixth (3:5 5:8) and so on. From a study of these consonances he also derived ratios which determined the heights of rooms, based on the arithmetical and harmonic mean, and the relationship of one part of a building to another and to the whole. It is therefore no flower of speech to talk of the harmony of Palladio's churches and villas. They are as mathematically complex and harmoniously satisfying as the fugues of Bach.

One of the aims of this study of mathematics and music was to unravel the secret of ancient Roman buildings which were considered the most perfect ever erected. Vitruvius's treatise provided, and the ruins of Rome illustrated, further laws which governed the practice of architects who wished to re-create the grandeur of Rome in sixteenth-century Italy. There were, however, many difficulties to be overcome in applying these laws to modern buildings, especially churches. For although the church was the lineal descendant of the pagan temple, it had to answer different requirements. Whereas the temple had contained only one *cella*, the church usually needed aisles with altars in them, and this meant that the façade would have to be wider than the classical pedimented temple front allowed. Ever since the fifteenth century, architects had wrestled with this problem, but Palladio found a perfect solution which he adopted for his three great church façades in Venice and which provided a model for later architects. Deriving his authority from an obscure remark in Vitruvius about the " double arrangement of gables " on the basilica at Fano, he superimposed two temple fronts, one based on the height of the nave and the other on that of the aisles.

Looking at the façade of **San Giorgio,** you will see that the two sections of the pediment on either side of the main block are the two ends of a pediment whose base is marked by the string-course between the central half-columns and whose apex would come in the centre of the main frieze. This arrangement prepares the visitor for the plan of the aisled church inside. Indeed, exterior and interior are closely linked and the, perhaps slightly awkward, raised half-columns in the centre echo the Greek columns which Palladio used on the inside of the façade.

The interior of San Giorgio strikes one first by its lightness, airiness and spaciousness. As in all truly great buildings, one is impressed more by the area of space enfolded by the structure than by the decorations of the shell. Here, nothing is cramped, nothing is fussed. Every detail of decoration forms an essential part of a single plan of logical clarity. And, of course, every measurement is determined by a system of proportions. The miracle is that such a scholarly church should also be deeply imbued with a sense of the numinous.

There are many paintings and sculptures of interest. Above the main door stand stucco statues of the Evangelists by Alessandro Vittoria—their slightly mannered movements providing a by no means displeasing contrast with the classical rigidity of the architecture. Over the second altar on the right there is a fine and moving carved wooden Crucifix dating from the first half of the fifteenth century. The high altar is dominated by Girolamo Campagna's vast bronze group of the Evangelists supporting the world with God the Father above (1591–3). The same artist was responsible for the rather heavy statue of the Virgin and Child above the first altar on the left. Several works in bronze deserve attention: a pair of romanesque candlesticks with an almost oriental air before the altar in the left transept, two magnificent candlesticks alive with *putti* by the master bronze worker Niccolò Roccatagliata, just inside the high altar rails and, on the high altar itself, six neo-classical candlesticks made by Francesco Righetti in Rome and given to the church by Pius VII.

In the nave the only painting of note is the dark *Adoration of the Shepherds* over the first altar on the right—a late work by Jacopo Bassano, painted with his usual rustic realism. The two large paintings in the transepts, *The Coronation of the Virgin* and *The Martyrdom of St. Stephen* are characteristic productions of the Tintoretto studio, fine in composition (probably roughed out by the master himself) but humdrum in execution. Their weaknesses become all the more apparent if they are compared with the two paintings on either side of the chancel, which are mainly from Tintoretto's hand, though even here he must have relied on some studio assistance. Painted between 1592 and 1594, in the last two years of his life, they represent *The Last Supper* and *The Gathering of Manna*. The daily gift of manna to the Israelites in the wilderness provided the Old Testament parallel to the institution of the Eucharist, and the two paintings were intended to be seen by the communicant from the altar rails. From here the bold rhythms of their compositions can best be appreciated. On closer inspection the eye is caught by many felicitous and realistic details—in *The Gathering of Manna* the figure of the man reaching down to the stream, and the two women thumping their washing against boulders, just as they do their laundering even to-day in Venetia, or, in *The Last Supper*, the cat peering cautiously into a basket, the Venetian glass flagons on the table and the beautifully painted still life of pears and peaches. Details such as these help to relate the cosmic mystery of the two scenes to the everyday world.

Behind the high altar is the **monastic choir** which was finished after Palladio's death. On the balustrade dividing it from the chancel stand two exquisitely beautiful statuettes of St. George and St. Stephen executed by Niccolò Roccatagliata in 1593 with an elegant delicacy which anticipates the eighteenth century. In striking contrast, the choir stalls, carved by Alberto van der Brulle and Gasparo Gatti between 1594 and 1598 have an almost Victorian opulence and fussiness which makes them look as if they had escaped from the Great Exhibition of 1851. There is a scene from

112

CARVINGS. *Above left,* Byzantine relief in the Cathedral at Torcello; *right,* a gothic capital on the arcade of the Doges' Palace. *Below left,* the renaissance well-head in the courtyard of Goldoni's house, Palazzo Centani; *right,* The Spy, a 17th century wood carving by Francesco Pianta in the Scuola di San Rocco

Looking down the Grand Canal from the Accademia bridge towards the domes of Santa Maria della Salute

the life of St. Benedict on the back of each stall, and in front there are more immediately attractive figures of *putti* riding dolphins.

A door to the right of the chancel leads to the **Cappella Superiore** (ask sacristan to open), the room in which the college of Cardinals met in conclave to elect a successor to Pius VI who had died a prisoner of Napoleon in 1799. Here they ruminated until March 1800, disturbed only by the visit of an English emissary bringing the welcome news that George III had agreed to give an annual allowance to his distant cousin, Cardinal York (alias Henry IX). Their choice fell, however, not on the soi-disant King of England but on Barnaba Chiaramonti who took the title of Pius VII and who is recorded in the chapel by a portrait and various relics, including his cardinal's hat. The altarpiece of *St. George and the Dragon* signed by Vittore Carpaccio and dated 1516 is a, largely studio, version of his painting in the Scuola di San Giorgio (see p. 73), and is notable mainly for the freely painted panels of the predella. Before leaving the church it is well worth while ascending the campanile to obtain one of the most beautiful views of Venice and the lagoon.

Outside the church, the door in the corner of the little quay-cum-*campo* opens into the former **monastic buildings,** now occupied by the Fondazione Giorgio Cini. (To visit these buildings it is necessary to write or telephone in advance to the secretary of the Foundation.)

Soon after its brief moment of Papal glory, when it housed Pius VII, the monastery fell on hard times. The Austrians turned it into a barracks, and thus it remained until 1951 when Count Vittorio Cini rescued it from decay. The buildings were in a sorry state; foundations were shaky, large rooms had been divided vertically and horizontally, windows had been bricked up and the whole place was surrounded by a rash of those hideous corrugated iron shacks which armies always seem to leave behind them. In a remarkably short time the monastery was restored and then brought back to life by the installation of a group of institutes named in memory of Count Cini's son, Giorgio, and devoted to the study of Venetian civilisation. Schools were also established for orphans and the children of sailors. And an open-air theatre with marble seats guarded by cypresses, where plays and operas are performed in the summer, was constructed in the gardens.

The first cloister, called the *chiostro dei cipressi* (though its only

The Companion Guide to Venice

tree now is a large *magnolia grandiflora*) was designed by Palladio, begun in 1579 and finished in 1614. The carpet bedding in the centre, which seems at first sight to be an anachronism, is carefully copied from an eighteenth-century print. The second cloister is about fifty years older and probably the work of Giovanni di Antonio Buora, the architects of the dormitory which runs along the east side. Though simpler than Palladio's cloister, it is no less serenely impressive. On the north side stands the Chapter House, with an elegant Renaissance doorway, now used by the institute of the history of art for exhibitions of old master drawings during the summer months. From the other side of the cloister, archways lead to the refectory built in 1560—Palladio's earliest work in Venice, and one of the most impressive rooms in Europe.

The **refectory** is approached through two ante-chambers, the first narrow and high with a monumental opening, on the scale of a Ptolemaic temple, which leads to the second of the same width but three times the length. At either hand are two gigantic aedicules sheltering red marble wash-basins. Two steps lead up through a second vast portal to the refectory itself. The dramatic effect of the spatial contrasts between the successive halls, each related to the others by a constant scale of proportions, cannot be conveyed in words: and it is difficult to suggest a parallel elsewhere, except perhaps in classical Greece.

It is, indeed, of Greece rather than Rome that one is immediately reminded by this great hall, though it resembles no other structure whatever. Of the utmost simplicity, its effect depends upon the exquisite adjustment of the proportions and fortuitously upon the breaks in the gargantuan cornice—created by the walling-up of two windows—which clasps the soaring vault in a sturdy yet tender embrace. Only one thing is missing—the vast *Marriage Feast at Cana* which Paolo Veronese painted for the end wall in 1563 but which was removed by Napoleon's army and is now in the Louvre. In its place hangs a Tintoretto-school painting of *The Marriage of the Virgin*.

From the first cloister a double staircase by Baldassare Longhena leads up to the first floor. Its baroque movement complements the classical solidity of Palladio's work and prepares the visitor for the opulent grandeur of the library which occupies the upper part of the range dividing the two cloisters. The library, designed by Longhena in 1641, is furnished with handsomely carved book-

114

cases and decorated with allegorical ceiling paintings by Giovanni Coli and Filippo Gherardi. It now contains one of the best collections of books on the history of Venetian arts and is frequented by scholars from both sides of the Atlantic and both sides of the iron curtain.

Motoscafi leave San Giorgio Maggiore every quarter of an hour for the **Giudecca.** This island, or rather series of eight little islands linked by bridges, was formerly a place of green quietude, the resort of those who wished to flee the hurly-burly of Venice. Michelangelo, an exile from Florence, stayed here in 1529 in order to live as a solitary. Three centuries later Alfred de Musset said he wanted to spend the rest of his life on the island (which he called by its dialect name):

> À Saint-Blaise, à la Zuecca,
> Dans les prés fleuris cueillir la verveine;
> À Saint-Blaise, à la Zuecca,
> Vivre et mourir là.

There are no meadows by the Fondamenta San Biagio now, and it would be difficult to find so much as a sprig of vervain, unless it be in one of the few enclosed gardens which still remain on this busy island or in the roof garden above Fortuny's factory.

The motor-boat makes its first stop outside the church of Santa Maria della Presentazione, usually known as **Le Zitelle** (the virgins) a very simple but satisfying church by Palladio. Its façade is flanked by the austere buildings of a convent where the nuns make fine lace, including the most cobwebby variety produced in Venice, *punto in aria.* A few doors down there is a fantastic house (No. 43) with vast Gothic-style windows, built by Marius Pictor, a landscape painter who enjoyed some renown in the early years of this century. Farther down the island, a street leads along a narrow canal to the largest private garden in Venice, laid out by an Englishman named Eden and thus known as the Garden of Eden (not open to the public). Facing it stands Palazzo Munster (No. 149) where that great writer and singularly tiresome individual, Frederick Rolfe—alias Baron Corvo—received the Last Sacrament in 1910. The house was then an infirmary for British sailors managed by Lady Layard (widow of the archaeologist) whom Corvo was to pillory in his posthumous book *The Desire and Pursuit of the Whole.*

The main monument on the Giudecca is Palladio's **church of** the Redentore. On approaching it you catch a glimpse of the minaret-like bell towers which serve as a reminder of the Veneto-Byzantine background to Palladio's classicism. The church was built as a thank-offering to commemorate the end of a plague which had ravaged the city. From the time of its foundation the Doge and Signoria made a pompous annual visit to the church, processing over a bridge of boats from the Zattere. The tradition is maintained to this day (it is one of the very few to survive from the Republic), and every year on the third Sunday of July the Venetians keep the festival of the Redentore. In the morning or afternoon they visit the church. In the evening there are firework displays and everyone in Venice who has a boat—gondola, sandalo, barge or motor-boat—spends the night on the water, feasting on mulberries (called *mori del Redentore*) and usually rowing over to the Lido to await the dawn.

The church, begun on 1577 and consecrated in 1592, is one of Palladio's greatest masterpieces. Its façade is a development of that which he designed for San Francesco della Vigna in 1568, based on a complex arrangement of superimposed temple fronts —derived from the Pantheon, which he had seen, as much as from the Basilica at Fano about which he had read in Vitruvius— with pediments over the door and central bay and the end sections of two hidden pediments on either side of the main block. As at San Francesco della Vigna, the whole scheme is regulated according to a complicated system of proportions.

The pilasters at the corners and the half-columns on either side of the door are two-thirds of the height of the main order: and the width of the central part of the façade is two-thirds of the entire width, representing a relationship of 2:3, a harmonic fifth. Now this ratio may alternatively be represented as 4:6 and subdivided 4:5 and 5:6 which, harmonically, represent a major and minor third. It is therefore not surprising to find that the height of the façade is four-fifths of its total width, and the width of the central part is five-sixths of its height. Inside, the proportions are governed by a still more complicated system which cannot be explained without numerous diagrams. Suffice it to say that the length of the nave is double its width and that each of the side chapels is one-third of the length of the nave.

Those nurtured on romantic notions of artistic inspiration may find this mathematical analysis saddening and distasteful. If a

116

system of mathematical ratios can produce a great work of art, they may ask, why have not all architects followed it? The answer is that many architects, especially in recent years, have followed harmonic rules but, lacking Palladio's genius, have failed to produce buildings as artistically satisfying (Le Corbusier with his similar rules has been the most successful). And, of course, Palladio was no slave to his rules, which he treated as guides rather than unbreakable laws. Indeed, much of the beauty of the Redentore is independent of them—the serene solemnity of the façade, the precision of such decorations as the wave-pattern stringcourse which ripples round the boldly simple interior. For an appreciation of such beauties, no knowledge of the arcane laws of harmonic proportions is necessary. Palladio himself probably agreed with Francesco Giorgi that " as the proportions of the voices are harmonies to the ears, those of the measurements are harmonies to the eyes. Such harmonies usually please very much without anyone knowing why, except the student of the causality of things." But an awareness of the rules of harmony is essential for those who wish to understand the characteristically late Renaissance mathematical-cum-mystical frame of mind in which the Redentore was created. Like many another man of his time, Palladio believed that the ideal ratios he employed captured in stone not merely the music of flute and viol but that celestial harmony to which Shakespeare alluded in the *Merchant of Venice*:

> There's not the smallest orb, which thou behold'st,
> But in his motion like an angel sings,
> Still quiring to the young-eyed cherubins;
> Such harmony is in immortal souls;
> But, whilst this muddy vesture of decay
> Doth grossly close it in, we cannot hear it.

I often wonder if it is entirely a coincidence that those lines are spoken in the garden of Belmont, a villa near Venice.

The **interior** of the Redentore is an improvement on that of San Giorgio Maggiore. The relationship of the dome to the nave, transepts and choir, is happier, and the semi-circular colonnade behind the high altar provides a much better climax. Palladio seems also to have paid more attention to the visual effect of the interior. From the door the church appears as a simple rectangular basilica with an apse. But as you walk towards the high altar, the majestic curves of the dome and transepts gradually reveal

117

themselves, giving an appropriate sense of elation and expansion rarely achieved by such simple and purely architectural means.

In this sonorous symphony of stone, the high altar strikes a discordant note and prompts one to wonder what form of altar Palladio intended—probably a very simple affair. But the present altar is a fine thing in itself. Executed in 1679, the marble reliefs of *Christ Falling Beneath the Cross* on the front and the *Deposition* on the back are by a Tyrolean sculptor, Tommaso Ruer; the bronze Saints by a Bolognese, Giuseppe Mazza. Two other works of bronze sculpture are worth noting: the elegant statuettes of Christ and St. John by Francesco Terilli (1610) in the holy water basins on either side of the main door. There are no paintings of much interest apart from a *Virgin and Child* by Alvise Vivarini and a *Baptism* by Veronese, both in the Sacristy.

From the landing stage in front of the Redentore you look across the canal to the **Zattere**. A little to the right of the largest of the three churches on that shore stands an undistinguished pink building, now the Pensione Calcina, where Ruskin stayed in 1877 when writing *St. Mark's Rest*. He liked it because it was cheap and, he wrote, " I look along the water instead of down on it and get perfectly picturesque views of boats instead of mast-head ones, and I think I shall be comfy." The view of the Redentore was no advantage to him, however. He regarded Palladio as one of the most baneful influences thrown up by the Renaissance and on the only occasion he brought himself to mention the Redentore he brushed it aside as ' small and contemptible, on a suburban island.' His venom he reserved for San Giorgio Maggiore: " It is impossible to conceive a design more gross, more barbarous, more childish in conception, more servile in plagiarism, more contemptible under every regard." These remarks serve to remind one that even the greatest and most sensitive critic can be resoundingly silly about works of art which fall outside his chosen period and which he cannot be bothered to understand.

A frequent motor-boat service connects the Giudecca with San Marco, the Zattere and the Piazzale Roma.

CHAPTER 9

The Accademia: Giorgione, Veronese and others

The contents of a great art gallery should be sipped, not gobbled.
A collection as rich as the Accademia cannot be taken in at a
single gulp without mental indigestion. Brief but frequent visits
are necessary to savour its quality. However, the present chapter
is designed for those who can spare time for no more than a single
visit. So it is not a survey of this wonderful collection but merely
some remarks on those, mainly secular, pictures which can be
studied better in the Accademia than anywhere else in Venice.
All the paintings are well labelled, and visitors with more time to
spare will have no difficulty in finding their way about the rest
of the collection.

From the door (10–4; holidays 9–1; closed Mondays) a double
staircase leads up to the impressive **Sala del Capitolo** of the old
Scuola di Santa Maria della Carità which, together with the adjoining church and monastery, were converted into the present art gallery
early in the nineteenth century. The rich ceiling of this room, all
aflutter with gilded cherubin, was carved in 1484 by Marco Cozzi.
The room is devoted to Venetian Gothic paintings by such masters
as Paolo da Venezia, Lorenzo Veneziano, Michele Giambono and
Antonio Vivarini. However, the greatest work of art here is not
a painting but a massive reliquary cross of silver and rock crystal,
made in the fifteenth century for the Scuola di San Teodoro.
Combining a love of richness and refinement with deeply emotional
religious feeling, it is a paragon of Gothic art.

The second room is devoted to eight large altarpieces, by
Giovanni Bellini, Cima, Carpaccio and Basaiti. They are works
of such high quality that they have retained nearly all their beauty
though stripped of the architectural frames specially designed
for them and torn from the churches for which they were painted.

119

All but three came from churches which have now been destroyed and I, for one, should like to see those three restored to their proper places in the church of San Giobbe (the Bellini *Virgin and Child with Saints;* the prototype of the large Venetian altarpiece, Basaiti's *Agony in the Garden* and Carpaccio's *Presentation of Christ in the Temple*).

A flight of steps leads up to a low dark room giving on to two small rooms (IV and V) which contains some of the greatest paintings in the collection. They are small in size—though in nothing else. Mantegna's *St. George* (588) has a statuesque monumentality which belies its tiny scale. It is one of the only two pictures in Venice by this artist who exerted such a vital influence on the young Giovanni Bellini and, as a consequence, the whole development of the Venetian school. There is a Cosmè Tura *Virgin and Child* (47), as hard and sinewy as the trunk of an olive tree—a fine example of the School of Ferrara, so near to and yet so far in feeling from Venice. From farther south comes the exquisite little *St. Jerome with a Donor* (47) depicted against the sunscorched landscape of Umbria by Piero della Francesca.

The next room (V) is hung with paintings by **Giovanni Bellini** and Giorgione. In five devotional pictures, Bellini plays a series of *adagio* variations on the *Virgin and Child* theme—varying the clothes, changing the backgrounds through a series of mountainous prospects, placing the figures in isolation or with Saints, and in one painting, alas, badly damaged—poignantly replacing the Child with the Dead Christ. Other Venetian artists could paint landscape backgrounds no less beautifully than Bellini, but none could so perfectly evoke the mood of the Magnificat in the Virgin's beauty, humility, tenderness, and her look of joy clouded by apprehension. In a very different vein are Bellini's five allegories representing Prudence (the nude woman with a dish), Summa Virtus (the blindfolded harpy), Inconstant Fortune (the woman in a boat), Perseverance or perhaps Sensuality and Virtue (the two male figures) and Slander, or according to other authorities, the Burden of Sin (the men with a monstrous shell). They were painted to decorate some piece of furniture, possibly a mirror like that owned by Catena and mentioned in his will as the work of Bellini. In point of subject matter, they are among Bellini's most uncompromisingly Renaissance paintings, for they appear to illustrate the arcane philosophical ideas of some humanist. Yet the general effect is curiously Gothic. For, like the majority of Venetian painters, and unlike the Ferrarese and the Florentines (there is no equivalent to the *Primavera* in fifteenth-century Venetian art), Bellini seems to have cared little for the intellectual ideas of the humanists. When late in life he was painting a mythological picture for Isabella d'Este he complained that he was working slowly because he found the pagan subject so distasteful. His aim was narrower and more conservative—to discover and depict the beauty of the world about him, to express the age-old concepts of the Church and to explore no further.

With **Giorgione's** *Tempesta* (915) we move into a later season where the skies are already overcast with the premonition of a summer thunder storm. The period of exploring the visible world is over: the world of imagination now lies before us. In point of subject the *Tempesta* is still more baffling than Bellini's allegories, but the explanation matters far less. For we accept this strange and haunting image of a soldier and a woman suckling a baby under an ominous sky simply as visible " poetry." Explanations of its literary meaning—and there have been many of them—are as irrelevant and as tedious as investigations into the identity of the dark lady of Shakespeare's sonnets. Giorgione's other picture here, the almost embarrassingly vivid portrait of a wrinkled old woman (272), is much more self-explicit. In her hand she holds a scroll inscribed *Col Tempo*, a warning to the young and fair of the ravages of time—an admonition that is for some more sobering than a *memento mori*. The idea is a familiar one, carrying with it the message of Marvell's "Coy Mistress," or Yeats's "When you are old and grey . . .," or indeed the old Venetian song which is much less subtle:

> Maridìte maridìte, donzela,
> Che dona maridada è sempre bela:
> Maridìte finchè la foglia è verde,
> Perchè la zoventù presto se perde.

(Get married, get married girl, the married woman is always beautiful: marry while the leaf is green, because youth is soon lost.) But it has seldom been expressed with such force, one might say with such savagery, and no artist before Giorgione could have expressed it in paint.

These two works reveal the modernity of Giorgione's genius and the part he played in the development of the Venetian school.

His paintings form a bridge between the early and the high Renaissance, between the hymns of Bellini and Cima and the solemn rhetoric of Titian, the elegant comedy of Veronese, the impassioned drama of Tintoretto. The very little that we know about him, amounting to no more than the fact that he was active in Venice in 1506 and died of the plague in 1510, has left ample room for romantic speculation. Something mephitic breathes from his works and maddens the judgment of the wisest and most cautious. Despite whole volumes of comment, explanation and hypothesis, the personality of Giorgione remains shrouded as if by some heavy and opaque exhalation from the lagoon. Only one documented work by him survives—an undecipherable fragment of fresco from the Fondaco dei Tedeschi (see p. 127 and p. 175). Only four of the pictures attributed to him have never been seriously doubted (and they do not include the *Col Tempo*); no more than another eight have won a measure of general acceptance. Yet there can be no question that he was greatly admired in his lifetime and exerted a fundamental influence on Venetian artists of the sixteenth century.

Returning to Room III and crossing the corner of Room VI— passing Paris Bordone's *The Doge and the Fisherman* with its splendid architectural setting—you reach Room VII. Here there are two paintings of special interest, both by artists strongly influenced by Giorgione. One, representing the hermits *St. Anthony and St. Paul* (328) painted in a sombre yet strangely sensuous colour scheme of greys and browns, is the work of Girolamo Savoldo of Brescia. The other is an arresting portrait of a pale young man in his study (912) by **Lorenzo Lotto,** dating from about 1524. His hands are long and white and delicate, his finely chiselled face is sensitive and almost *fin de race*. Looking up from his book, he stares at us with a gaze that seems pregnant with the hopes, doubts, and fears of youth. To find a portrait of similarly revealing intimacy half a century earlier would be as impossible as to find a *Tempesta*. For Lotto may justly be considered as the first truly psychological portrait painter in the history of European art. As Berenson remarked " his spirit is more like our own than is, perhaps, that of any other Italian painter of his time "; and in the faces of the people he portrayed with such rare understanding we are able to recognise across the centuries kindred spirits to ourselves.

Room X (up the stairs from Room VII), the grandest in the

Accademia, is dominated by **Paolo Veronese's** vast painting which fills the end wall. This work was the subject of a *cause célèbre* which throws as much light on the artist as on the ecclesiastical attitude to the arts in the period of the Counter Reformation. Veronese completed the painting, then called *The Last Supper*, for the refectory of Santi Giovanni e Paolo in 1573 and was promptly called before a tribunal of the Inquisition. Here he was cross-questioned about certain figures he had inserted without warrant of the Gospels. " What signifies the figure of him whose nose is bleeding? " asked the Inquisitor. " He is a servant who has a nose bleed from some accident," Veronese replied. " What signify those armed men dressed in the fashion of Germany with halberds in their hands? " " We painters," said Veronese, " use the same licence as poets and madmen, and I represented those halbadiers, the one drinking, the other eating at the foot of the stairs, but both ready to do their duty, because it seemed to me suitable and possible that the master of the house, who I was told was rich and magnificent, should have such servants." " And the one who is dressed as a jester with a parrot on his wrist, why did you put him into the picture? " pursued the Inquisitor. " He is there as an ornament, as it is usual to insert such figures." After further questions they reached the core of the problem and the Inquisitor asked: " Do you know that in Germany and other countries infected with heresy, it is habitual, by means of pictures full of absurdities, to vilify and turn to ridicule the things of the Holy Catholic Church, in order to teach false doctrine to the ignorant? " To which the painter replied, " I agree that it is wrong, but I repeat what I have said, that it is my duty to follow the examples given me by my masters." By this time it had become clear that Veronese was no heretic, and the Inquisitors released him on condition that he promised to correct the picture. This he did, not by tampering with any of his beautifully painted figures of halbadiers and Germans and buffoons but by changing its title to *The Supper in the House of Levi*. The whole affair sharply reveals the conflict between the new, rather solemn and dogmatic ecclesiastics of the Counter Reformation and an artist brought up in the Renaissance tradition who thought less of historical truth than sensuous beauty and whose aim was not to illustrate a sacred story but to produce a magnificent pageant painting.

It is hard to imagine a more magnificent or less spiritual picture.

The Companion Guide to Venice

Yet Veronese was not an irreligious man—and his rendering of the Last Supper is no more unlike the actual event than a Papal High Mass. But were it not for the Inquisition one would hardly concern oneself with the subject of this eminently unintellectual work. It is pleasure enough to let the eye roam over it, revelling in the luxury of silks, satins, gold and Murano glass, exploring the fantastic architectural prospect, wondering at the beautifully composed patterns of cool colour, and marvelling at the sharpness of Veronese's observation in the rendering of one figure after another—the youth leaning over the balustrade, the gesticulating man with the Negro page, the portly major domo, not to mention the dog and the cat beneath the table.

With the exception of Pordenone's tightly packed *St. Lorenzo Giustiniani with Six Saints* (316), all the other paintings in this room are by **Titian** and **Tintoretto**. And all are masterpieces which deserve the closest attention. The Tintorettos reveal further aspects of this artist's mystical personality, further exercises in the art of foreshortening and showing figures in movement. His *Transport of the Body of St. Mark* (831) is perhaps the most successful evocation of the mystery of a supernatural event ever painted. But he is still better represented elsewhere in Venice, especially in the Scuola di San Rocco (see p. 62).

Although the contrast between Tintoretto's mysticism and Titian's worldliness is generally a valid one, Titian's *Pietà* (400) reveals that he could touch chords of the profoundest spiritual feeling. It is a very late work, executed in an " impressionistic " manner at a time when, according to Palma Giovane, " he painted much more with his fingers than his brush." Left unfinished at his death, it was completed by Palma Giovane. The works of most artists in old age have an air of quiet resignation, but here the calm of the central group is shattered by the cry of the Magdalen rushing towards us—and it is significant that this figure is an after-thought, added as if Titian was dissatisfied with the conventional idea of the peace of death.

In the next room (XI) the paintings range in date from the sixteenth to the eighteenth century. There are further works by Veronese including an *Annunciation* (260) as cool and as freshly coloured as an Alpine meadow in spring, and *The Marriage of St. Catherine* (883), a variation on Titian's richly harmonious Pesaro Madonna (see p. 60) transposed into a higher key. Luca

Giordano's melodramatic *Deposition* (643), Strozzi's *Supper in the House of Levi* (777), with its earthy realism which contrasts so strangely with Veronese's rendering of the same subject, and Solimena's sultry *Rebecca and Jacob* (871) introduce us to the world of the Baroque. While Tiepolo's *Invention of the Cross* (642) reveals the elegance of the *settecento* and its author's debt to Paolo Veronese.

A corridor (XII) lined with eighteenth-century landscapes leads to a number of small rooms each of which contains a few paintings of interest. The first (XIII) has a group of portraits of Venetian dignitaries by Tintoretto, works which leave a stronger impression of red damask than of human personality. More interesting are three paintings by **Jacopo Bassano**, *St. Eleutherius Blessing the Faithful* (401), *St. Jerome* (652) and *St. Jerome in the Wilderness with the Virgin in Glory* (920) which includes a view of the country around the painter's native city, Bassano del Grappa. A Venetian of the mainland, not of the lagoon, Jacopo da Ponte, called Bassano, derived much from his three great contemporaries, Titian, Tintoretto and Veronese. He translated their style into a more rustic idiom, replacing their silks and jewels with no less well painted homespuns and flowers of the mountain. In the course of time he developed a personal style, rich in the use of colour, free in the handling of paint, and a rustic realism which foreshadows the seventeenth century. Several of his pictures have been attributed to the young El Greco whose genius took fire from contact with his personality.

Room XIV is devoted mainly to the two most distinguished painters working in seventeenth-century Venice—both of them foreigners—**Jan Liss** from Holstein and **Domenico Fetti** from Rome. The great sixteenth-century flowering seems to have exhausted the art of painting in Venice. The city became a museum visited by connoisseurs and painters of all nations—Poussin, Rubens and Van Dyck were among them—but producing only sedulous imitators. Foreign artists who settled in Venice were able to learn from the masters whom the Venetians were content to copy. These delicately coloured and sensuously painted works by Fetti and Liss could not have been executed without the example of the great Venetians of the sixteenth century, yet they are original productions of the baroque age which owed so much to Titian and Tintoretto.

Four large mythological pictures by **G. B. Tiepolo** decorate Room XV. They are, alas, in poor condition and a better estimate of this artist's abilities may be gained from some small *bozzetti* in Room XVI. One is a sketch for a *Glory of St. Dominic* (810), the other a *Transport of the Holy House to Loreto* (911) for a ceiling in the Scalzi church (destroyed 1915). Affording a vivid glimpse of the creative process, they have the spontaneity and freshness of a letter from a great writer.

This room also contains paintings by **Canaletto** and **Francesco Guardi**. Most people derive their first impression of Venice from Canaletto whose views of the city are to be found in museums and private collections throughout the world. And they may be surprised to discover that only two of his pictures are now to be found in Venice. He worked largely for export, painting his serenely beautiful architectural prospects for grand tourists. Guardi, on the other hand, worked mainly for Venetians and—so far as may be discovered—Venetians of the middle class. The two painters reveal the contrasting strains in the Venetian character which had, in an earlier period and on a much higher plane, been expressed by Titian and Tintoretto. Canaletto was interested mainly in static, monumental qualities, the richness of colour and the clarity of light. Invariably the more competent of the two, he rose to heights of poetry only on rare occasions. Guardi is a painter of movement who attempted to catch the flicker of sunshine on water or marble, to represent the lurch of a gondola, the rustle of a domino, or the lapping of the lagoon. Little concerned with topographical accuracy, he aimed to capture a mood, to represent the essential feeling of Venice. The buildings he painted are never monumental, they are dissolved in corruscations of light. Here there is one of his many views of San Giorgio Maggiore, looking like a *fata morgana*. The Canaletto is a *capriccio*, a view of an imaginary courtyard, painted with such solidity and lit with such limpid light that one can hardly believe that it had no reality outside the painter's mind.

At the end of the room there is a group of *genre* pieces by Pietro Longhi, similar to those in the Galleria Querini-Stampalia (see p. 94). There are also some delicate pastel portraits by **Rosalba Carriera,** the most famous female artist in history. All her women are either beautiful or distinguished: all her men are handsome. Very rarely does a hint of personality peep through these inanimate faces which might as easily be carnival masks. Perhaps that was why Rosalba was so popular with the eighteenth-century visitors to Venice whom she portrayed by the drove.

Room XVIa, on the other side of the corridor, contains more eighteenth-century pictures. There is a fascinating *genre* piece by the Neapolitan Gaspare Traversi, representing a scene after a duel. Painted with a hard attention to detail, it might well be taken as an illustration for some novel of *galanterie*. The story is as explicit as in any Victorian Academy picture. A striking contrast is provided by **G. B. Piazzetta's** masterly *Fortune Teller* (483) in which the subject has no more importance than in a late Rembrandt. Everything here depends on the brilliantly accomplished realisation of the human figure, the fluid handling of the paint, and the rich colour scheme of reds, browns, turquoise and white.

The corridor ends in a little tribune where a vitrine contains models by **Antonio Canova.** Two of these terra-cottas are early works, a reduced copy of the antique group of the Wrestlers in Florence and a little statue of Apollo which he presented to the Accademia on his election in 1779. The third is a *bozzetto* for the *Pietà* which he began to model in 1819 for the new church he was building in Possagno, but he died before he completed it.

This group of works by Canova brings the history of the Venetian school to an end. But the resources of the Accademia are not yet exhausted. To your right a door leads into a large Gothic room, formerly the church of Santa Maria della Carità. Just inside the door an area of pink and white plaster represents all that remains of Giorgione's one documented work, the frescoed façade of the Fondaco dei Tedeschi (see p. 122 and p. 175). Otherwise the room is devoted to fifteenth-century altarpieces, many of them works of great beauty. From the other side of the little tribune a corridor leads to two rooms which contain cycles of paintings from Venetian *scuole*.

The paintings in Room XX come from the Scuola di San Giovanni Evangelista (see p. 55) and are the work of various artists: Carpaccio (566), Gentile Bellini (563, 567, 568), Giovanni Mansueti (562, 564), Lazzaro Bastiani (561) and Benedetto Diana (565). They represent incidents from the story of a relic of the True Cross which is still preserved in the Scuola di San Giovanni Evangelista

and record the miracles performed in its presence: how a mad man
was cured when the patriarch of Grado carried it into his room
(566), how a victim of quartan fever recovered when he touched
a candle which had stood by it (563) and, most enchantingly, how
it dropped into a canal and bore above the waters the man who
valiantly jumped in to rescue it (568). But the true subject of all
these paintings is Venice—Venice in the late fifteenth century in
all her pride and pomp and opulence. They record the beauty
of the buildings many of which remain little changed, and the
richness of the clothes worn by the patricians (it is worth mentioning
that the plump, crowned lady kneeling on the left in 568 is almost
certainly Caterina Cornaro, ex-Queen of Cyprus). Gentile
Bellini's *Procession in Piazza San Marco* (567) might almost be that
witnessed by Sir Richard Guylforde and his astonished chaplain
from Yorkshire on Corpus Christi Day in 1505: "the most solempne
procession that ever I sawe. . . . It wold make any man joyous
to se it. And over that it was a grete marueyle to se the grete
noumbre of relygious folkes, and of scoles that we call bretherheds
or felyships, with their deuyses, whiche all bare lyghte of wondre
goodly facyon, and betwene every of the pagentis went lytell
children of bothe kyndes, gloryously and rychely dressyd, berynge
in their hande in riche cuppes or other vessaylles some plesaūt
floures or other well smellynge or riche stuffe, dressed as aungelles
to adorn the sayde processyon. The forme and maner therof
ecedyd all other that ever I sawe so moche that I can not write it."
The background is immediately recognizable, yet much has
changed since 1496 when this picture was painted—all the mosaics
on the façade of San Marco have been replaced save that over the
door on the left, while the clock-tower has been built on the
left and the Procuratorie Nuove on the right. Another painting—No. 566—shows how the Rialto bridge looked before the
present stone one was erected, with a draw-bridge in the centre
to let through tall-masted ships or to interrupt the passage of
walkers.

Every time one sees these pictures, the attention is arrested, the
eye enraptured by some previously unnoticed detail—a Negro
preparing to dive into the canal, two women discussing a calamity—
as Venetian women so love to do—the row of chimney-pots above
the Procuratie Vecchie, a little dog sitting in the prow of a
gondola, or the washing hanging out on poles from palace windows.

The Ca' d'Oro, or house of gold, so called because of the lavish use of gilding on the façade. The gold has now vanished but it is still one of the richest Venetian gothic buildings

Santa Maria dell'Orto maintains a cloistered peace, in a part of Venice usually ignored by the tourist but full of delights

It is the sum of such down-to-earth details that give the paintings
their peculiar fascination. For nothing could be less mystical than
these pictures. Every supernatural implication is elbowed out by
some homely detail from real life. One has only to compare them
with paintings of miracles executed in Siena fifty years earlier, or
by Tintoretto fifty years later, to appreciate how Venetian artists
of the late fifteenth century were obsessed by their exploration of
the world in which they lived.

The cycle of paintings in Room XXI is the work of **Vittore
Carpaccio** and was painted between 1491 and 1498 for the
Scuola di Sant' Orsola. It illustrates scenes from the life of St.
Ursula—from left to right—the apotheosis of the Saint (576): the
Ambassadors of the King of England ask the King of Brittany to
give the hand of his daughter Ursula to their master's son, while she
in an adjoining room lays down the conditions of the marriage, that
the Prince shall be baptised and accompany her on a pilgrimage
(572); the Ambassadors take their leave (573); they tell the
King of England the conditions of the marriage (574); Ursula
and the English Prince set out on their travels (575), the engaged
couple are greeted by the Pope in Rome (577); Ursula dreams
that she must undertake a pilgrimage to the shrine of the martyrs
(578); she arrives with the Pope and her thousand virgin atten-
dants at Cologne, besieged by the Huns (579); the martyrdom and
funeral of St. Ursula outside Cologne (580). Once again the eye
is caught by many details of pageantry or everyday life. The
elegant bowmen in the martyrdom scene must have been inspired
by the young Venetians who were required to practise archery on
the Lido. Many a Venetian bedroom must have looked like the
Saint's, though without the crown at the foot of the bed. But
here there is something more than realism. For this is less the
picture of a room than a picture of light and air flooding into
a room. Carpaccio was fascinated by the problem of rendering
light and colour. And in painting the peculiar quality of Venetian
light he has only one rival—Canaletto.

Returning along the corridor to the neo-classical tribune, and
turning left, you go down a flight of stairs to the last room of the
Accademia, the former Albergo of the Scuola della Carità. The
wall facing you is covered with **Titian's** *Presentation of the Virgin*,
painted for this room in the 1530s. There is a record here of the
late fifteenth century anecdotic interest in *genre* painting, especially

notable in the figure of the old woman with a basket. But the scene
is no longer episodic. Every line of the composition directs the
eye to the main figure—the tiny child Virgin ascending the staircase. The room also contains an interesting reliquary for a fragment of the True Cross, partly Byzantine and partly fifteenth-
century Venetian.

CHAPTER 10

The Mercerie and Mannerism

The Mercerie—San Giuliano—San Salvatore—Campo and church of San Bartolomeo—San Lio—Santa Maria della Fava—Ponte della Guerra— Calle Larga San Marco

The Mercerie, leading from the clock tower in the Piazza to the Rialto, is the busiest street in Venice (*merceria* is Italian for haberdasher, hence the name of this street which is divided into three parts—Merceria dell' Orologio, Merceria di San Giuliano, and Merceria di San Salvatore). Picking their way through a crowd of international window gazers, with many a *permesso* and *scusi*, an occasional *Buon giorno, Commendatore* or *Ciao*, the Venetian men of affairs hurry between the two main centres of business life in the city. It has always been a busy thoroughfare and shopping street. In the sixteenth century artists sometimes displayed their pictures here in the hope of attracting commissions. John Evelyn in 1645 described it as "one of the most delicious streets in the world for the sweetness of it . . . all the way on both sides as it were tapestried with cloth of gold, damasks and other silks which the shops expose and hang before their houses from the first floor. To this add the perfumes, apothecaries' shops, and the innumerable cages of nightingales which they keep, that entertain you with their melody from shop to shop." Nowadays the shops offer leather, clothes, jewellery, glass. The nightingales have vanished but you may catch the strains of Callas singing *O Casta Diva* or some tenor rendering the latest pulsingly sentimental Neapolitan love song, from the doors of the gramophone dealers.

So bright and gay are the window displays of the Mercerie that few visitors look upwards at a strange little relief above the first archway on the left after the clock tower. At first sight it appears

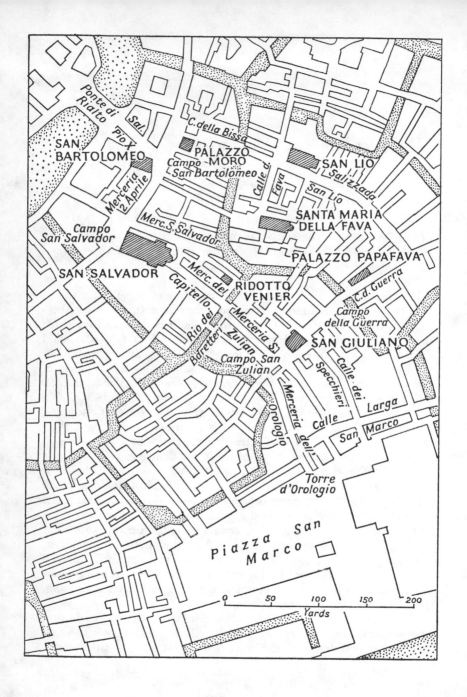

to represent a woman emptying a chamber pot out of her window, and some have supposed it to be a visual equivalent to the " gardy-loo " shout which used to echo through the streets of old Edinburgh. In fact it records a far more solemn and romantic occasion. In 1310 Bajamonte Tiepolo led a revolt against the government of Venice, intending to establish a different type of oligarchy if not a tyranny. By the dawn light of the 15th June, his forces advanced by two columns on the Ducal supporters in the Piazza. The smaller column entered from the west while the other, led by Bajamonte, went along the Mercerie. The timing was perfect and Bajamonte might well have won the day by surprising the Doge's army from the rear while it was engaged by the other column. But at the vital moment, just as Bajamonte was reaching the Piazza, an old woman peering out of her window to see what was going on, knocked a mortar from the ledge and felled the rebel standard-bearer. In confusion, Bajamonte and his troops turned and fled back to the other side of the Rialto. The last revolt against the *Serrata del Maggior Consiglio* had been defeated. When the Doge offered to reward the old woman who had played so important a part in the day she asked no more than the promise that her rent should never be raised and the privilege of hanging the standard of St. Mark from her window on the anniversary of the event. Every year until the fall of the Republic a banner was hung from the window on the 15th June, and when the original house was demolished in the nineteenth century the present relief was put up.

So much for the *vecchia del morter*. The first part of the Mercerie —Merceria dell' Orologio—leads to the church of **San Zulian** (Giuliano), notable for its architecture and several works of art. The façade, designed by Jacopo Sansovino between 1553 and 1555, is of a simple classical form enriched with allegorical reliefs and inscriptions in Greek and Hebrew. It was built at the expense of Tommaso Rangone, a physician who steered a somewhat dubious course between science and charlatanism and won considerable fame in Venice. He must have been a man of great vanity for he began this monument to himself at the age of sixty, choosing the inscriptions and commissioning from Sansovino the striking statue which is placed above the main door and shows the doctor seated in his study, among his books and terrestial and heavenly spheres (it has recently been called " the greatest and most elevated High Renaissance sculptured portrait "). He must also have been

133

unusually preoccupied with death. With great care he planned the route that his funeral cortege should take to San Giuliano where no fewer than three orations were to be made in his honour—it would not be surprising to find that he wrote them himself. His most famous book was a treatise on how to live to the age of 120. He himself managed to reach only eighty.

The interior of the church is agreeably rich, with gold glittering from the carved wood cornice and ceiling and with velvety late sixteenth- and early seventeenth-century paintings. The central panel of the ceiling, representing the apotheosis of St. Julian, was painted in about 1585 by Jacopo Negretti, a nephew of Palma Vecchio usually known as **Palma Giovane.** Though trained in Rome where he picked up many tricks of the mannerist style—which had come into existence partly as a reaction against the classical perfection of Raphael and partly as an expression of the spiritual disturbances of the Counter Reformation—Palma Giovane sought above all to follow in the footsteps of Titian and Tintoretto. A remarkably prolific painter, he left works of greatly varying quality in practically every Venetian church. The San Giuliano ceiling is one of his best—Tintorettesque in inspiration, though with a slightly disorganised composition. He appears in a Titianesque mood in the *Assumption* (second altar on the right) where the drama of the great Frari altarpiece degenerates into the merely theatrical. On either side of this painting stand long-limbed statues of St. Daniel and St. Catherine, and on the altar frontal there is a relief of *The Birth of the Virgin*, with lively dancing figures, all by Alessandro Vittoria. Another sixteenth-century painting of interest is Veronese's sadly damaged *Pietà with Three Saints* over the first altar on the right (only the upper part is by the master). In the Sacramental Chapel to the left of the chancel there is a very elaborate marble altar designed by Giovanni Antonio Rusconi with terra-cotta statues painted to simulate bronze and a relief by Girolamo Campagna.

The two vast pictures on either side of the high altar, *A Miracle of St. Julian* and *The Martyrdom of St. Julian*, by **Antonio Zanchi,** represent Venetian baroque painting at its not very excellent best. Although intentionally realistic, with an abundance of solid figures shown in violent movement, the two paintings have a curious touch of Venetian fantasy and the two soldiers in that on the left have an almost spectral quality. In the top right corner of the other picture, there is a portrait of the donor who observes the horrifying scene with a smugly complacent air, as if he had ordered the martyrdom as well as the painting of it.

To leave the quiet church of San Zulian and return to the bustle of the Mercerie is like descending from the mountains to the plain. This part of the street is called the Merceria San Zulian. The Libreria della Serenissima on the left is one of the best book shops in Venice, much patronised by artists and intellectuals. Crossing the Ponte dei Baretteri you will see straight ahead the brick built apse of San Salvatore with a little tabernacle which traditionally marks the place where Pope Alexander III slept in the open on the first night of his incognito visit to Venice in 1177. If you turn right after the bridge, go under the *sottoportico* then turn left and ring the bell of No. 4939 you may, if fortunate, be admitted to see one of the most elegant stuccoed interiors of eighteenth-century Venice —the Casino Venier which transports one to the very heart of Casanova's city. At the very end of the street, where the Merceria San Salvatore opens into the *campo* of the same name, there is a nice example of early twentieth-century Venetian fantasy—a monstrous iron bird holding in its beak a lampshade in the form of three glass umbrellas. But we must turn to more serious matters.

The white façade of **San Salvatore,** a solid and relatively simple example of Venetian baroque architecture, was built in the late seventeenth century to the design of Giuseppe Sardi. The interior, begun by Giorgio Spavento in 1506, continued by Tullio Lombardo and completed by Sansovino in 1534 is a very fine specimen of Venetian Renaissance architecture: it marks a stage in development between Pietro Lombardo and Palladio, between the early and the high Renaissance.

In the early days of the Renaissance, Tuscan architects formulated the centrally planned Greek cross church in which one wall echoed another in perfect harmony and where the combination of square base and circular dome symbolised man's relation to the universe. One such church, San Giovanni Grisostomo (see p. 174) had been built in Venice. The central plan posed numerous practical problems, however—it was often difficult to fit into an existing site and it was less well suited to the liturgy than the basilica. At San Salvatore the little known Spavento therefore compromised by running three Greek cross plans together (see plan). To satisfy the conservatism of the religious authorities, who had long regarded

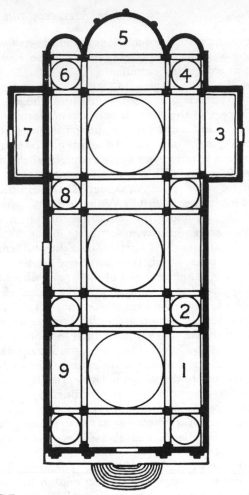

S. SALVATORE

1. Statue of Christ by Giulio Moro
2. Monument to Doge Francesco Venier by Sansovino and Vittoria (*c.* 1556)
3. Monument to Catherine Cornaro by Bernardino Contino (1580-4)
4. *The Annunciation* by Titian (1566)
5. The Transfiguration by Titian (1560s)
6. *The Supper at Emmaus* by a follower of Giovanni Bellini
7. Monument to Cardinals Marco, Francesco and Andrea Cornaro by B. Contino (1570)
8. Statues of St. Roch and St. Sebastian by Alessandro Vittoria (*c.* 1600)
9. Monument to Doges Girolamo and Lorenzo Priuli designed by Cesare Franco (1578-82)

the short-armed Latin cross as the ideal symbolical plan for a church, he tacked on slightly awkward transepts. The decorative scheme relies for its effect on bold grey stone mouldings which stand out against the white walls, as in Palladio's churches. And the relation of column to arch is perfectly adjusted to provide a sense of static classical solemnity, solidity and repose.

The same classical qualities mark Sansovino's noble monument to Doge Francesco Venier (2) of 1556–61. Here Sansovino took over the triumphal arch type of monument—like that used by the Lombardi—but reduced its sculptural decoration to the bare minimum of an effigy and two graceful, ineloquent, allegorical statues. It was against the sense of unquestioning security expressed in such a monument as this that certain mid-sixteenth-century architects and sculptors reacted. For want of a better name they are usually called Mannerists.

There are several mannerist monuments in this church. The outer walls of the two transepts, for example, are filled with vast monuments to members of the Cornaro family, designed by Bernardo Contino and erected in the 1570s. That on the right is to Catherine Cornaro, Queen of Cyprus, who is shown in a low relief handing over her kingdom to the Doge: that on the left commemorates three cardinals. A curious sense of insecurity, not to say *angst*, is given to them by the architectural framework. Instead of crowning the simple Ionic colonnade with a triangular pediment, Contino used the two arcs of broken curved pediments at either side and superimposed on them a triangular pediment which juts awkwardly into their lines. In the monument to Doges Lorenzo and Girolamo Priuli in the nave (9), designed by Cesare Franco and erected between 1578 and 1582, the effect is still more uncomfortable. Instead of making one homogeneous monument, the architect placed two double storied aedicules side by side in such a way that there is a cluster of columns in the centre between the niches. If you try to analyse this monument in classical terms you will find that the relations between the various parts are jarring, and intentionally so. Within the classical framework nothing happens quite as one would expect in a classical design. This wilful breaking of the classical rules is the essence of mannerist architecture. For the style is a highly sophisticated one, based on the assumption that everyone knows what the rules are.

The Priuli monument is decorated with recumbent effigies of the

137

Doges proudly dressed in cloth of gold. Above there are statues of St. Lawrence and St. Jerome, by Giulio Moro, which reflect the tendency of mannerist artists to distort and contort the human form in order to obtain effects of physical elegance or spiritual feeling. The athletic St. Lawrence is just too elegant by half. With his wasp waist, his well developed biceps and calves, he is an ideal of mannerist health and efficiency. On the other side of the church there is a statue by the same sculptor of the Redeemer (1). But here he wished to give the figure an appearance of ascetic spirituality which he achieved by the attenuation of the limbs and face.

One may notice a similar mannerism in two statues by a much greater sculptor **Alessandro Vittoria,** the St. Roch and St. Sebastian flanking an altarpiece by Palma Giovane (8). These figures seem to be struggling to dissociate themselves from the architectural framework. The writhing St. Sebastian is derived from one of the famous Slaves by Michelangelo who was the first Renaissance sculptor to abandon the canons of classical restraint and whose work anticipates not merely Mannerism but also the Baroque. Carved in about 1600 these statues reveal Vittoria's style at its most mature.

Alessandro Vittoria was the most prolific and by far the ablest sculptor in sixteenth-century Venice. For many years he worked under Jacopo Sansovino and, indeed, contributed the relief lunette to that master's Venier monument in this church (2). But he broke away from Sansovino's classicism under the influence of Michelangelo whose works were known to him, as to Tintoretto, by terra-cotta models. He shared with Tintoretto a preoccupation with the problem of rendering the human body in movement. His statues of Saints also display a similar strain of mysticism. Very little is known about him as a personality, except that he was something of a solitary devoted to his flower garden near San Giovanni in Bragora.

There are three outstanding pictures in the church. In the chapel to the left of the high altar there is a *Supper at Emmaus* painted in clear bright colours and flooded with Venetian light but much restored. It has been attributed to Giovanni Bellini, though most authorities now assign it to a follower. Of greater interest are two masterpieces by **Titian,** an *Annunciation* in the chapel to the right of the high altar, and a *Transfiguration* which serves to cover the silver-gilt dorsal of the high altar itself. (Ask sacristan to turn on light.) They are both fairly late works, painted in the 1560s when Titian's handling was becoming broader and more " impressionistic " and when he was beginning to paint religious subjects with greater spirituality. The rich deep tones of the *Annunciation* contrast with the luminous light colours of the *Transfiguration*. In the latter the exaggeratedly foreshortened tumbling figures seem to suggest the influence of Tintoretto.

Next to San Salvatore stands the cloister of the old monastery, now the telephone exchange, a pleasant classical construction by Sansovino. On the other side of the *campo* stands the Scuola di San Teodoro which, like the church, has a baroque façade by Sardi with statues by Bernardo Falcone. Inside this building, now used as an exhibition hall, there is a handsome double staircase leading to the upper floor.

From the Campo San Salvatore the Merceria Due Aprile (the name commemorates the Venetian " last ditch " proclamation to resist the Austrians at all costs on 2nd April 1849) leads to the **Campo San Bartolomeo.** During working hours this square is always swarming with business men in immaculate dark suits and sparkling white shirts clutching morocco brief-cases. They appear, very sensibly, to transact most of their affairs over cups of espresso coffee and glasses of vermouth in the surrounding cafés which echo with the words—*centinaia, millioni, milliardi.* Presiding over this animated scene is Carlo Goldoni who, if he returned to Venice, would find that life on the Rialto has altered little save that the talk is of lire instead of *zecchini.* The statue vividly presents Goldoni's humorous and humane if rather scornful personality. It is by Antonio del Zotto (1883) and one of the best pieces of late nineteenth-century Italian sculpture to be found anywhere.

In the Salizzada Pio X, leading towards the Rialto bridge, stands the church of **San Bartolomeo.** Here there are two magnificent paintings of St. Alvis and St. Sinnibaldo executed by Sebastiano del Piombo as shutters for the organ. There is not much else of interest in the church. But at the base of the campanile beside it there is one of the best grotesque heads in Venice—reminiscent of photographs of Irving in the role of Shylock. Leaving the *campo* from the other side, down the Calle della Bissa which opens beside the fourteenth-century Gothic Palazzo Moro, you reach the Ponte Sant' Antonio where you have a good view (to the right) of a small palace with slender round-headed windows, a little masterpiece of early Renaissance architecture.

The Companion Guide to Venice

The Calle della Bissa—called after a type of silk which used to be sold here—leads on to the Campo **San Lio**. Inside the church the rather low ceiling is painted with an attractive *Apotheosis of St. Leo* by Domenico Tiepolo, son of the more famous Giovanni Battista. The early Renaissance chapel to the right of the high altar was designed by the Lombardi and has exquisitely carved pilasters alive with foliage and birds. Above the altar there is an agonised *Pietà* relief, possibly by Tullio Lombardo, which retains traces of its original gilding. To the left of the high altar there is a large painting of *The Crucifixion* by Pietro Muttoni, nicknamed della Vecchia on account of his facility as a copyist of older masters. It was painted in 1633 and combines the twin strains of fantasy and earthy realism so typical of Venetian baroque painting. The very prominent soldiers dicing in the foreground are dressed in the costumes of the *Landsknechte* who descended to ravage northern Italy at every swing of the political pendulum in the early seventeenth century. At the base, portraits of three staring donors introduce a note of almost surrealist incongruity. It is a disturbing work, possibly the best that Muttoni ever painted, but not very appealing. Over the first altar on the left there is a painting of St. James by Titian, but so badly damaged as to be hardly recognisable as his.

From the Campo San Lio the Calle della Fava leads to the church of **Santa Maria della Fava** (so called from a type of sweetmeat in the form of *fave* or beans made in a *pasticceria* here in former times). It is an eighteenth-century building of little architectural merit. Statues and reliefs by Giuseppe Bernardi—interesting mainly as the master of Antonio Canova—line the nave. The church is, however, worth visiting for two outstanding eighteenth-century paintings. The earlier is **G. B. Piazzetta's** *Virgin and Child with St. Philip Neri* (second altar on left) executed between 1725 and 1727. Painted in a colour scheme of rich browns and dull reds with a slash of dark turquoise sky across the top, it is an autumnal vision rather than a religious painting. As in Piazzetta's secular pictures (see p. 127) the subject matter seems of slight importance in comparison with the artist's bravura handling. Subject matter plays a far more important part in the other great *settecento* altarpiece: **G. B. Tiepolo's** charming *Education of the Virgin* of 1732, over the first altar on the right. The influence of Piazzetta, which marked Tiepolo's youthful style, is still evident

140

here, but he has already adopted a much brighter, lighter, palette. And the altarpiece relies for its effect more on the delicate relationship between St. Anne and the young Virgin Mary than on purely painterly elements. Above the second altar on the right, Jacopo Amigoni's *Visitation* is an attractive minor work notable for its pale pastel colours of a tonality which Tiepolo used in his mature paintings, though with much greater subtlety and sensitivity.

If you turn right on leaving Santa Maria della Fava, go down the *calle* which runs alongside the church and take the first turning to the left you will reach the Salizzada San Lio, more or less opposite an attractive Veneto-Byzantine house of the thirteenth century. The Salizzada is another busy shopping street but with an atmosphere quite different from the Mercerie only a few hundred yards away. For here we are in the poor Castello *sestiere* and most of the shops offer only the simplest wares—stout shoes and thick clothes, wooden spoons and other household utensils which are all the more attractive for being unpretentious. There is, however, one shop which caters for a more sophisticated clientèle, selling nothing but tassels and fringes which are produced in a barely credible variety of colours, shapes and sizes.

If you turn right on entering the Salizzada San Lio and right again at the end, the narrow Calle della Guerra will lead you past the Palazzo Papafava, with a fine early sixteenth-century doorway, to the Ponte della Guerra. This is one of the several bridges on which pitched battles used to be fought by members of the two sections of the Venetian *popolo*, the Castellani and the Nicolotti. The touch lines are marked by white marble soles let into the pavement. Straight ahead, the *calle* leads back to San Giuliano. From here you can return to the Piazza along the Calle dei Specchieri which, as its name suggests, was once inhabited by vendors of looking glasses.

But before returning to the Piazza it is worth pausing in the **Calle Larga San Marco,** another busy shopping street. A few doors down to the left stands the Farmacia G. Mantovani al Redentor, one of the most attractive of the several eighteenth-century chemists' shops still functioning in Venice, with a handsome carved rococo counter and huge and mysterious bottles of elixirs on the shelves. Italian pharmacies—one can hardly call them by a less dignified name—are often very elegant. In the eighteenth century they were informal clubs, rather like coffee houses. The

Farmacia Mantovani was particularly famous as the resort of learned patricians, priests, academicians and lawyers who met there to converse with the apothecary while his apprentices pounded drugs in bronze mortars or distilled liquids from great retorts. It is satisfying to record that this *farmacia* maintains its intellectual tradition for the owner is one of the leading critics and collectors of modern art in Venice. Farther down the Calle Larga stands the Ristorante All' Angelo, a favourite meeting place of artists. Its walls are hung with an impressive collection of contemporary paintings, drawings and etchings. Every other year it becomes particularly lively during the week before the opening of the Biennale when it is thronged with critics, artists and dealers of all nationalities. Feelings run high at this moment when, I am told, angry artists and critics have been known to come to fisticuffs in the Piazza. There are also some more entertaining incidents. On the eve of the opening of a recent Biennale word ran round the Piazza that a certain painter had won the main prize. Promptly, his friends—and many others who hoped to become his friends— carried him off and feasted him with champagne and caviare and every delicacy Angelo could provide. Next morning the official list of prize winners was published without his name and he gaily confessed that he had started the rumour. It was an incident which Goldoni would have relished.

CHAPTER 11

Dorsoduro: Venetian Baroque

Santa Maria della Salute—Pinacoteca Manfrediana—Guggenheim collection —Zattere—Gesuati—a squero—*San Trovaso*

If you come to Venice by sea—and any other approach is like entering a palace through the back door—the most prominent of the myriad architectural marvels that greet you is the church of **Santa Maria della Salute.** As if riding at anchor at the entrance to the Grand Canal, with its balloon-like dome weighed down by great baroque scrolls, this fabulous building dominates the scene even more than the Palazzo Ducale or San Giorgio Maggiore. It is the supreme masterpiece of the Venetian Baroque—and of its author Baldassare Longhena, one of the few Venetian architects whose personality is strong enough to glimmer through the mists of history. Contemporaries tell us that he was a short dapper man, always dressed in black, of quiet and gentle manners. He had the embarrassing habit of asking everyone he met their opinion of whatever work he then had in hand. But this apparent lack of self-assurance finds no echo in the magnificently extrovert and ebullient buildings he designed, least of all in Santa Maria della Salute.

The church commemorates a terrible plague which ravaged Venice in 1630. A few months after it had begun the Senate determined to build an *ex voto* church dedicated to Santa Maria della Salute (the word signifies both health and salvation). A site was chosen, the buildings on it were demolished, no fewer than 1,156,627 wooden piles were driven into the mud to make a solid foundation, and architects were invited to compete for the commission. In a memorandum the prerequisites were summarised as follows: the church should be so designed that its whole ample

143

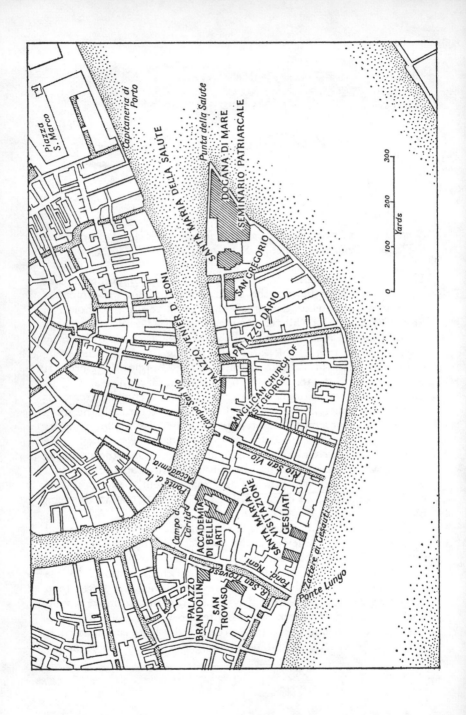

structure might be visually understood as it was entered, that there would be an equal distribution of bright light, that the high altar would dominate the view from the main door and the other altars should come into sight only as the visitor approached the chancel. The architect was also required to construct a building which would harmonise with the site and—a typically Venetian note— which would make a grand impression or " *bella figura* " without costing too much. Among eleven entries only two were found worthy of consideration by the Senate and that by Longhena was accepted. Work was begun promptly, but the church was not completed until 1687, more than half a century later and five years after the death of the octogenarian Longhena.

By much the simplest way to reach the church is to take the *tra-ghetto* from Harry's Bar (at the end of Calle Valaresso, just by the San Marco motor-boat station) to the Punta della Salute—the point of the Dorsoduro *sestiere* which is occupied by the long low building of the Dogana or customs-house. (The name Dorsoduro, " hard back," refers to the hard clay sub-soil of this part of Venice). From the water you may best appreciate the picturesque grouping of cupolas which echo in a major key those of San Marco. Walking along the *fondamenta* past the customs-house—where *carabinieri* may be seen guarding the bales and crates in the central halls—you reach the shallow square from which the grandiose steps rise up to the church. The central theme of the complex frontispiece is a triumphal arch flanked by two receding church façades derived from Palladio's little church of Le Zitelle on the Giudecca. It is a remarkably powerful composition, but its full effect can be judged only on the rare occasions when the main doors are open to reveal a perspective of arches leading to the high altar. Longhena seems to have derived much from theatrical design, especially the Palladian theatre at Vicenza with its proscenium like a triumphal arch which affords a view up a central vista of columned, be-statued buildings. The great central doors are, of course, thrown open on the Festa della Salute (21st November) when most Venetians walk across a bridge of boats to visit the church.

Longhena kept constantly in mind not merely the terms of the commission but also the purpose and significance of the church as an *ex voto* offering. " The mystery contained in its dedication to the Blessed Virgin," he wrote, " made me think, with that little talent which God has given me, of building it in a circular form,

that is to say in the shape of a crown to be dedicated to the Virgin."
He was clearly thinking of the invocations to the Queen of Heaven
in the Venetian litany which was recited in times of plague, and also
of the reference in *Revelation* to " a woman clothed in the sun, and
the moon under her feet, and upon her head a crown of twelve
stars." A statue of the Virgin with these attributes stands on the
lantern above the cupola. At a lower level, on the great scrolls,
stand statues of the Apostles—the twelve stars in her crown. The
symbolism is maintained inside the church by an inscription in
the centre of the pavement—*unde origo inde salus* (whence the
origin, thence the salvation and health) referring to the origin of
Venice under the Virgin's protection—one of the several accounts
of the foundation of the city relates that the Virgin led the people
of Altinum to the islands in the lagoon.

On entering the church one is again reminded of the terms of
the commission. If you stand with your back to the main door
you look through the arches to the grandiose high altar which bears
a statue of the Virgin and Child, with Venice praying on the left
and an angel chasing away the plague on the right. It is the only
altar in sight until you advance to the large octagonal space under
the cupola. Yet you are from the first aware of the extent of the
whole church. In the centre of the pavement you find yourself
surrounded by eight equal archways, six of which lead through
the circuit of the ambulatory to the minor altars. The ingenuity
of the plan reveals a further debt to theatrical design, for the eye is
never left to wander but always directed down one of the carefully
arranged vistas, through the wedge-shaped groups of pilasters and
half-columns which carry the dome.

Beyond the main octagon, Longhena built a chancel with apsidal
ends on a transverse axis, and beyond that an oblong choir. On a
plan these two rooms look as if they were awkwardly tacked on to
the octagon as mere appendages. But although each is designed
as a separate entity, the visitor is aware of no more than a slight
change of scale as he passes from one to another. To achieve this
effect, Longhena resorted to Palladio, especially the Redentore
(see p. 116). It is therefore hardly surprising to find that the three
parts are designed according to Palladian rules of harmonic proportions. The influence of Palladio is one of the factors which differ-
entiates Longhena's baroque style from that practised at the same
time in Rome. With its complex scenic and spatial effects, Santa

Maria della Salute could hardly be farther in feeling from such a contemporary Roman building as the Gesù. But Palladio does not entirely account for the difference. Longhena, like Palladio, looked back to the Veneto-Byzantine tradition which makes itself felt in the cupola over the chancel no less than in the octagonal plan which may owe something to San Vitale at Ravenna. From these sources he derived a scenographic, picturesque and dynamic style which is as uncompromisingly baroque as it is essentially Venetian. Indeed, he developed an alternative to the Roman baroque which was destined to influence later architects as far afield as Naples and Spain.

In decoration Longhena followed the Palladian scheme of grey stone against white-washed plaster which gives a pleasantly cool appearance to the interior. But he allowed himself some colour in the intricately patterned floor, using a spiral design which emphasises the dynamism of the whole construction, and seems to have intended a richly painted interior to the dome. The most prominent of the many works of sculpture is the high altar group by Giusto Le Corte who, with a team of assistants, was responsible for most of the statues inside and outside the church. Although ponderous as a whole, it is well and freshly carved—and the figure of the old hag representing the plague is among the best baroque statues in Venice.

Paintings, which would have occupied a much more important part in the decorative scheme of a Roman church, are here limited to six minor altarpieces. The three on the right are all by the prolific Neapolitan baroque painter, Luca Giordano. Above the first altar on the left there is a *Pentecost* by Titian. This work was executed in the 1550s for Sansovino's church of Santo Spirito (demolished 1656) and it is therefore no more than a coincidence that the window through which the dove descends should echo that in the wall above (unless the picture influenced Longhena's design).

Other paintings by Titian from Santo Spirito adorn the ceiling of the sacristy (door to left of high altar). They represent *Cain and Abel, The Sacrifice of Abraham, David and Goliath* and busts of Evangelists and Fathers of the Church, and date from the 1540s. Like Tintoretto's masterly *Marriage at Cana* (1561) on the wall below, they reveal a preoccupation with the rendering of movement and dramatic presentation which anticipates the Baroque. The sweeter, more sensitive and delicate Titian of some thirty years earlier is represented by the richly coloured altarpiece of *St. Mark Enthroned between Saints Cosmas, Damian, Roch and Sebastian* painted to commemorate the plague of 1510.

The tabernacle on the sacristy altar contains a fine twelfth-century icon originally in Agia Sophia, Constantinople. Below it there is an exquisitely embroidered fifteenth-century Venetian altar frontal, worked on a design inspired by Mantegna. In the adjoining antesacristy there are two *bozzetti* by Luca Giordano for his altarpieces in the church—brilliant sketches which are in many ways more satisfactory than the finished pictures.

The large building between Santa Maria della Salute and the Dogana is the **Seminario** which houses the Pinacoteca Manfrediana's strange jumble of masterpieces and *croste*—that is to say mere " crusts " of paint of certain antiquity but doubtful artistic merit. (Not officially open but usually accessible). You reach it through cloisters crammed with sculpture of all periods, and up a monumental staircase by Longhena. The greatest treasure of the collection is the painting of *Apollo and Daphne* (Room II) executed in the first decade of the sixteenth century, probably for the front of a *cassone*. It is one of those problematical works over which the pundits have argued for years, some attributing it to Giorgione and others to the young Titian. After changing his mind once or twice, Berenson said that it was partly the work of Giorgione. And there can be no doubt about the Giorgionesque inspiration of this elegiac vision of the Venetian countryside at that golden moment when spring merges with summer. It is a charmingly Venetian interpretation of Ovid, with a chubby village boy, thinly disguised as Apollo, chasing Daphne through the *foresto* of some little town in the foothills above the plain. The collection also includes a profile of St. Lorenzo Giustiniani by a follower of Gentile Bellini, a lunette of God the Father by Cima and a fragment of fresco by Veronese which once decorated Palladio's Villa Soranza. Among several non-Venetian paintings the most notable are the *Penelope* by Domenico Beccafumi (all hot smoky colours, as if the figure were about to smoulder into flame), a *Deposition* by Domenico Puligo, a diptych by Filippino Lippi, with *Christ and the Woman of Samaria* on one panel and the *Noli Me Tangere* on the other, and from a much later period, the portrait of Abbot Zaghis by Sebastiano Ceccarini (1739)—a sharp piece of eighteenth-century characterisation. Sculptures include an attractive little *Nativity* relief by a follower of Lombardo and several busts by Vittoria, notably a terra-cotta of the sad-eyed Procuratore Pietro Zen and a marble of Doge Niccolò da Ponte in the glory of a rich brocade mantle. A vivid later bust in terra-cotta, of Gian Matteo Amadei, has been attributed to Canova but is probably by some other sculptor working in the 1770s. The attributions on the labels in this collection can rarely be trusted. Before leaving the Seminario it is worth pausing in the Oratorio della SS Trinità, by the main door, to see Gian Lorenzo Bernini's busts of Agostino and Pietro Valier, though they are fairly early works which reveal little or nothing of his later brilliance.

On the other side of the Salute façade a bridge and *sottoportico* lead into a narrow *calle* with the disused red-brick Gothic church of San Gregorio on the left and its former monastic buildings on the right. Should the door (No. 172) be open you can catch a view of what Ruskin considered " the loveliest cortile I know in Venice." The *calle*, or rather succession of *calli*, leads on past the Guatemalan consulate and the American consulate to No. 701, the home of Mrs. Peggy Guggenheim who has arranged a choice collection of modern art in a pavilion in her garden (open in summer, Mon. Wed. Fri. 3–5). As it contains few works by Venetians this gallery might be thought to fall outside the scope of the present book, but it cannot be ignored by anyone seriously interested in the arts. The room is dominated by a large polished bronze sculpture *Bird in Space*, an emblem of powerful elegance by Constantine Brancusi. The collection is particularly strong in surrealist paintings especially by Max Ernst and Yves Tanguy.

The *calle* winds on to the **Campo San Vio** which opens on to the Grand Canal, affording a splendid view of the palaces on the other side, notably Sansovino's imposing Palazzo Corner (see p. 218). In the *campo* stands the prim little Anglican church of St. George, one of the many churches built in the diocese of Gibraltar for the benefit of travelling and expatriate Englishmen. There was a time when it was well attended throughout the year, when gondolas brought loads of English ladies in feathered hats and gloves and English gentlemen in billycocks and starched collars for Matins every Sunday. A vivid, if unkind, picture of this English community just before the first war is to be found in Corvo's *Desire and Pursuit of the Whole*. But now that the English

149

colony has dwindled to a fraction of its former size, St. George's is served by a chaplain for no more than a few months each summer. During the rest of the year it is closed, except for an occasional funeral.

In the hey-day of the English colony this part of Dorsoduro was a fashionable district. It still retains a pleasant residential air, distinctly middle-class in comparison with the various *sestieri* on the other side of the Grand Canal. You can absorb some of its atmosphere by following the Rio San Vio to the Zattere, the long *fondamenta* which looks across to the Giudecca and is named after the *zattere* or lighters that used to unload wood here. The *rio* joins the Zattere by the Ponte degli Incurabili. On the corner stands a pink house which was occupied in the early years of this century by Horatio Brown who appeared in Corvo's novel as Hector McTavish. He was the author of several attractive books about Venice—*Life on the Lagoons, In and around Venice* and the more scholarly *Studies in Venetian History*—all of which repay attention as much for their factual matter as for the charm of their style and the picture they give of Venice fifty years or so ago. (It is heart-rending now to read his descriptions of an unspoilt Lido and Jesolo). But this place has a more important and rather surprising historical connection. It was here, in the hospital for incurable diseases, that St. Ignatius Loyola and St. Francis Xavier worked during their brief visit to Venice. The Jesuit order which St. Ignatius founded was never to enjoy much success in Venice.

Further along the Zattere, to the right, past the Pensione Calcina where Ruskin stayed in 1877, stands the church of Santa Maria del Rosario, usually known as the **Gesuati** (from the order of Poveri Gesuati merged with the Dominicans in 1668). It was begun in 1736 and harmoniously combines outstanding examples of Venetian eighteenth-century architecture, painting and sculpture. The architect was Giorgio Massari who, like Longhena before him, derived inspiration from Palladio. But whereas Longhena had dramatised his model, Massari prettified and elaborated it. Gesticulating statues of Prudence, Justice, Strength and Temperance animate the façade. The interior is also rich in sculpture—Evangelists and Prophets (the turbanned Aaron second on the right is perhaps the best), and reliefs of New Testament scenes by Giovanni Maria Morlaiter, one of the ablest sculptors in early eighteenth-century Venice. He came from beyond the Alps and his works have a touch of the elegant exuberance of Bavarian rococo sculpture.

The ceiling is decorated with paintings by G. B. Tiepolo (1737–9). A number of grisailles, which look like stucco reliefs when the light is dim, surround three larger panels representing *The Apotheosis of St. Dominic*, *The Institution of the Rosary* and *St. Dominic Blessing a Dominican Monk*. The central panel is particularly attractive, with the Virgin and Child hovering in the sky above St. Dominic who has just caught the rosary from their hands and holds it out to a group of gaily dressed supplicants. A miracle of sparkling light and delicate colour, it is one of the most successful of Tiepolo's ceiling paintings. But unfortunately it is poorly lit and none too clean.

Tiepolo's easy mastery of bright clear colours may more easily be appreciated in the first altarpiece on the right, a vision of the Virgin and Child with Saints Catherine of Siena, Rose and Agnes. It is suffused with the gay unmystical and unquestioning piety of eighteenth-century Italy—and the solemnity of the figures is relieved by several little *scherzi*, a chaffinch perching on the cross-bar of the arcade and St. Rose's habit tumbling out of the frame. The third altarpiece on the right is by G. B. Piazzetta and represents three Saints of the Dominican order—Vincent Ferraris, Hyacinth and Lawrence Bertrando—painted in a subdued colour scheme of blacks and whites enlivened by the turquoise of the sky and some flashes of chestnut brown. Opposite Tiepolo's altarpiece there is another eighteenth-century painting, of *Pius V with St. Thomas and St. Peter the Martyr* by Sebastiano Ricci—a work full of the airs and graces of the early *settecento* but with few of its solid merits. Ricci was a great plagiarist and in this picture you can see his scissors at work, snipping elements from Veronese and Tiepolo.

If you leave the church by the main door, turn right, then right again along the Fondamenta Nani you will see on the other side of the *rio* one of the most picturesque scenes in all Venice. It is a **squero**, one of the few remaining yards where gondolas, *sandali* and other craft are built and repaired by traditional methods which can hardly have changed at all in centuries. Smoke nearly always rises from some part of the yard as paint is burnt off a hull by the simple process of lighting a bonfire beside it! An antiseptic smell of pitch mingles with the less savoury smells of the canal. Describing such a place, Henri de Régnier remarked that the gondolas

The Companion Guide to Venice

"*rapiéciées, mortes, noires, le ventre à l'air, ressemblant à la fois à des poissons morts ou à des sombres tranches de melon.*" The *squero* is a surprisingly busy place, for although few Venetians can afford to maintain a gondola (a motor-boat is cheaper and more practical nowadays) and the number that ply for hire diminishes every year—those in use call for constant attention since their hulls must be scraped and tarred every three weeks or so. Gondolas are still built, however—for export to America. The owner of a nearby yard tells me that he carries on a brisk export trade with the oil magnates of Texas, though he was unable to enlighten me on the use to which gondolas are put on the other side of the Atlantic. Do millionaires build canals for them in their arid gardens so that they can float among the prickly pears? Or do they use them to decorate their halls, filled with potted hydrangeas and cinerarias?

Farther down the *rio* stands the church of **San Trovaso**. It is in fact dedicated to Saints Gervasius and Protasius whose names have by some mysterious process been concertinaed into the mythical Trovaso. An attractive though not very distinguished building, it has two equally important façades derived from that of the Zitelle, with the addition of a few flourishes. Tradition states that there are two façades because the church stands on neutral ground between the territories of the two rival factions of the *popolo*, the Castellani and the Nicolotti. Even as late as the nineteenth century great rivalry persisted between these two groups, though they expressed themselves in competition for prizes in the regatta rather than the street brawls and pitched battles on bridges which their ancestors had enjoyed. San Trovaso was the only church common to both. When there was a wedding between members of different parties, the Castellani entered, and left, by the south door, the Nicolotti by that on the west façade.

Inside the church there are several fine paintings. Two are by Tintoretto: a *Last Supper* on the right wall of the Sacrament chapel and a very spirited *Temptation of St. Anthony* (1577) in the chapel to the left of the high altar. In the chapel on the other side of the chancel there is one of the finest Gothic paintings in Venice, Michele Giambono's *St. Chrisogono* dressed in the height of early fifteenth-century knightly fashion and mounted on a richly caparisoned charger. But the most notable work of art in the church is the group of three marble reliefs on the front of the altar in the

152

Clary chapel (west side of south transept). The outer panels are carved with the figures of angelic musicians while the central one contains a number of similar angels holding the instruments of the Passion. They have the crisp April morning freshness of the best *quattrocento* sculpture, and in the treatment of the swirling draperies, which clearly reveal the form of the child-like bodies, they are reminiscent of reliefs in the Tempio Malatestiana at Rimini. It seems probable that they were carved in about 1470, but their authorship remains a mystery and they are usually assigned to "The Master of San Trovaso."

The Rio di San Trovaso is flanked by some handsome palaces. A house next to the church has some Byzantine reliefs encrusted in its walls. On the opposite side of the *rio* stands the fifteenth-century Palazzo Nani with ogee windows and flamboyant Gothic coats of arms. Near it, there is a pretty little chemist's shop with an iron gallery running round the upper part of its main room. Further down (No. 1075), on the other side, stands the rather grim sixteenth-century Palazzo Brandolin which once boasted frescoes by Tintoretto on its façade. If you continue to follow the *rio* and turn right at the end, the Calle Contarini Corfu will lead you to the motor-boat station in front of the Accademia.

CHAPTER 12

The Settecento: Tiepolo and Guardi

Palazzo Rezzonico—Campo Santa Margherita—Scuola di Santa Maria del Carmine—Santa Maria del Carmelo—Palazzo Zenobio—San Niccolò dei Mendicoli—Angelo Raffaele—San Sebastiano

Of all the many magnificent palaces on the Grand Canal, the vast **Palazzo Rezzonico** is one of the richest, both outside and in. It was begun in the 1660s for the ancient Bon family to a design by Baldassare Longhena. But the architect died before it had risen above the first floor, and early in the eighteenth century the Bon family fell into financial difficulties and sold the unfinished building to the Rezzonico—a newly rich family better able to support this *folie de grandeur*. The Rezzonico were bankers of Genoese origin who bought their way into the Venetian aristocracy in 1687 for the very considerable price of 100,000 ducats (about 2% of the entire annual revenue of the Republic!) in addition to some 60,000 ducats given to charity. They commissioned Giorgio Massari to complete the building and employed the best artists available to decorate the interior.

The Palazzo Rezzonico can be reached by *vaporetto* or on foot from the Accademia (notice boards point the way). But the pleasantest means of approach is certainly by the *traghetto* from the *diretto* motor-boat station in the little Campo San Samuele, beside Massari's Palazzo Grassi (a fine palace where exhibitions of modern art are shown in the summer). From water-level you can best appreciate the architectural merits of the Palazzo Rezzonico with its heavily rusticated basement supporting the sculptured and be-columned structure above. It is a triumph of monumentality given a typically Venetian insubstantial-pageantry appearance by its deep recesses which dissolve the wall surface into a pattern of

154

flickering light. The ferry takes you to the Calle del Traghetto leading up to the Campo San Barnabà, near the main entrance to the palace which now houses the civic museum of eighteenth-century art (9.30–4; holidays 9.30–12.30).

This is one of the most delightful museums I know. So skilfully is it arranged that it seems to have the authentic atmosphere of a great eighteenth-century house, and one is seldom made aware that many of its furnishings and pictures, including whole ceilings, have been brought together from a number of different palaces. To wander through its many rooms is to enter the carnival world of eighteenth-century Venice.

A great stone staircase leads up to the **ballroom** and other state apartments on the *piano nobile*. Rooms such as these were, of course, built not for daily use but to make a *bella figura*, to impress visitors on great occasions. Even the grandest of grand Venetian families lived mainly on the floor above or below the *piano nobile*, in rooms much more simply decorated and furnished.

The chairs and vase stands in the ballroom of the Palazzo Rezzonico and a room leading out of it are among the most showy ever produced. The arms of the chairs, in the form of gnarled tree trunks, are supported by little Negro boys with ebony heads, hands and feet and patches of ebony flesh glinting through the slashes in their box-wood breeches. Some of the vase stands or *guéridons* are upheld by slender Negroes with chains around their necks, others by *putti* scrambling on top of one another, while the largest incorporates classical deities clutching at fragile *famille verte* vases. But to describe such objects as furniture is a little misleading, for they are pieces of sculpture which happen to have a practical function. It is hardly surprising to find that they are the work not of a cabinet maker but of a sculptor, **Andrea Brustolon** from Belluno. In the throne room there are some carved and gilt tables and chairs which, though they may look sobersides in comparison with Brustolon's suite, are elaborate enough—all alive with wriggling *putti* and giggling mermaids. They too are the work of a sculptor—Antonio Corradini.

During the eighteenth century there was also a vogue in Venice for lacquered furniture of which several fine examples are in this palace—chairs, tables, doors, beds, high-bosomed commodes. Most of these pieces are decorated with chinoiseries—Venetian interpretations of how the distant and flowery Empire of Cathay

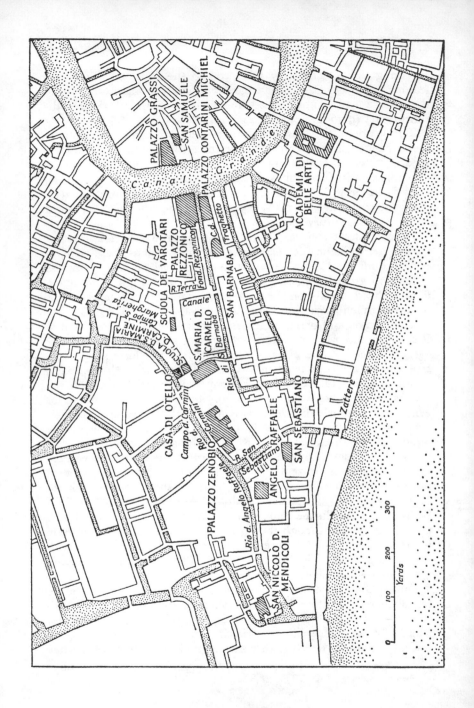

ought ideally to look. But in making this furniture Venetian craftsmen barely troubled themselves to emulate the hard refulgent glossiness of true oriental lacquer. Indeed, the surface is distinctly coarse and the furniture itself is often of poor, sometimes slipshod, craftsmanship. To eyes trained on the solid worthiness of a Chippendale or meticulous perfection of a Riesener, most Venetian furniture will appear gimcrack and gaudy. But it compensates in liveliness of form and decoration for what it lacks in technical proficiency. With an exuberant vitality, none the less appealing for its want of conventional good taste, it reflects the breathless gaiety of the carnival at a time when it was said " the Venetians do not taste their pleasures, they swallow them whole."

The charge of incompetence is the last that could be levelled at the decorative painters of the city. So accomplished were they that with no means other than paint they could convert a barn-like room into an apartment fit for the most sumptuous ball with marble panelling and reliefs, pilasters and colonnades, rich draperies and proud heraldic achievements, and with a whole Parnassus of immortals conducting their athletic amours on the ceiling. Even to-day it takes the visitor to the ballroom in Palazzo Rezzonico a few moments to realise that, with the exception of the columned entrance doorway, all the architectural decorations are painted flat. When the paint was fresh the effect must have been still more deceptive. The artists responsible for this triumph of *trompe l'oeil* were G. B. Crosato who painted the luminous ceiling and a team of assistants who carried out the more humdrum tasks.

Most of the rooms on the *piano nobile* have **painted ceilings.** The earliest are those in the Sala del Brustolon (leading out of the ballroom by the door on the left) and the library next to it, painted by Francesco Maffei, a seventeenth-century artist whose works often anticipate the gaiety and elegance of the *settecento*. The first of the rooms leading out of the ballroom on the other side has a ceiling by G. B. Tiepolo. It was painted in 1758 to celebrate the greatest event in the annals of the Rezzonico family—not, surprisingly enough, the election of Carlo as Pope Clement XIII but the marriage of his nephew Lodovico to Faustina Savorgnan the daughter of one of the oldest Venetian noble families. Fame trumpets this social " arrival " while Apollo drives the young couple across the sky in the chariot of the sun to a group of allegorical figures, one of whom brandishes the arms of Rezzonico impaling Savorgnan.

On another ceiling (room VI) Tiepolo showed Merit—a laurel-crowned ancient—between Nobility and Virtue. And on another (room VII), painted in 1744–5 for Palazzo Barbarigo, he depicted Strength and Wisdom. Nowadays we tend to dismiss the allegorical meaning of these works, regarding their complicated programmes as mere excuses for Tiepolo's voluptuous compositions, his visions of an eighteenth-century Olympus where the rarest silks are used not to cover but enhance the firmly youthful naked bodies of supercilious deities and agreeably seductive virtues. But these ceilings had a more than decorative significance. They were literally intended to glorify the patrons who commissioned them, to celebrate their lineage, to proclaim their merit and, perhaps, to compensate the rulers of an impotent Venice for the slights they received from other more powerful aristocracies.

A large number of *settecento* paintings has been gathered on the second floor. In the central *portego* there is a darkly dramatic *Death of Darius* by G. B. Piazzetta, where the theatrical gesture of Alexander seems to deflate the heroics of the scene—perhaps intentionally. On the other side there is a glittering *Mucius Scaevola* by G. A. Pellegrini, one of the several Venetian artists who worked for a while in England. Room XVIII, furnished with green lacquer of unusually good quality, has a *Triumph of Diana* ceiling, all sparkling with flickers of light, by Gian Antonio or perhaps Francesco Guardi. The Guardi brothers are also represented by three rather damaged frescoes (room XIV) and two glimpses of high life, the masked figures in the Ridotto and a fashionable assembly in the parlour of a nunnery (room XX). Room XIX, which has a Tiepolo ceiling, is devoted mainly to Pietro Longhi's little scenes of everyday life enacted by doll-like figures. An equestrian portrait represents William Graeme, a Jacobite General who commanded the Venetian army for a period in the mid-eighteenth century.

Rooms XXIII to XXIX are devoted to a series of frescoes from the Tiepolo family house at Zianigo, near Mestre. **Domenico Tiepolo** had already decorated the chapel of this attractive but modest villa before his father bought it in the 1750s. The other frescoes were painted by Domenico for his own amusement in the last three decades of the century. In the entrance hall there is a panel of *Rinaldo and Armida* illustrating an incident from Tasso but almost a parody of a great history painting with the hero swooning before the faintly comic statue of his beloved. One room is devoted to the Punchinellos which Domenico so loved to draw. Here they are up to their usual tricks, turning somersaults, gossiping, courtings while one disports himself on a swing overhead. There are more Punchinellos in the grisailles; and here it becomes clear that the artist was poking fun at the vogue for grandiose decorations. For at this period such grisailles were normally painted in imitation of classical reliefs of Grecian gods and Roman senators. Another room is devoted to centaurs, satyrs and fauns— graceful, lively and libidinous.

In the largest room, painted in the 1790s, Domenico turned his attention to the follies of dress. With the exception of a preposterously overclad buck and belle who mince across the scene, all these figures have their backs to us. A group of people in their Sunday best stand gazing or waiting to gaze into a peepshow which represents *Il Mondo Nuovo*. In another scene a fashionable trio takes a country walk accompanied by a servant and dogs. They appear to be walking away towards the new world of the Rights of Man, of liberty, equality and fraternity, though the man in an old-fashioned tricorne turns his head as if to catch one last glimpse of the dying fires of the eighteenth century. Inevitably one is reminded of Goya whose early works were to be seen in Madrid while Domenico was there with his father (he later acquired a copy of the *Caprichos*). But there is nothing savagely ironical in Tiepolo's wit. Like his contemporary Carlo Gozzi he was amused by the absurdities of humanity just as he was amused by satyrs, centaurs and punchinellos. And he invested his drawings and paintings of them with a sense of poetry which is again reminiscent of Gozzi's fairy-tale dramas.

On the top floor, the Palazzo Rezzonico becomes more obviously a museum. Several rooms are devoted to a collection of ceramics which includes coarse if characteristic specimens of the Venetian Cozzi porcelain factory and the *faience* factories of Bassano and Este. There is a room of terra-cotta *bozzetti* for sculpture, a marionette theatre, a chemist's shop and a collection of costumes.

While returning down the vast staircase to the ground floor, it is worth recalling that the Palazzo Rezzonico was for a while the home of Robert Browning who grandly described it as " a corner for my old age." Here he died in 1889. Of all English poets he was the one who loved and understood Italy best. His son, Pen,

159

continued to live in the palace for some years, allowing one room to be used as the Anglican church.

Just behind the palace stands the church of San Barnabà. In this parish the impoverished noblemen of Venice were given apartments by the Republic. Too proud to work—and lose their patent of nobility—too stupid to play any part in the government, they led lives of shabby gentility, preying on the state for lodgings and a small dole which they augmented out of the pockets of tourists. Yet every one retained his hereditary seat in the Great Council which members of recent families like the Rezzonico and Grassi could enter only on payment of vast sums.

In the Rio San Barnabà you will usually find an exotic green-grocery barge with a vast orange awning which calls to mind Gautier's description of " *ces barques, encrustées de légumes verts, de raisins, de pêches, laissent derrières elles une suave odeur de végétation qui contraste avec le senteur âcre des embarcations chargées de thon, de rougets, de poulpes, d'huitres, de pidocchi, de crabes, de coquillages.*" From the Rio a right turn along the Rio Terrà Canale, will take you to the sprawling **Campo Santa Margherita.** Here there is a picturesque market which does a brisk matutinal trade in fish and vegetables. At the far end, on the right, a truncated campanile stands next to the old church of Santa Margherita, now a cinema which seems to specialise in the more sensational types of film. The little building isolated in the centre used to house the Scuola dei Varotari (tanners). At the other end of the *campo* stands the **Scuola di Santa Maria del Carmine**—a handsome seventeenth-century building of white stone with elaborate iron grilles covering the windows.

The *scuola* (9–12 and 3–6 except holidays when 9–12 only) is very richly decorated with eighteenth-century paintings among which G. B. Tiepolo's ceiling in the *salone* upstairs is by far the best. Painted in 1744 for the modest fee of 400 *zecchini* (£200), the ceiling so pleased the Confraternity that they made the artist an honorary member. It represents St. Simon Stock receiving from the Virgin the scapular of the Carmelite Order—two pieces of white cloth joined by strings. A Papal Bull, which may be a forgery, promised that all who wore this scapular in life would be relieved of the pains of purgatory on the first Sunday after their death or, at any rate, " as soon as possible." St. Simon Stock had his vision at Cambridge, surprisingly enough, but Tiepolo set it in sixteenth-century Venice where all historical events had, for him. taken place. In this airy vision of the Mother of Mercy shimmering in silken drapery, **Tiepolo** testified his faith. For despite the lightheartedness, the frivolity even, of some of his religious paintings, there can be no doubt that he was a man of quiet unquestioning piety. Several pictures, painted in his last, sad, disillusioned years attest the depth and sincerity of his religion. It is characteristic that we should know this only by deduction from his paintings. Otherwise his personality is as dim as that of any other great Venetian artist. The few of his letters that survive reveal only his devotion to his painting and his healthy scepticism of artistic theorising.

The son of fairly well-to-do parents he was born in 1696. As a painter he began by working in the tenebrist style fashionable in the baroque period. But soon he looked back across the gulf of the seventeenth century to Paolo Veronese who inspired him to work with a lighter touch, a brighter and clearer palette. By the time he began to paint the Carmine ceiling he was generally recognised as the leading artist in Venice. Soon after finishing it he was summoned to work at the courts of princes. In 1762 he went unwillingly to Madrid at the command of the Senate who used him as a pawn in their diplomatic intrigues. (The Republic needed to appease Spain, a traditional enemy, and the new king of Spain wanted to secure Tiepolo rather than any other painter. The whole affair was transacted at ambassadorial level.) He has been called the greatest painter of the eighteenth century, and he was certainly the greatest among the Italians. If his work lacks the elegiac pathos of Watteau and the emotional depth of Goya it is perhaps a more faithful mirror of the spirit of the age—of its elegant refinement, its civilised wit, its optimism and faith in human reason.

The church of **Santa Maria del Carmelo** stands beside the *scuola*, with a tall seventeenth-century campanile crowned by a statue of the Virgin which is a conspicuous Venetian landmark. It is a large brick building dating mainly from the fourteenth century but with many later additions. The interior is very rich, with gilt wood statues crowning the arcades of the nave and supporting a series of baroque pictures. These canvases, which illustrate stories from the history of the Carmelite Order, are by such artists as Gregorio Lazzarini (Tiepolo's first master), Gaspare Diziani, and G. A. Fumiani. Only one is of outstanding merit, the fifth from the altar on the left, *The Virgin Appearing to Pope Honorius III*, a strange fantasy with iridescent figures floating to and fro like exotic fish in an aquarium. It is by the Florentine painter and poet Sebastiano Mazzoni who settled in Venice in the mid-seventeenth century.

Above the second altar on the right there is a placid *Nativity* by G. B. Cima, painted shortly before 1510 and showing the influence of Giorgione. On the other side of the church there is a still more Giorgionesque picture of two decades later: Lotto's *St. Nicholas of Bari* with a landscape of a sleepy port shimmering in a noon-day heat haze. On the two choir lofts, just above the high altar rails, there are paintings of *The Annunciation, Adoration of the Shepherds* and *Epiphany* by Andrea Schiavone touched with a delicate lightness which looks forward to the *settecento*. A bronze relief of *The Lamentation over the Dead Christ* in the chapel to the right of the high altar is by the Sienese sculptor and architect Francesco di Giorgio (*c.* 1475). A graceful statue of *Virginity* by Antonio Corradini (1721), with the same proud beauty as Tiepolo's Madonnas, stands on the left of the third altar on the right.

The west door of the church leads into the **Campo dei Carmini.** Legend associates the house no. 2615 with Othello. But although Shakespeare is known to have taken his plot from a Venetian story by Cinthio, and archivists have shown that more than one Venetian husband loved his wife " not wisely but too well " and murdered her lest she " betray more men "—none of them is known to have lived here. Nor, alas, is Cinthio's story set in this part of Venice. From the Campo dei Carmini the **Fondamenta Foscarini** leads to the church of the Angelo Raffaele. On the way you pass Palazzo Zenobio (no. 2593), now an Armenian boys' school run by the monks of San Lazzaro (see p. 236), a simple late seventeenth-century building with little grotesque heads peering out of the façade. Here Luca Carlevaris, the townscape painter who prepared the way for Canaletto and Guardi, lived for a while as the tame artist in the Zenobio household. Though the building is not officially " open to the public " the porter is often willing to take visitors upstairs and show them a sumptuous ballroom bright with allegorical frescoes painted by a French artist, Louis Dorigny, shortly before 1700. No. 2590 occupies the site of a home for fallen women founded by the ex-courtesan Veronica Franca whom Montaigne encountered after she had retired, reformed and won some reputation as a poetess. In the famous catalogue of courtesans she appeared as " 204, Veronica Franca . . . 2 scudi." You pass also the Centro Marinario Cini, with a headless antique statue in the garden, and no. 2376, Palazzo Ariani, with very delicate fourteenth-century Gothic windows—among the earliest in Venice —much admired by G. E. Street on account of its irregularity.

Before visiting the church of the Angelo Raffaele, it is worth walking to the end of the Fondamenta and turning right to see the little church of **San Niccolò dei Mendicoli,** one of the most appealing in Venice. Begun in the seventh century it was added to from time to time during the next millennium. The stocky campanile dates from the twelfth century, the loggia at the west end—once a dwelling place for poor religious women—from the fifteenth and the main doorway from the seventeenth. Inside it has the quiet cosy atmosphere of a remote village church. Above the squat columns of the nave, with heads too big for their bases, there are wooden statues similar to those in the Carmini. The apse dates from the twelfth century and has a Byzantine style cornice, but the *Glory of Angels* above was painted in the eighteenth. This confusion of works of many periods gives the church a peculiar charm.

The church of the **Angelo Raffaele** contains one important work of art—a series of scenes from the story of Tobias and the Angel on the balcony of the organ loft above the main door. All aglitter with sparkling dewy light, they are clearly by a member of the **Guardi** family. Scholars have argued long and loud as to whether they are by Gian Antonio, who is known only as a painter of religious pictures, or by his younger brother Francesco who is known mainly for his Venetian views. The dispute has rivalled the intensity of the feud between the Castellani and the Nicolotti in the Middle Ages; and if the adherents of the two schools of thought have not yet come to blows, they are known to have cut each other dead in the narrow *calli*. But as a more than usually thick biographical blanket shrouds both of the Guardi brothers— the most interesting thing known about them is that their sister married G. B. Tiepolo—the point is a purely academic one which should not be allowed to distract attention from the beauty of these pictures. Painted in colours of unusual brillance, even for Venice, with the light shimmering on the elegant figures, the technique almost anticipates that of the French Impressionists.

(It is significant that Guardi has been rediscovered in the age of the Impressionist cult.) The paintings seem to be illuminated by the last flames from the embers of the Venetian school while reminding us of the almost continuous influence that Venice has exerted on the art of Europe since the sixteenth century.

From the *campo* on the north side of the church a short *calle* leads to the Rio and Fondamenta **San Sebastiano.** On the corner, just by the bridge, stands a very pretty little red Gothic house, for many years the home of Filippo de Pisis, one of the few modern painters who has successfully caught the flicker of Venetian light. The bridge is one from which, despite all laws, Venetian boys as brown as Renaissance bronzes like to dive into the canal on hot summer days.

A short way along the *rio* to the right stands the early sixteenth-century church of San Sebastiano, which has one of the most beautiful interiors in all Venice, glowing with the opulent colour of **Paolo Veronese's** paintings. The earliest of these pictures are *The Coronation of the Virgin* and the four panels of the Evangelists on the ceiling of the Sacristy. Painted in about 1555 they are still rather immature. Though no more than a year later, his next works, on the ceiling of the church, are far more accomplished. They represent: *Esther Taken to Ahasuerus, Esther Crowned Queen by Ahasuerus,* and *The Triumph of Mordecai.* (Esther was regarded as the Old Testament prototype of the Virgin—her intercession for the Jews providing the parallel for the Virgin's intercession for humanity.) After completing this ceiling which introduces us to his sumptuous world of silken dalliance, he frescoed the frieze with sibyls seated between white barley-sugar columns, though here he relied a fair amount on the help of his studio which had begun to grow in size with his fame. In 1558 he painted *St. Sebastian before Diocletian* and *The Martyrdom of St. Sebastian* in the upper choir at the east end. The luminous high altarpiece of *The Virgin in Glory with Saints Sebastian, Peter, Catherine and Francis* was finished a few years later. At about the same time he painted the doors of the organ with *The Purification of the Virgin* outside and *The Pool of Bethesda* inside, decorating the front of the organ loft with a *Nativity.* In 1565 he began the two vast scenes from the life of St. Sebastian which flank the chancel.

Vasari called one of Veronese's pictures " joyous, beautiful and well conceived." And joyous is perhaps the best word to describe
164

these paintings which manifest an uninhibited sensuous delight in the beauty of the world, in stalwart men and buxom women, in boldly patterned silks and satins, gold and silver plate and clear Murano glass, and in gleaming white marble palaces with abundance of columns, and statues and towers. He loved the richness of pageantry and tended to convert every subject he painted into a pageant. St. Sebastian goes to martyrdom with as sprightly a step as any well-dressed young patrician walking in the Corpus Domini procession. It is perhaps significant that Veronese died from overheating himself while following an Easter procession. He is said to have been of a frank, gay, generous disposition, though a trifle choleric. Born in Verona he adopted Venice as his home and became so attached to the city that he refused an invitation to go and work for the Spanish court. His career must have been a very successful one for he bought a sizeable house in Venice and a country estate near Treviso. But he remained a modest man and sent his son to study under Jacopo Bassano, saying, " Carletto will be a better artist than I am." Of the trio of great Venetian *cinquecento* painters he is the most immediately appealing though he never achieved the emotional intensity or depth of feeling of either Titian or Tintoretto.

Very appropriately, Veronese was buried in San Sebastiano. His tomb is marked by an indifferent seventeenth-century portrait beside the organ. The church contains a few other notable works of art. There is an impressive monument to Livio Podocattaro, Bishop of Cyprus, by Sansovino in the third chapel on the right. An attractive group of the Virgin and Child with St. John over the second altar on the right is by Sansovino's pupil, Tommaso Lombardo. In the first chapel on the left there is a portrait bust of Marcantonio Grimani and a very elegant little statue of St. Anthony the Abbot, both by Vittoria. The blue and white maiolica tiled floor in the chapel to the left of the high altar is also noteworthy: it dates from about 1510.

If you turn right after crossing the bridge in front of the church you will soon reach the motor-boat station on the Zattere.

CHAPTER 13

A House of Gold and a Church of Damask

Ca' d'Oro—Fondamenta Nuove—Gesuiti—Santi Apostoli—San Giovanni Grisostomo

" The rychesse, the suptuous buyldyne, the relygyous houses, and the stablysshynge of their justyces and councylles, with all other thynges yt make a cytie glorious, surmouteth in Venyse aboue all places yt euer I sawe." So wrote the chaplain of Sir Richard Guylforde in 1505, comparing the gilded and marbled magnificence of Venice with the weathered manor houses and dark city wynds of his native Yorkshire. A decade earlier the cosmopolitan diplomatist Philippe de Commynes, from a still medieval Paris, had been no less struck by the aspect of " *la plus triumphante cité que j'aye jamais veue.*" In the fifteenth century Venice stood at the height of her prosperity, and her citizens were able to indulge to the full their love for opulent and ostentatious magnificence. How gaudily they displayed their wealth may be seen in the richly decorated façade of the **Ca' d'Oro** on the Grand Canal, though it is but a shadow of its former self. Originally every flower-shaped crocket on its roof was gilt and there was more gilding on every one of the carved capitals and numerous relief decorations. The glitter of all this gold was set off by a lavish use of colour, especially cinnabar red and ultramarine blue which must have given the house a distinctly fair-ground appearance. Nowadays it is as difficult to imagine what the effect can have been as to picture Greek temples in their original garish painted state.

The Ca' d'Oro, which can be reached by the slow Grand Canal *vaporetto* (in about twenty minutes from San Marco), is the finest example of Venetian Gothic domestic architecture to survive. Yet one hesitates to use the word Gothic for a building which shares

166

so little, apart from the pointed arch, with Gothic buildings outside Venice. Its lacy open-work screens, its ogee windows and surrounds which seem to emulate the design of Muslim prayer rugs, its equally oriental pinnacles on the parapet, are a far cry indeed from the Gothic decorations of Chartres, or Canterbury or Cologne. The Ca' d'Oro fits into no international pigeon-hole. It is not Gothic but Venetian—as Venetian as the waters of the Grand Canal which are echoed in its rippling traceried decorations. When the sun strikes the canal, sending up reflections of sparkling light which play on the stonework and break the dark recesses of the loggias, the whole building seems an incandescent vision. All the elements which distinguish the Venetian school are here combined—colour, light, opulence and exotic fantasy.

Originally built for the Contarini family between 1420 and 1434, the Ca' d'Oro has had many vicissitudes—frequent changes of ownership, alterations made to adapt it for the great ballerina Taglioni and division into separate apartments. Finally it was rescued by Baron Franchetti who restored it, filled it with a large collection of paintings, sculpture and furniture, and left it to the Italian State in 1922. You will be well advised to visit it on a clear bright morning for there is no electric light (renovation in progress so, alas, unlikely to be open for some time).

The entrance is in the Calle del Ca' d'Oro. On the ground floor there is a picturesque courtyard with a fifteenth-century well-head carved by Bartolomeo Bon. A stone staircase, built out of the remnants of the original one—which was destroyed in the late nineteenth century—leads up to the **main floor** *portego*, a long and rather dark room running from front to back, character-istic of Venetian houses. The collection displayed in the rooms on either side and on the floor above is distinguished mainly for its bronze statuettes and other works of sculpture which may be studied here better than anywhere else in Venice.

From the loggia looking on to the Grand Canal a door leads into Room I, called the Sala del Carpaccio on account of an *Annunciation* and *Death of the Virgin* painted by Carpaccio, with much studio assistance, for the Scuola degli Albanesi. As in Renaissance times, silky Turkish carpets hang among the tapestries on the walls. A huge late sixteenth-century Venetian table stands in the centre. Facing you as you enter, there is an early fifteenth-century *cassapanca* —a *cassone* or chest which may also be used as a seat. On the

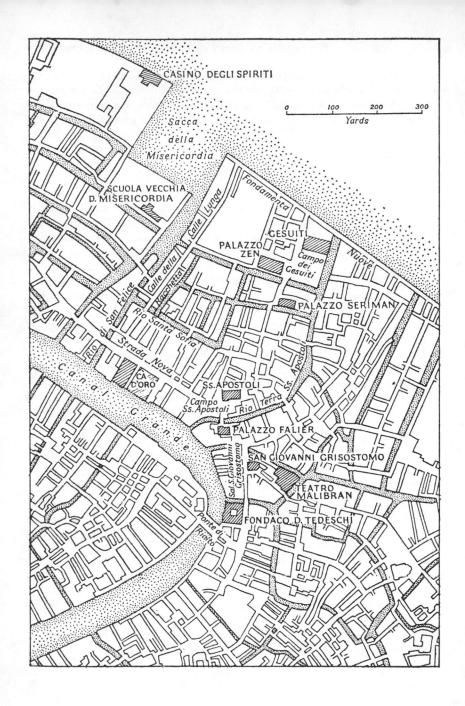

CASINO DEGLI SPIRITI

100 200 300

Yards

Sacca
della
Misericordia

SCUOLA VECCHIA
D. MISERICORDIA

Fondamenta

Calle Lunga

GESUITI

PALAZZO
ZEN

Campo
dei
Gesuiti

Nuove

Calle della

Racchetta

San Felice

Rio Santa Sofia

Rio d.

Strada Nova

PALAZZO SERIMAN

Ss. Apostoli

CA'
D'ORO

Ss. APOSTOLI

Campo
Ss. Apostoli

Rio Terrà

PALAZZO FALIER

Sal. S. Giovanni
Grisostomo

SAN GIOVANNI GRISOSTOMO

TEATRO
MALIBRAN

Ponte di
Rialto

Canal Grande

FONDACO D. TEDESCHI

wall above it there are four bronze reliefs made in 1511, by the great Paduan sculptor, Il Riccio, for a reliquary of the True Cross. Riccio's main Venetian follower, Vittore Camelio, is represented on the opposite wall by two reliefs of battles between muscular bearded giants and satyrs, pagan glorifications of virility which were made in the 1530s for the sculptor's own tomb.

The room leading out of the Sala del Carpaccio is remarkable mainly for a very delicate fifteenth-century staircase (not one of the original furnishings of the house). The room nearest the loggia on the other side of the *portego* is devoted to sculpture: an appealing fifteenth-century bust by Gian Cristoforo Romano of a little Gonzaga prince; an almost painfully realistic sixteenth-century *Pietà* in terra-cotta; and a marble relief of two heads by Tullio Lombardo, in direct emulation of ancient Roman funerary sculpture. But the work which most catches the attention is the bust of an ageing parish priest with crows' feet beneath his eyes, by Alessandro Vittoria. It is a work which demonstrates the sculptor's abilities far better than his familiar official portraits of unnaturally sage and solemn Doges and Procurators, which suggest nothing more than the " *grand bela presenza, e'l gran bel tratto* " of the old song.

In the next room, with a gilded ceiling, there is a *Venus* by Titian—a studio replica of a much greater picture. Most of the other paintings here are Florentine. In Room V there is a *Virgin and Child with a Donor*, notable mainly for the cool landscape background—by a follower of Giovanni Bellini. Next door there is a little oratory which contains one of the greatest treasures of the collection—Andrea Mantegna's agonised *St. Sebastian*, left unfinished at his death in 1506.

On the upper floor the room above the oratory is dominated by a full length portrait of a man in black—possibly a member of the Genoese Brignole family—by Antony Van Dyck who, like so many northern artists, visited Venice in the seventeenth century to study the works of Titian and Giorgione. In Room X to the right of the loggia, there is an attractive little *Virgin and Child* by Michele Giambono, and a pair of sparkling Venetian views by Francesco Guardi. Two large paintings by G. B. Cima (with a fair amount of studio help) hang in the *portego*, both notable for their landscapes. They represent *St. Mark enthroned between St. Andrew and St. Louis* and *The Lion of St. Mark with Saints John the Baptist, John the Evangelist, Mary Magdalene and Jerome*.

Room XI, to the left of the loggia, is devoted mainly to small works of sculpture. Perhaps the most notable is the bronze relief of St. Martin on horseback dividing his cloak with a beggar, by Andrea Briosco, called **Il Riccio.** This artist began his career as a goldsmith, which helps to account for the exceptionally fine surface quality of his works. He was friendly with several humanist scholars of Padua University whose passion for the antique world he shared. Under the guidance of one of them, in 1507, he decorated the paschal candlestick for the Santo at Padua with a whole mythology of sphinxes, satyrs and centaurs of thoroughbred pagan descent. For him and for his humanist friends no gulf divided pagan from Christian art. Their aim was to revive the splendours of the ancient world. In the St. Martin relief with its elegant swags and rams' heads, its muscular beggar and handsome young rider, there is nothing to show that the subject was taken from Christian hagiography rather than the writings of Livy or Tacitus. It was as natural for Riccio to represent St. Martin in this fashion as it was for Marcantanio Sabellico—a Venetian who associated with the Paduan humanists—to compose a history of Venice in good Ciceronian Latin.

On the cupboard between the windows there are two terracottas of labours of Hercules by the Roman Stefano Maderno: they date from the first years of the seventeenth century and remind one of the persistence of classical inspiration in the baroque period. The cases in the centre of the room contain medals, including some by Pisanello which are among the earliest and the greatest of Renaissance portraits. The medal itself was, of course, yet another instance of the Renaissance revival of antique forms.

From the loggia, which gives a wonderful view of the Grand Canal, a door leads into a series of rooms filled mainly with seventeenth-century Dutch and Flemish pictures of slight interest. But in the first room there are some of the finest **bronzes** to be seen in Venice. The bronze statuette was perhaps the most revealing of all Renaissance revivals. In this period collectors became so addicted to antique sculpture that they wished to have pieces literally to hand, pieces which they might fondle in their studies. On the whole they preferred nudes. At this time, however, Roman bronzes were hard to find and the few that had been dug up lacked the perfect finish demanded by the Renaissance connoisseur. So sculptors not unwillingly supplied the need in countless little figures of gods and mythological beings, derived from classical statues and modelled with exquisite refinement. In this room there is one of the finest, a statuette of Apollo derived from the Apollo Belvedere, with gilt drapery and silver eyes. It was modelled by Pier Jacopo Alari Bonacolsi, usually called Antico, and cast in 1501 for Lodovico Gonzaga of Mantua, the patron of Mantegna. In the same case there is a little Marsyas, also derived from a classical statue; the forearms were either omitted or deliberately broken off to give it an antique appearance. In a strikingly different vein there are two reliefs by Bartolomeo Bellano, a Paduan follower of Donatello; one represents three horses with rich saddle cloths, the other a cow seen from behind. In the third room there is another Labour of Hercules by Maderno and two brilliant bozzetti by Bernini for allegories on the Fontana Navona, Rome.

The Calle del Ca' d'Oro leads to the wide and busy Strada Nuova with its many market stalls selling fish, vegetables and fruit. If you turn left, take the first on the right—through the Campiello Testori—and go down the Calle della Racchetta (the name is derived from a rackets court frequented in the fifteenth and sixteenth centuries by the young Venetians including the members of the Compagnie della Calza, dressed in parti-coloured hose, who make such an elegant appearance in paintings of Carpaccio and Gentile Bellini) and Calle Lunga you will eventually reach the Fondamenta Nuove. On the way you cross two bridges both of which afford attractive views of palaces and small houses. To the left of the second bridge—Ponte Molin—stands the mid-fifteenth-century Scuola Vecchia della Misericordia. The façade was originally much richer with a magnificent relief of the *Madonna della Misericordia* (now in the Victoria and Albert Museum) over the main door.

From the **Fondamenta Nuove** (which was new in 1589) you can see to the left, on the far side of the stretch of water called the Sacca della Misericordia, a little pink house standing in a garden planted with cypresses. It was built in the sixteenth century and acquired the name of the Casino degli Spiriti, from the literary luminaries of spirits who met to talk and while away the summer afternoons in the quiet solitude of this delightful place. But on account of its proximity to the cemetery island of San Michele a ghost story was later invented to explain the name. Looking out towards the Lagoon, the island of Murano lies straight ahead with

The Companion Guide to Venice

San Michele nearer in to the right. Nearly every morning a funeral procession of gondolas, led by the black velvet-hung, elaborately carved and gilded hearse, emerges from under the bridge on its way to the cemetery—an eerie and deeply moving spectacle.

If you turn to the right and walk along the Fondamenta for a hundred yards or so you come to a *calle* which leads to the church of Santa Maria Assunta, usually known as the **Gesuiti,** with a riotous baroque façade and sea-blanched statues seemingly leaping from the pediment. It was built for the Jesuits between 1714 and 1729. On account of its subjection to the Papacy, the Society of Jesus had never been very popular in Venice and the Senate refused to allow its members to set foot in the city for about fifty years during the seventeenth century. So when they came to build their church, with money provided by the Manin family, they took care that it should appeal to the Venetian taste for magnificence while soft-pedalling their ownership.

The interior is extraordinary. At first it appears to be uphol-stered from floor to roof in a dark green and white damask which is gathered in tasselled flounces over the pulpit. But it is in fact all green and white marble. Many other churches in Italy are decorated with marble intarsia, but in none of them is the pattern so bold or the general effect so startlingly rich. It was designed by Domenico Rossi. The ceiling has paintings by Francesco Fonte-basso set in an elaborate surround of white and gilt stucco. Giuseppe Pozzo designed the high altar which enshrines a tabernacle of glittering lapis lazuli and a marble group of God the Father and Christ seated on the world, probably by Giuseppe Torretto. The same sculptor carved the elegant statues of Archangels which stand at the corners of the crossing. On the altar in the right transept there is a fine statue of St. Ignatius by Pietro Baratta who also carved the reliefs on the altar frontal. Above the main door stands a vast monument by Sansovino to three Procurators of the da Lezze family, a weighty left-over from an earlier church on the site.

A still more notable survivor from the previous church is Titian's *Martyrdom of St. Lawrence* in the first chapel on the left (a switch for the electric light is behind the column on the right). Painted in the 1540s, it is among Titian's finest works. In this virtuoso night piece, the beam from heaven, the torches and the glowing fire beneath St. Lawrence's grille, illuminate the pagan idol, flicker on the marble temple and glint on the soldiers' helmets. One is even inclined to suspect that the painting is an excuse for these pyrotechnic effects and the use of dark, rich colour rather than an attempt to render the Saint's agony. Apart from a fresco by Raphael in the Vatican, it is the first successful nocturne in the history of art. Like the *Assumption* in the Frari it anticipates the baroque style. It therefore exerted considerable influence when night-pieces became so popular throughout Europe in the seventeenth century.

From 1531 until 1576 Titian lived in this part of Venice, in a house just beyond the east end of the present Gesuiti church. There was no *fondamenta* then and he had a garden which stretched to the water's edge. The Florentine grammarian Priscianese describes an August evening he spent here in 1540 with Titian, Aretino and Sansovino. " As soon as the sun went down," he recorded, " the lagoon swarmed with gondolas, adorned with beautiful women, and resounded with the varied harmony and music of voices and instruments, which till midnight accompanied our delightful supper."

At the end of the Campo dei Gesuiti farthest from the Fondamenta Nuove stands the Palazzo Zen—a strange building of 1538 in which the ogee window is used in a barely disguised form among Renaissance ornaments. On the other side of the bridge stand houses once owned by the Scuola della Carità and still decorated with its emblem—a relief of the Virgin sheltering the devout beneath her cloak. If you walk along the Salizzada Seriman—which takes its name from the handsome Gothic palace No. 4851—and turn right at the end you will reach the Campo dei Santi Apostoli.

The church of the **Apostoli** has an undistinguished exterior. But inside there is one little gem of Renaissance architecture, the Corner family chapel on the right of the nave, with columns rising from finely carved bases to support a little cupola of great delicacy. It dates from the late fifteenth century and was probably designed by Mauro Coducci. On the altar there is a painting by G. B. Tiepolo of *The Communion of St. Lucy* (1746–8) which combines a sense of true piety with a love of pastel coloured silks and a lighthearted wit revealed in such details as the Negro page and the figure peering down curiously from the balcony. The only other painting

173

of note is *The Guardian Angel* by Francesco Maffei in the chapel to
the left of the high altar, placed there as a thanks offering by
someone who was rescued from a shipwreck. Though painted in
the mid-seventeenth century it glistens with a nacreous light which
seems to anticipate Francesco Guardi. Just outside the chapel
there is a fine rococo processional standard, carved with figures of
souls in purgatory, gilded and inlaid with fish scales of mother-of-
pearl.

A series of *calli* and *campielli* winds from the Campo dei Santi
Apostoli towards the Rialto bridge. From the Ponte dei Santi
Apostoli, the way goes under the Palazzo Falier, a thirteenth-
century building with Byzantine style windows and incrustations
of reliefs. If you follow the signs pointing to the Rialto—or the
lines of white marble in the pavement which have served the same
purpose for many centuries—you will reach the trim red and
white church of **San Giovanni Grisostomo.**

This church was designed by Mauro Coducci and built between
1497 and 1504. The plan, a Greek cross with a central cupola,
was one particularly admired by Renaissance architects no less
for its beautiful simplicity than its symbolism—a combination of
the square and circle representing the relation between man and
the universe and the cross standing for the redemption. There
are two pictures of outstanding importance. Above the first altar
on the right is Giovanni Bellini's *St. Jerome with St. Christopher and
St. Augustine*, painted in 1513 when he was an octogenarian. The
treatment of the soulful St. Christopher and the gentle hilly landscape reveal how the old artist fell under the spell of Giorgione
who had died three years before; while the elegant marble pilaster
in the centre, which looks like the jamb of a chimney-piece, seems
to have been taken from the work of another of his younger contemporaries, Tullio Lombardo. The influence of Giorgione marks,
still more strongly, Sebastiano del Piombo's *St. John Chrysostom and
Six Saints* on the high altar (1508–10). Indeed, the somewhat plump
St. John the Baptist and St. Liberale who stands behind him were
probably laid in by Giorgione himself shortly before his death.
The third great work of art in the church is the relief of *The Coronation of the Virgin*, over the second altar on the left, carved between
1500 and 1502 by Tullio Lombardo who also decorated the pilasters
in the chapel. With its carefully modulated rhythm of draperies
and its serious self-possessed figures, this strongly classicising relief

was destined to exert great influence on Venetian painters, notably
Bellini and Cima.

On the south side of the church, an archway next to the Nane
Mora restaurant leads to the Corte Prima del Milion and the Corte
Seconda del Milion. It was near here that the Polo family lived
(a plaque marks the place on the Fondamenta beyond the second
courtyard) and the two courts are called " del Milion " after
Marco Polo's book known to Italians as *Il Milione* on account of
the million marvels—or lies—it contained. **Marco Polo,** the
son of a Venetian merchant, returned here after working for some
twenty-five years as a civil servant in China under the great Tartar
Emperor Kublai Khan. Here he held Venetians spell-bound with
his stories of the wonders and riches of the East. The Veneto-
Byzantine archway in the Corte Seconda must have been a familiar
sight to him, and one wonders if he recognised the Far Eastern
origin of the birds and monsters which adorn it. He probably did
not, for these motifs have been transformed in their journey across
Asia and retain no more than a whiff of the oriental exoticism of
their ancestors in Persia and China. Besides, Marco Polo's book
reveals that he had little interest in the arts.

The Salizzada San Giovanni Grisostomo leads to the large square
building, the **Fondaco dei Tedeschi** or German factory, now the
main post office. Built in 1505 to replace a predecessor which
had perished by fire, this great grim pile was originally enlivened
by frescoes by Giorgione and Titian on two of its façades. The only
scrap that remains of Giorgione's work is now in the Accademia
(see p. 127). But on the side of the building facing towards the
Rialto bridge you may still discern the last pale glimmer of Titian's
Judith and Holofernes—his earliest documented work—high up on
the wall above the central lion-crowned door.

In the fifteenth and sixteenth centuries the Venetians carried on
a considerable trade with the various German states—as Shakespeare seems to have been aware when he made Shylock refer to
a diamond that cost him two thousand ducats in Frankfurt.
The Fondaco dei Tedeschi was provided by the Venetians as a
block of apartments, offices and warehouses in which the German
merchants were obliged to live and conduct their affairs. Everything was arranged for them. All the servants and higher function-
aries were appointed by the State. The merchants were allowed
to transact business only with born Venetians and only through

the brokers who were allotted to them and who took a percentage on every deal. Originally the broker was expected to be present at every transaction, but in time it became usual for him to delegate his authority to a clerk. By the end of the fifteenth century the office of broker was a sinecure in the gift of the Senate but, by typically Venetian ingenuity, financed out of the pockets of the foreigners. Both Giovanni Bellini and Titian were rewarded with brokerages in the Fondaco dei Tedeschi, apparently in payment for work in the Palazzo Ducale which thus cost the Senate nothing.

The Fondaco dei Tedeschi was restored rather severely in the early years of this century. The great internal courtyard, which was originally open to the sky, is surrounded by three tiers of sturdy arcades, as simple and forthright as the most hard-headed merchant could desire. Always filled with busy, hustling crowds, posting letters, collecting mail from the *poste restante* or arguing vainly with customs officials about import taxes levied on parcels from abroad, the place still retains some of the brusque activity of a great business centre. And, of course, the staccato clatter of German voices can still be heard here—more appropriately than in any other part of Venice.

CHAPTER 14

Churches and Theatres: Music and Fantasy

San Moisè—San Fantin—Teatro La Fenice—Santa Maria Zobenigo—
San Vitale—Palazzo Pisani—San Stefano—Palazzo Pesaro—San Luca—
Palazzo Contarini del Bovolo

The busy **Salizzada San Moisè** leads from the Napoleonic end
of the Piazza to the *campo* and church of San Moisè. Near the
beginning there is one of the city's best newspaper kiosks with an
international stock of papers and magazines. Italy has only two
national newspapers: *L'Osservatore Romano*, published by the
Vatican, and *L'Unità*, the organ of the Communist Party. Shades
of political feeling between these two extremes are expressed in
a vast number of local papers. The Venetian paper is the
Gazzettino, of a moderately conservative Christian-Democrat complexion which appeals to the majority of its readers who are members
of the middle class—though Venetian intellectuals tend to be left
wing and the gondoliers, who profit almost exclusively from
capitalist visitors and Italian millionaries, are said to be Com-
munists to a man. But it is not at all provincial in comparison
with, say, the newspapers of Chicago or Cleveland, Ohio. Most
of the space is devoted to international and national news and
there is usually an arts page with general essays and reviews of
books and exhibitions.

Several of the more fashionable shops are in the Salizzada—
dress shops, glass shops, an antique dealer and a photographer's
where you may buy photographs and colour reproductions of the
celebrated works of art in and around Venice. Leading down to
the Grand Canal on the left, the Calle Valaresso passes Palazzo
Dandolo (No. 1362) which gained notoriety as the Ridotto or
gambling house between 1768 and 1774 when it was closed to

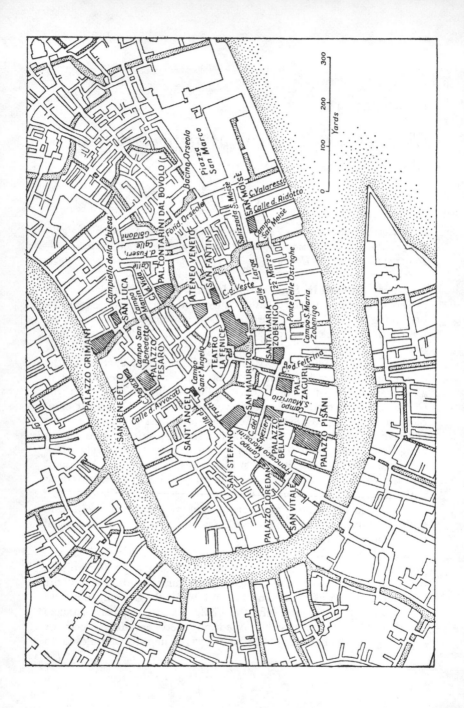

Yards

300

200

100

0

Piazza San Marco

Bacino Orseola

Fond. Orseola

SAN MOÏSE

C. Valaresso

Calle d. Ridotto

Salizzada S. Moïse

Campo San Moïse

Campiello della Chiesa

Calle Goldoni

PAL. CONTARINI DAL BOVOLO

Calle d. Fuseri

Calle d. Vida

ATENEO VENETO

SAN FANTIN

Calle Larga

22 Marzo

Ponte delle Ostreghe

Calle S. Maria

C. d. Veste

SANTA MARIA ZOBENIGO

Campo S. Maria Zobenigo

SAN LUCA

Campo San Marin

PALAZZO PESARO

Campo San Benedetto

PALAZZO GRIMANI

SAN BENEDETTO

Calle d. Avvocati

Campo Sant'Angelo

TEATRO LA FENICE

SAN MAURIZIO

Fond. Feltrina

PAL. ZAGURI

Campo S. Maurizio

SANT'ANGELO

Calle del Frati

Campo Francesco Morosini

SAN STEFANO

Calle del Spezier

PALAZZO BELLAVITE

PALAZZO LOREDAN

SAN VITALE

PALAZZO PISANI

prevent the Venetian nobility from losing all their money to foreigners (a sign of decadence if ever there was one). There were other gambling hells in Venice but this was the most famous. The curious rules admitted to its tables only those of noble birth or people who were masked—and as masks were inexpensive, people of all classes and all nations gathered here. A similar assembly, comprised partly of Venetians, partly of café society and partly of those who wish to be mistaken for one or other of these · categories, is nowadays to be found nearby in Harry's Bar, not gaming but sipping gin fizzes and dry martinis.

No one has ever had a good word for the façade of **San Moisè**. " It is notable," said Ruskin, " as one of the basest examples of the basest school of the Renaissance." Even the most fervent devotee of the baroque must admit that it is too heavy, too over-crowded in ornament and too coarse in detail. It was built in the 1660s to the design of Alessandro Tremignon and, a couple of decades later, decked with statues (some of which have been removed) by the northern sculptor Heinrich Meyring—or Arrigo Merengo as he is known in Venice. Yet it is not entirely to be despised. If freed of the pigeon droppings (pigeons are, alas, sacred birds in Venice, supposedly descended from those released in the Pentecost ceremonies each year) it might well present a sparkling, *mouvementé* effect of light and shade. (The unusual dedication to Moses derived from Byzantium where churches were often dedicated to prophets.)

Once one's eyes have become accustomed to the gloom inside the church, they are caught by what appears to be a rock garden where one would normally expect to find the high altar. It is in fact a gargantuan piece of sculpture by Meyring, representing Moses on Mount Sinai receiving the tablets of the law. A similar spirit of fantasy, though here rather morbid, invests the skeleton-adorned monument to Canon Ivanovich by Marco Beltrame, over the north door. Opposite there is a fine eighteenth-century *Pietà* by Antonio Corradini, with a very elegant figure of the Virgin. The outstanding work of sculpture in the church is, however, the exquisitely cast and tooled bronze altar frontal by Niccolò and Sebastiano Roccatagliata (1633) in the sacristy. It represents the angels carrying the dead body of Christ and is strongly marked by Tintoretto's influence which was seldom so beneficial in seventeenth-century Venice.

The Companion Guide to Venice

On the right wall of the chancel there is a vast canvas of *The Plague of Serpents* by Giovanni Antonio Pellegrini, the best of the eighteenth-century Venetian painters errant who travelled across Europe brightening walls and ceilings with southern colour. This is one of his relatively few works in Venice. The organ balcony over the main door is decorated with a series of glittering rococo paintings by Francesco Migliori and Francesco Pittoni. A simple tomb stone in the nave floor commemorates John Law, the financier and adventurer. He was a Scot who killed a man in a duel in London in 1694, was sentenced to death but escaped across the Channel, established the first bank in France, and eventually gained control of the entire French economy until, in 1720, he fell into disgrace and was forced to flee the country. He spent the remaining nine years of his life in Venice.

Leaving the church by the main door you are confronted on the left by the recent façade of the Bauer-Grünwald Hotel which now receives as much abuse from connoisseurs of architecture as San Moisè did in Ruskin's day. It is, indeed, an even less distinguished example of the style of its period. But the hotel is a comfortable one and boasts the most famous hall porter in Europe—Signor Tortorella who is said to be able to provide (for those who know him) the best seats at the opera, the best cabins on the Lido, and air-line bookings to anywhere at a moment's notice. He is also the author of popular songs which are often to be heard on the Italian wireless.

The Ponte San Moisè leads into one of the widest streets in Venice, the **Calle Larga XXII Marzo** built in 1880. The name commemorates the day on which the Venetians, under Daniele Manin (no relation of the last Doge) rose and expelled the Austrian garrison in 1848. For seventeen months Manin headed a new Venetian Republic. But in August 1849 blockade and bombardment forced the rebels to surrender.

The street is flanked by banks, travel agencies and antique shops which usually fill their windows with elegant trifles of eighteenth-century porcelain and furniture. One of the shops, no. 2251, is the agent for the Fortuny silks so highly praised by Proust. They are made in a factory of the Giudecca and frequently repeat the patterns of textiles in paintings by Veronese and Tiepolo. Several narrow *calli*, alive with slinking cats, lead down to the hotels on the Grand Canal. That called Calle del Teatro San Moisè records the long-vanished

180

theatre where Claudio Monteverdi's opera *Arianna* (now known only from the hauntingly beautiful *Lament*) was first performed in 1640.

The Calle della Veste leads to the Campo San Fantin where there are three notable buildings: a church, a *scuola* and a theatre. The church of San Fantin is of interest mainly for its noble chancel built to the design of Sansovino (1562-4). The Scuola di San Girolamo (now occupied by the Ateneo Veneto society of arts and letters) is a late sixteenth-century building with some seventeenth-century embellishments, like the curious curly pediments over the windows. Inside there are ceilings by Palma Giovane and Antonio Zanchi and one of the finest of Vittoria's bronze busts, representing Tommaso Rangone. The members of this *scuola* assumed the unhappy duty of accompanying condemned criminals to the scaffold and giving their bodies decent burial.

The **Teatro La Fenice** is now the oldest and largest theatre in Venice. Designed by Giovanni Antonio Selva in 1790, it was burnt down in 1836 but rebuilt with only slight alterations. (Unkind critics of the architect construed the word *Societas* on the façade as an acrostic: *Sine ordine cum irregularitate erexit theatrum Antonius Selva*). The auditorium, all gilt and pink plush with cherubs swooping and soaring on the ceiling, provides a perfect setting for any opera by Bellini, Donizetti or the early Verdi. It is an unforgettable experience to attend a gala performance when periwigged and gold-embroidered flunkeys meet the gondolas, when the boxes, each with a bunch of scarlet carnations on its balcony, glitter with diamonds, and when the many reception rooms echo with the rustle of silk dresses and the lisp of soft Venetian voices. Performances vary considerably at the Fenice, but the décor of the theatre itself never fails to come up to scratch.

During the Austrian occupation the Fenice was often a rallying point for malcontents. Symbolic red, white and green bouquets would be thrown on the stage. And occasionally some patriot would add a bunch of flowers tied with ribbons of the Austrian colours for the pleasure of seeing the *prima donna* kick it aside. In these years the operas of Verdi were particularly popular both for their hidden *risorgimento* significance and because they gave the audience an opportunity to chant " Viva Verdi "—for his name stood for the slogan: *Vittorio Emanuele Re d'Italia*.

Several notable operas were written specially for the Fenice and performed there for the first time—Rossini's *Tancredi* (1813) and *Semiramide* (1823), Vincenzo Bellini's version of Romeo and Juliet, *I Capuleti e i Montecchi* (1830) and *Beatrice di Tenda* (1833). But the most important operas which had their world premières here were all by Verdi—first *Ernani* (1844), then *Rigoletto* (1851) which was an immediate success. Surprisingly enough, *La Traviata*, first performed in 1853, was a spectacular disaster—due partly to the modern dress, partly to indifferent singers and, to some extent, to its absence of *risorgimento* symbolism. Saddened, but not seriously grieved, Verdi wrote one more opera for the Fenice, *Simone Boccanegra* which was received with enthusiasm when it was first performed in 1857. Of recent first nights the most memorable was that of Stravinsky's *The Rake's Progress* in 1951.

If you return to the Calle Larga, turn right, then left by the shop with an engaging display of old prints and books, then right again and cross the Ponte delle Ostreghe (bridge of the oysters), you will reach Campo **Santa Maria Zobenigo** also called Santa Maria del Giglio. The façade of the church shocked Ruskin profoundly, for not only is it a baroque construction—built by Giuseppe Sardi between 1678 and 1683—but amongst its profusion of sculptured ornaments it includes not a single Christian symbol. Designed and paid for by Antonio Barbaro who served under Francesco Morosini in the war of Candia but was dismissed for incompetence, this façade is an outrageous piece of self-glorification and self-justification erected—as Barbaro pointed out with glee in his will—within sight of Morosini's palace. In the centre a statue of Antonio Barbaro in his general's uniform stands above his sarcophagus. He is flanked by statues of Honour, Virtue, Fame and Wisdom. In the niches below there are statues of his four brothers. On the plinths of the columns there are relief plans of the towns where he had served the Republic: Zara, Padua, Rome, Corfu, Spalato and, of course, Candia.

Inside, the church is much less secular, lit by a particularly dim religious light and crowded with painted and sculptured images. By the main door there is an elegantly attenuated statue of Christ by Giulio del Moro. After the first altar on the right a passage leads to a dark chapel where a very fine eighteenth-century ivory crucifix with a kneeling figure of St. Mary Magdalene dramatically shines out of the gloom. The last chapel on the right of the nave is a little eighteenth-century Baptistery—a riot of stucco cherubs and draperies and barley-sugar columns around a font with a cover of gilded waves on the crest of which St. John the Baptist pirouettes. Among the paintings the finest are two of the Evangelists by Tintoretto (1552–7) behind the high altar. In the Sacristy there is a *Virgin and Child* attributed over-optimistically to Rubens. Of higher quality is the nearby painting of *Abraham Dividing the World* by Antonio Zanchi—as fine a piece of baroque bravura in paint as can be found in Venice. All around the church there is a series of Stations of the Cross painted by such masters as G. B. Crosato, D. Maggiotto, G. Diziani and F. Fontebasso, each one an exquisite minor work of art.

The Ponte della Feltrina, a *campiello*, another bridge and a brief *calle* lead to the **Campo San Maurizio**. On the left, as you enter, stands the fifteenth-century Gothic Palazzo Zaguri and on the opposite side the simple and somewhat severe Palazzo Bellavite (no. 2760) where Alessandro Manzoni—author of the greatest Italian novel *I Promessi Sposi*—lived from 1803–4. On the left side a picture dealer spreads his wares outside his shop. Facing him stands the neo-classical façade of San Maurizio by G. A. Selva, decorated with solemn statues and reliefs, and just beyond it, the early sixteenth-century Scuola degli Albanesi which once contained a cycle of paintings by Carpaccio.

The *calle* between the *scuola* and the Palazzo Bellavite leads over a bridge, past one of the most tempting cake shops in the city and emerges in the large **Campo Francesco Morosini**. This is one of the more important centres of Venetian life, distinctly bourgeois in comparison with either the mondaine Piazza or such haunts of the populace as the Campo Santa Margherita. There are always children playing in the centre—and one of the unfailing joys of Italy is the constant presence of inquisitive, bright-eyed, sun-tanned children playing their complicated games with complete absorption and a lack of restraint which would gladden the heart of any London psychiatrist. Should you ever wish to escape the grandeurs, the international crowd, and the bands of the Piazza, you cannot choose a better place to drink your *aperitivo* or coffee than the Campo Morosini.

In the centre stands a not very interesting nineteenth-century statue of Nicolò Tommaseo—a *risorgimento* figure—usually graced by a pigeon perching on his head. (Do the pigeons, I sometimes wonder, retreat here from the Piazza for reasons similar to my own?) Around the *campo* there are several notable buildings.

At the far left end stands the early eighteenth-century church of **San Vitale** with a façade derived from Palladio. It is now disused but you can usually gain admittance through the art gallery next door. Inside there is a painting by Carpaccio of St. Vitalis riding what is unmistakably one of the bronze horses of San Marco, an attractive *Annunciation* by Sebastiano Ricci and some good eighteenth-century sculpture by Antonio Tarsia. Next to San Vitale stands the long low Palazzo Loredan (No. 2945) which has on its main door a handsome bronze knocker in the form of Neptune and two sea horses, by some follower of Vittoria. Opposite, the small Campo Pisani opens out of the Campo Morosini. Here the **Palazzo Pisani** rises up like some vast stranded ship. The façade dates from the eighteenth century and was probably designed by Girolamo Frigimelica. If you ask permission from the porter you may be allowed to go up the imposing staircase to see several grandiose frescoed and stuccoed apartments. Since 1897 this palace has been a conservatory of music which has included among its directors Ermanno Wolf-Ferrari (composer of *I Quattro Rusteghe* best known for its lilting barcarolle intermezzo which perfectly expresses the movement of a gondola) and Gian Francesco Malipiero (the editor of *Monteverdi*). In the mornings you can usually catch from its windows the hoarse piping of oboes, the scraping of fiddles, hesitant tinklings on pianos and soprano trills which never quite touch top C.

At the other end of the Campo Morosini stands the large Gothic church of **Santo Stefano,** which now has a peaceful air though it records more turbulent times. It had to be reconsecrated on no fewer than six occasions because of bloodshed within its walls. In the early sixteenth century the attached monastery was famous for the plays performed by the monks. The entrance to the church is through a fifteenth-century door luxuriant with Gothic foliage.

The architecturally simple interior is richer in sculpture than in paintings. Indeed, apart from the pretty *Birth of the Virgin* by Nicolò Bambini, over the first altar on the right, the only pictures of note are in the Sacristy (east end of south aisle). Here there are two late paintings by Tintoretto, dating from about 1580: *The Agony in the Garden* with wraith-like figures glimpsed through the olive trees and *Christ Washing the Disciples' Feet*. A *Last Supper* which has an enchanting detail of a child playing with a cat, is by a member of his school. Over the door there is a vast *Massacre of*

184

the Innocents (1733) painted in clear bright colours, probably the masterpiece of an otherwise dull minor painter, Gaspare Diziani. Rather rigid fifteenth-century statues by a sculptor of the Lombardo school, which originally graced an altar screen, stand around the chancel. The high altar has a brilliantly coloured *pietre dure* frontal dated 1661. In front there are two elaborate bronze candlesticks, one made in 1577, probably in Vittoria's studio, the other a seventeenth-century copy of it. The monks' choir, behind the altar, has stalls carved with a rank growth of Gothic vegetation by Marco Cozzi who also carved the stalls in the Frari and a ceiling in the Accademia.

On the right side of the door to the Sacristy there is a bronze relief of *The Virgin and Child with Saints and Donors* attributed to Alessandro Leopardi, the artist who cast Verrocchio's Colleoni monument. In striking contrast, on the other side of the door, there is a preposterous baroque monument to a judge, Lazzaro Ferri, all flustered periwig, fluttering cherubs and flounced curtains with an eagle clutching a scroll in its claws.

The third altar on the left is decorated with three crisply carved little statues one of which is signed by Pietro Lombardo; they probably stood originally on the altar screen. Pietro Lombardo and his sons were also reponsible for the monument on the west or entrance wall to Giacomo Surian a physician from Rimini. It has a recumbent effigy of Surian, a relief of him kneeling before the Virgin, and a beautifully carved podium with deaths' heads, festoons of fruit, shields carved to the texture of damask, and a charming little relief of a farmyard scene. Next to it stands Antonio Canova's monument to his first patron, Giovanni Falier. The monument is of a type derived from Greek stele by Canova and reduced to a cliché by his numerous followers. The carving is very fine, especially in the rendering of the textures of the dress of the mourning figure and the parchment face of Falier. Canova carved some of his first works in the cloister of San Stefano where he had a studio.

In front of the first altar on the left a slab records the burial place of Giovanni Gabrielli, organist of San Marco from 1585 to 1612 and one of the best of the early Venetian composers who have been rediscovered in this century. Another notability buried in the church is Francesco Morosini whose vast tomb slab is in the centre of the nave.

185

A door at the east end of the north aisle leads into the sixteenth-century cloister where the last relics of a frescoed frieze by Pordenone can still be seen. This cloister is not the peaceful other-wordly place it used to be, however. The Ministry of Finance has offices in the monastery and quick footed, harassed faced, tax payers and tax gatherers have replaced the shuffling, benign old monks who once sauntered here. A door leads from the cloister into the Campo Sant' Anzolo (or Angelo).

On an island in the middle of the *campo* stands the Oratory of the Archangel Michael. Next to it there is a shop advertising apartments and houses to be let but, in true Italian fashion, making no mention of prices, so that none of the fun of bargaining shall be lost. In the quietest corner of the *campo*, at no. 3555, a brass plate indicates the office of private detectives—though I am told that these sleuths of the lagoons are much less in demand now that the days of *cicisbeatura* are over. At the other end stands the Gothic Palazzo Duodo (no. 3584) where the composer Domenico Cimarosa died in 1801. Behind the Oratory there is a handsome eighteenth-century palace (no. 3831) with great Goliath heads—of the type so popular in Venice—frowning out above the doors and windows. Next door there is a simple Gothic house by the entrance to the Calle dei Avvocati.

If you go down this *calle* and take the first turning to the right (Calle Pesaro) you will reach a bridge beneath the early fifteenth-century Gothic façade of Palazzo Pesaro, with ogee windows and little marble balconies. The *calle* leads on to the Campo San Beneto (Benedetto) one side of which is filled by another façade of **Palazzo Pesaro**—about a half a century later and much more richly decorated with all the florid refinements of cusps; crockets and poppy heads. In the late eighteenth century it was the seat of a musical society and is sometimes known as Palazzo degli Orfei. Some decades ago it was restored by a Spanish painter, Mariano Fortuny y de Mandrazo whose widow bequeathed it to the city of Venice in the vain hope of preserving it and making it available to the public.

The little church of **San Benedetto** contains several notable paintings—*St. Francis of Paola* by G. B. Tiepolo, a dramatic *St. Sebastian* by Bernardo Strozzi, and two pictures of St. Benedict, one with a fantastic shrouded figure, by Sebastiano Mazzoni. But unfortunately it is rarely open.

If you leave the Campo San Beneto by the Salizzada del Teatro and turn down the Calle delle Muneghe you will soon reach the door of Palazzo Contarini (no. 3980) with a magnificent covered seventeenth-century staircase in the *cortile*, an attractive little fountain and, under the arcade, a group of eighteenth-century *casapanche* with elaborate backs. This palace is now the headquarters of the Venetian waterworks company. Continuing along the *calle* you reach the Ponte del Teatro Rossini which takes its name from one of the oldest theatres in Venice, recently rebuilt as a jazz-modern cinema. It was originally called the Teatro San Benedetto and, like the several other theatres in Venice, financed by a noble family (in this instance the Grimani). Here the castrati piped their coloratura arias and buffoons enacted the age old plots of the Commedia dell' Arte.

To the left, on the Grand Canal, stands the Palazzo Grimani, now the Court of Appeal. In front of the bridge stands the church of **San Luca** with a dull early nineteenth-century façade. There is little of interest inside apart from a fifteenth-century relief of the Virgin and Child over the first altar on the right, and a painting of *St. Luke in Ecstasy* by Paolo Veronese—with a good deal of studio assistance—above the high altar. It was in this church that Pietro Aretino was buried in 1556, but no stone marks his resting place. A writer of genius, a connoisseur of rare discrimination, he was the friend of Titian and Sansovino. But he was also the most notorious *mauvaise langue* in history, of whom it was said that he had a bad word for everyone except God, and that only because they were unacquainted. Twin talents for the most effusive flattery—applied to those who rewarded him with gifts—and the most abusive satire —applied to all who did not—won him a comfortable livelihood. In Venice he prudently refrained from attacking the powerful senators, reserving his venom for those who could do him no harm in the city (especially the wives of unimportant patricians) and the rulers of other states who refused to buy his silence, notably Isabella d'Este " the monstrous great Marchesa of Mantua who has ebony teeth, ivory eyebrows, is dishonestly ugly and *arcidishonstamente* made up, and gives birth to children in senility." In his crude and clumsy epigrams all women are whores and all men impotent cuckolds. He surveys the scene smacking his moistened lips and crying like Thersites " Lechery, lechery, nothing but lechery." Strange as it may now seem, his satires were thought to be amusing and gained him innumerable imitators in Venice (unfortunately his letters which are often beautifully written were less imitated). He appealed strongly to the strain of savage mockery in the Venetian character. His heirs are the dissatisfied intellectuals of to-day who will tell you with some relish of the corruption in Church, State, local government, education and business and who succeed in taking in visitors of a like mind.

In the *campiello* behind the church there is an unusual thirteenth-century Gothic door case (no. 4038) decorated with a pattern of moulded bricks. The Ramo della Salizzada leads into the **Campo Manin,** dominated by Luigi Borro's bronze monument to Daniele Manin. The Cassa di Risparmio (savings bank) on the right-hand side is built on the site of the printing shop founded by Aldus Manutius in the fifteenth century. Here the famous Aldine classics were produced. Above the door there was a monitory notice " Whoever you are and whatever you may want, Aldo requests you to ask it in a few words and depart, unless like Hercules, you come to lend the aid of your shoulders to the weary Atlas. In that case something will always be found for you to do, however many you may be." Erasmus of Rotterdam was one of those who lent his shoulder when he came here to see his *Proverbs* through the press. An unfriendly report says that when he stayed with Aldus, he ate for three and drank for many without doing the work of one. But then, Erasmus defined the ideal man as *homo quadratus*—a square.

The Calle della Vida leads from Campo Manin (first left, first right) to the Corte **Contarini del Bovolo** where, through a rusty fence, you can see one of the most remarkable and fantastic examples of late *quattrocento* architecture in Venice. This is the spiral staircase (*bovolo* in Venetian) of Palazzo Contarini, built shortly before 1500 probably to the design of Giovanni Candi. Mercifully this building has escaped the attention of the floodlighters and it is well worth seeing when the light of a full moon glitters on its marble arcade. In front of the palace there is a group of old well heads gathered from various parts of Venice and including one fine eleventh-century Byzantine specimen.

The Calle della Vida leads into the Calle dei Fuseri (turn right) and from there the first alleyway on the left leads to the Calle Goldoni which (turn right) takes you past the **Bacino Orseolo** to the Piazza San Marco.

The Albergo del Cavaletto, on the far side of the *bacino*, stands on the site of one of the most ancient hotels in Venice. It was called the Cavaletto on account of its proximity to stables which provided horses for visitors in the fourteenth century. For at that date the horse had not yet been superceded by the gondola as the normal means of transport in the city. The *bacino* is now one of the main gathering places for gondolas and echoes with the cries of gondoliers. To my ears these seem to be limited to an unmusical *OLE!* But nineteenth-century visitors distinguished greater variety—*Stalì, premè* and *sciàr*. Ruskin devoted an appendix of *The Stones of Venice* to them and Richard Monckton Milnes worked one into each stanza of an attractive little poem which must have been recited in many a Victorian drawing-room. It begins:

When along the light ripple the far serenade
Has accosted the ear of each passionate maid,
She may open her window that looks on the stream—
She may smile on her pillow and blend it in dream;
Half in words, half in music, it pierces the gloom,
" I am coming—*stalì*—but you know not for whom!
Stalì—not for whom!

CHAPTER 15

Cannaregio

San Marcuola—La Maddalena—Campo San Fosca—San Marziale—
Tintoretto's house—Sior Antonio Rioba—Madonna dell' Orto—San
Alvise—Ghetto—Palazzo Labia—Gli Scalzi

However large the crowds of tourists who visit Venice every
summer, several surprisingly large sections of the city remain quiet
and undisturbed.   The swarms of scantily clothed day-trippers,
smelling strongly of sunburn lotion, who pour out of motor coaches
at Piazzale Roma, wedge themselves into *motoscafi* and *vaporetti* as
tightly as St. Ursula's virgins and sail down the Grand Canal,
seldom venture very far from Piazza San Marco.   Those who
arrive by train may be found walking along the *calli* from the
station to the Rialto but very rarely do they stray northwards
into the large municipal district of Cannaregio, called after a canal
once green and shady with bamboo canes.   It is always pleasant
to wander through the narrow *calli* and along the undisturbed
backwaters of these districts where you can still savour that tranquil
melancholy atmosphere of old Venice so powerfully evoked by
Henry James in *The Aspern Papers.*
   It is as well to begin at the church of **San Marcuola** which can
be reached by the Grand Canal *Vaporetto.*   This is one of the very
few unfinished churches in Venice.   For unlike the Florentines,
who left four of their five main churches without façades, the
Venetians attached as much importance to the exterior as the
interior of a building.   Built between 1728 and 1736 by Giorgio
Massari, the church has a handsome interior.   The plan is unusual,
with twin pulpits over the north and south doors and altars clustered
in the corners.   Of the many statues by Morlaiter and others,
those of St. John the Baptist and St. Anthony the Abbot in the

north-west corner are perhaps the best. The two on the high altar
represent Saints Ermagora and Fortunato to whom the church is
dedicated and whose names have, by some peculiar process, been
concertinaed into Marcuola. By far the finest work of art in the
church is Tintoretto's *Institution of the Eucharist* on the north wall
of the chancel, painted in 1547 just as he was emerging from the
shadow of Titian to develop his own style. A curious old legend
relates that a priest of San Marcuola was dragged from his bed
one night and kicked and pummelled by all the corpses buried
beneath the church, because he had rashly preached against the
existence of ghosts and remarked " where the dead are, there they
stay." It is worth noting that the Venetians are almost the only
Italians who indulge in ghost stories.

If you leave San Marcuola by the north door, turn right over
the bridge and then, at the back of Palazzo Vendramin where a
plaque records the death of Wagner, turn left along the Calle
Vendramin you will reach the busy Rio Terrà della Maddalena.
This is an important shopping centre for the Sestiere di Canareggio
and is lively with stalls selling provisions besides several decked
with gondolier hats, Murano glass beads and silk scarves to tempt
tourists on the way to the railway. Turning right, you pass two
handsome palaces on the way to the Campo della Maddalena:
No. 2347, the Gothic windowed Palazzo Contin, and No. 2343,
with a monstrous hirsute head leering out from the key-stone over
the door, Palazzo Donà delle Rose (one of the most beautiful of
all Italian surnames, equalled only by the Veronese Giusti del
Giardino).

The **Campo della Maddalena** is surrounded by a huddle of
old houses with stocky Venetian chimneys triumphing over the
spindly television antennae on the sky line. No. 2143 has an ogival
door with a curious fifteenth-century relief of a saint and two
angels. In the centre there is a sixteenth-century well-head
decorated with acanthus leaf carving. The late eighteenth-century
church of the Maddalena, built by the historian of Venetian architecture Tommaso Temanza, has a very beautiful interior but is
securely locked against the visitor.

The Ponte Sant' Antonio leads into the Campo Santa Fosca.
In the centre there is a late nineteenth-century statue of one of the
greatest of all Venetians, **Pietro Sarpi,** a Servite monk known to his
contemporaries as Fra Paolo. In 1579, at the age of twenty-seven,

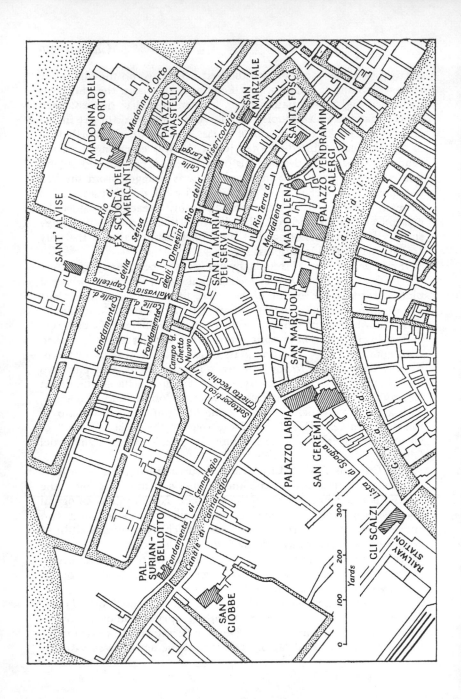

he was elected Venetian provincial of the Servite Order. The rest of his life he devoted to the study of theology, science and history, and to the service of his Order and the Venetian Republic. A convinced humanist and a devout Catholic, he is the patron of all modernists. " I never venture to deny anything on the grounds of impossibility," he once wrote, " for I am well aware of the infinite variety in the works of nature and of God." He also made a more famous remark which has become a Venetian proverb: " *Non dico mai buggie, ma la verità non a tutti* " (I never tell lies but I don't tell the truth to everyone). His work is impressive. He wrote the standard history of the Council of Trent (praised by Gibbon and Dr. Johnson) and he assisted Galileo in the construction of the telescope. He was the first to notice the expansion of the uvea in the eye and probably discovered the working of the valves in the veins. He was also reckoned an authority on magnetism. In his treatise on " human knowledge " he anticipated the philosophy of Locke.

Sarpi was also the first Catholic theologian to remark that the territorial ambitions of the Vatican ran counter to the spiritual aims of the Church. And here, naturally enough, he came into conflict with the Papal Curia. When, in 1606, the Pope put Venice under an interdict the Senate turned for advice to Sarpi who councilled resistance, encouraged the clergy to continue their functions, and fought the interdict in a series of manifestoes. Fulminating anathemas, the Pope prepared for war but, unable to find a single European state to support his battle for temporal supremacy, was eventually forced to yield and to sheathe the rusty weapon of the interdict for ever. It was generally recognised that Sarpi was responsible for this victory of State over Church—the first of the series that was to lead to the imprisonment of Pius IX in the Vatican—and thereafter he was a marked man. His books were put on the Index and no efforts were spared to entice him to Rome where a pyre would have welcomed him. Assassins were set on his tracks and one night in 1607 as he was returning from the Palazzo Ducale to his cell in the Servite convent he was waylaid, knifed and left for dead. Happily the wounds were not fatal; he recovered and continued to give the Senate the benefit of his advice for another sixteen years.

The bridge on which Sarpi was knifed is the Ponte di Santa Fosca. From it you can see to the left the high brick gateway to the old Servite monastery. Nearby lived the English ambassador, Sir Henry Wotton, who vainly hoped to wean Venice from the Roman to the Protestant communion but reckoned without Sarpi's orthodoxy in all matters save the temporal power of the Vatican.

From the Ponte di Santa Fosca the Calle Zancani leads to the Campo **San Marziale.** In the church there are four ceiling paintings—one of St. Marcellinus soaring up to heaven—by Sebastiano Ricci and among his best works. On the exuberant baroque altar to the right of the south door there is a painting of St. Marcellinus by Tintoretto (heavily restored). The high altar which looks like a celestial rock garden with St. Jerome and two friends (Faith and Charity) picnicking under a table is one of the more endearing if most preposterous baroque fantasies in Venice.

If you cross the Ponte San Marziale and turn left along the *fondamenta* you will see on the other side of the *rio* the garden wall of the Servite monastery, with a fig tree towering above it and a pretty little statue of the Virgin protected by a metal canopy at the corner. There are cafés here, little frequented save at midday and in the evening, where it is pleasant to sit and sip a cup of coffee or that popular Venetian drink, a glass of iced water flavoured with a few drops of *anisetta*. The Calle Larga (fifth on the right) leads to the Ponte dei Mori. From this bridge you catch a glimpse, straight ahead, of the onion dome on the campanile of the Madonna dell' Orto, almost Islamic in form but of a reddish colour which makes it look like some deep sea crustacean. To the right there is an enthralling view down the Rio della Sensa; in the distance you can see the high façade of the Gesuiti with white statues agitating their draperies on the skyline. Nearer at hand, just to the right of the bridge, stands the little Gothic palace (No. 3399) where Tintoretto lived for the last two decades of his life, surrounded by his collection which included oil sketches by Titian, casts of antique marbles and models of statues by Michelangelo and Giovanni Bologna which helped him in his lifelong study of the human figure. Here he gave little musical parties, accompanying the songs of his favourite daughter Marietta who was also his pupil, his assistant and his companion in old age and whose features may well be immortalised in several of his canvases (though only the most romantic can identify them).

As you go down the steps of the bridge you are met by a stone figure fixed to the corner of a building: he is known as Sior Antonio

Rioba. Two other statues are embedded in the wall of the same building, Palazzo Mastelli, looking on to the **Campo dei Mori** which takes its name from them. They are said to date from the late thirteenth century and traditionally supposed to be portraits of three mercantile brothers who hailed from the Morea (hence the *Mori* which has nothing to do with Negroes) and settled in Venice in 1112, taking the name Mastelli. If you follow the Calle dei Mori you can see into one of the courtyards of the palace encrusted with more rough carvings. On the fine Gothic façade, facing the Rio della Madonna dell' Orto there is a charming relief of a man leading a heavily laden camel.

Though smaller than either the Frari or Santi Giovanni e Paolo, the **Madonna dell' Orto** is perhaps the finest of the Gothic churches in Venice. It was built on the site of an earlier church to enshrine a miraculous image of the Virgin which was discovered in a nearby garden. The façade dates from the early fifteenth century with the exception of the two large windows which were put in some fifty years later. Built in warm brick and richly ornamented with statues, it is the only ecclesiastical counterpart to the opulence of the Ca d'Oro and the Porta della Carta. Purists have never approved of its elaboration, so reminiscent of a glowing Persian prayer rug. " Pseudo-pointed, flat, hard and awkward," the English Gothic Revival architect, G. E. Street called it. But he noted that the windows in which the delicate tracery is independent of the glazing, though " incongruous and unsatisfactory here " were " suggestive of an obvious opening for the use of decorative windows in domestic work." As his thoughts sped to his practice he no doubt dreamed of using this device on some house in north Oxford or some stronghold in the Chilterns. His comments remind one how difficult it is to look at Venetian Gothic buildings without recalling their numerous and monstrous progeny in England.

Inside, the Madonna dell' Orto is simple, with pink painted brickwork and Greek marble columns which have the appearance of grey watered silk. In the first chapel on the left there is a little *Virgin and Child* by Giovanni Bellini, a fairly early work. Over the first altar on the right there is another of G. B. Cima's exquisite visions of pensive Saints standing under a somewhat improbable Renaissance colonnade in an idyllic landscape with a distant view of a hill town.

This was **Tintoretto's** parish church—he is buried with his

195

family in the chapel to the right of the high altar—and it is rich in
his works. On either side of the high altar there are vast paintings
of *The Worship of the Golden Calf* and *The Last Judgement*, each about
fifty feet high. Tintoretto, his fingers itching to fill the empty
spaces on these chancel walls, is said to have asked no recompense
other than the cost of the materials. With its numerous diving and
swooping figures, *The Last Judgement* has a nightmarish quality
which provoked one of Ruskin's apocalyptic passages: " Bat-like,
out of the holes and caverns and shadows of the earth, the bones
gather, and the clay heaps heave, rattling and adhering into half-
kneaded anatomies, that crawl, and startle, and struggle up among
the putrid weeds, with clay clinging to their clotted hair. . . ."
The damned who, as in Dante and Milton, always seem more
interesting than the blessed, fill the greater part of the picture. In
The Golden Calf Tintoretto shows a similar interest in erring humanity
even while he protests, maybe, at the Midas cult of his fellow
Venetians. There are more paintings by Tintoretto behind the
high altar, on the walls between the chancels and the chapels, and
in the fourth chapel on the right of the nave. Of greater interest is
the *Presentation of the Virgin* (1551) which hangs over the Sacristy
door in the south aisle. It is a work of great dramatic intensity,
painted in an opalescent colour scheme, with the child Virgin
silhouetted against the sky as the Hope of Humanity. (It is best
seen in the afternoon light). The picture is often compared with
Titian's *Presentation* in the Accademia (see p. 129) to which it
owes something. But there is a world of difference between
Titian's sensuously realistic work and Tintoretto's mystically
sacramental treatment of the same theme. The shadowy figures
standing or lying on the stairs have been variously interpreted as
the poor and infirm or as representatives of the Old Testament—
the world before Redemption. The obelisk, by the way, which
also appears in the Titian, is derived from the Tragic Scene in
Serlio's book of perspective, a work much used by Venetian artists.
   Attached to the façade of the church stands the former Scuola
dei Mercanti with an early sixteenth-century relief of the Virgin
and Saints above the door. Immediately opposite, on the other
side of the *rio* there is an undertaker's premises which usually has
one or two carved and gilt gondola hearses moored outside it. A
little farther down to the right there is one of those intriguing
walled gardens, proclaimed by a flamboyant bignonia which

flourishes its brick-red trumpets over the water throughout the summer.

If you continue along the *fondamenta*, cross the wooden bridge, turn right along the Fondamenta della Sensa, and right again up the Calle del Capitello, you will reach the *campo* and church of **Sant' Alvise**—one of the quietest places in all Venice. The church dates from the late fourteenth or early fifteenth century with later embellishments. Inside there is an agreeably higgledy-piggledy arrangement of paintings and sculpture.

A striking early fifteenth-century portrait of a priest named Filippo, by Jacobello del Fiore, hangs above the font. In the middle of the right wall of the nave there is an imposing eighteenth-century altar enshrining an early sixteenth-century polychrome wood statue of St. Alvis. The three best pictures in the church are G. B. Tiepolo's *Christ Falling Beneath the Cross* on the right wall of the chancel, *The Flagellation* and *The Crowning with Thorns* in the nearby corner of the nave. They were painted in the 1730s and intended to be hung as a vast triptych. Despite the great beauty of individual figures, these are not among Tiepolo's most successful works. To paint them he turned from the inspiration of Veronese to Tintoretto whom he clearly found less congenial. But he reduced Tintoretto's cosmic dramas to the scale of the Venetian theatre. It seems that at this period of his life he had not yet reached that profundity of feeling needed to represent the supreme tragedy of the Passion.

If you return along the Calle del Capitello, take the Calle del Malvasia (named after the wine from Monemvasia which we call Malmsey), turn right along the Fondamenta degli Ormesini (called after a fabric imported from Ormuz in Persia) and cross the iron bridge you will reach the Campo del **Ghetto Nuovo**. The word Ghetto is derived from *gettare*—to cast in metal—and this district was named after the foundries in it. But in 1516 it was set apart for the residence of the Jews, and the word Ghetto was subsequently applied to the Jewish quarter in other cities.

Partly on account of Shylock, the Jews in Venice have long excited special interest. Their relations with the Republic were probably happier than with any other state until the seventeenth century. As early as 1132 there were more than 1300 Jews in Venice, apparently free to trade and to practise medicine, living either on the Giudecca, named after them, or on *terra firma* at

Mestre. In 1374 a number of them were given permission to settle in Venice itself on payment of a fee every five years. They applied themselves to usury with such success that by 1395 they had most of the gold, silver and jewellery of the city in their hands. They were expelled to Mestre but gradually returned and spread themselves over Venice. They were obliged to wear distinctive clothes; they were forbidden to own real estate, to marry Christians or indeed to have carnal intercourse with Christian women even if whores; and they were allowed to practise no profession other than medicine in which they excelled. In 1516 the Senate decreed that they should all live in the Ghetto district—an island then cut off from the rest of Canareggio by wide canals—and here, except for a brief period of expulsion between 1527 and 1533, they remained until the end of the eighteenth century with their pawn shops and old clothes shops. As the area of the Ghetto was limited the Jews were forced to build very high tenement blocks many of which survive. Napoleon had the gates of the Ghetto thrown down in 1797 and thereafter Jews were allowed to live where they pleased. But many have clung to the Ghetto. There are still two synagogues in use here, a meeting hall, a school and an old people's home.

In the Campo del Ghetto Nuovo there is also a small Jewish museum (9.30–12.30 and 3–6). It contains a few fine fifteenth-century manuscripts, some magnificently embroidered vestments and a number of pieces of ritual silver. On the upper floor there is a synagogue—a graceful eighteenth-century room with an oval gallery.

The Ponte del Ghetto Vecchio leads into the *calle* which passes the main synagogue, a seventeenth-century building with handsome iron grilles to its windows and finely carved doors. Opposite, a pathetic plaque records the death of 200 Venetian Jews among the six million from other parts of Europe massacred by the Nazis. The *calle* leads under a *sottoportico* to the Fondamenta di Cannaregio.

To the right, just before the triple-arched bridge designed by Andrea Tirali in 1688, stands the eighteenth-century Palazzo Surian-Bellotto (No. 975-7), at one time the French embassy. Here from 1743 to 1744 Jean-Jacques Rousseau worked as secretary to the ambassador, Comte de Montaigu. He liked Venice as little as he liked his master—not an unusual situation for him—but he enjoyed the music of the theatres and charitable institutes, especially the latter, declaring that he had heard "*rien d'aussi touchant que cette musique.*" He also had a typically unsatisfactory love affair which he described with clinical detail in his *Confessions*. On the far side of the canal stands the seventeenth-century Palazzo Savorgnan with two vast baroque coats of arms on its façade. To the left the canal is crossed by the Ponte delle Guglie, so called from the four tall obelisks that adorn it.

From this bridge, looking towards the Grand Canal, you have a good view of **Palazzo Labia,** with a frieze of proud eagles on the attic story. Built between 1720 and 1750 to the design of Andrea Cominelli, it is one of the richest *settecento* buildings in the city—a fit home for the Labia family whose extravagance was proverbial. On one occasion a Labia gave a dinner party and, to amuse his guests with the worst and most expensive pun on record, threw every one of the heavy gold plates on the table into the canal, crying "*L'abia o non l'abia, sarò sempre Labia*" (whether I have it or not I shall always be Labia). Inside the palace there is one of the most beautiful rooms in all Venice, frescoed with scenes from the story of Antony and Cleopatra by G. B. Tiepolo. But unfortunately you cannot see it without special permission which may usually be obtained from the Soprintendenza alle Gallerie (Accademia).

Next to the palace stands a twelfth- or thirteenth-century brick campanile, one of the oldest in the city, and the nineteenth-century façade of **San Geremia.** The interior of this church, inspired by Santa Maria della Salute and built in the 1750s, is handsome and spacious, with pink marble altars capped by gently curving pediments. There is nothing very grand in the way of painting and sculpture apart from a few pleasant eighteenth-century statues on the altars. The chapel in the north transept enshrines the body of St. Lucy of Syracuse, and is decorated with architectural elements from Palladio's church of Santa Lucia which was demolished when the railway station was built.

The north door of the church opens on to the Campo San Geremia, once used by young Venetians for the game of *pallone* —a local type of football. In the Lista di Spagna, No. 233, formerly the Palazzo Morosini, has a good ogival doorway with low reliefs of *putti*. The somewhat severe eighteenth-century palace, No. 168, was once the Spanish embassy from which the street takes its name. The Venetians insisted that all embassies should be gathered in this district so that they could more easily be watched. Great restrictions were imposed on ambassadors who were permitted to have no social contacts with Venetian patricians. (Though this rule was occasionally broken, notably by Mgr. de Bernis.) They were in fact treated in much the same way as ambassadors from the West in modern Moscow.

The Lista di Spagna leads to the church of Santa Maria di Nazareth, usually known as **Gli Scalzi,** with an elaborate sculptured façade designed by Giuseppe Sardi and built in the late seventeenth century. The Scalzi, a very strict off-shoot of the Carmelite Order, first came to Venice in 1633. Missionary work which they undertook in the Peleponnese endeared them both to the nobility and to the soldiers who served in the Greek wars. When they came to build their new church, patricians competed for the privilege of paying for parts of it. The façade alone cost 74,000 ducats paid by Conte Cavazza who had just bought his way into the patriciate and wished to rival the magnificence of older families.

Inside, the church is very dark and very opulent, the walls covered in marble and liberally decorated with statues and busts. The crowning glory was Tiepolo's ceiling painting of *The Transport of the Holy House to Loreto,* destroyed by an Austrian shell in 1915. (The present ceiling was painted by Ettore Tito in 1934.) There are, however, minor frescoes by Tiepolo in the second chapel on the right and the first on the left.

Among several works of sculpture the most notable are the elegant sybils by Giovanni Marchiori, standing on either side of the chancel and reclining on the rich baldachin. The rather more forceful statues of St. John of the Cross (first altar on right) and St. Sebastian (third altar on left) were carved by a Roman sculptor, Bernardo Falcone, in the 1660s. Heinrich Meyring's *Ecstasy of St. Theresa* in the second chapel on the right is a clumsy imitation of Bernini's famous group in Rome. The anonymous baroque Crucifix over the first altar on the left is a fine piece of work. Beneath it there is a glass case containing alarmingly life-like wax effigies of Christ between two tormentors, dating from the early eighteenth century. Critics hostile to the baroque have often suggested that all seventeenth-century sculpture strove towards such effects. But, in fact, the best baroque sculpture is less theatrically realistic than that produced in the late Gothic period, and wax images of this type continue a tradition of the Middle Ages. Baroque sculptors sought to elevate the mind before they deceived the eye.

The church of the Scalzi is one of the most popular in Venice and I have never seen it without at least a handful of worshippers. For the Venetians have always been, and continue to be, a pious people. They were also more tolerant of Jews, Schismatics and Protestants than other Italians—and more openly hostile to the temporal power of the Papacy and the spiritual power of the Jesuits. If some of their religious works of art from Carpaccio to Tiepolo lack solemnity, it should not be supposed that they were painted in a spirit of flippant scepticism. But as they refrained from religious persecution—the Inquisition had little power in Venice which partly accounts for the city's popularity with English and German tourists in the seventeenth century—so they rarely indulged in the vast and horrifying paintings of martyrdoms which were popular elsewhere in Italy. It is significant that of the relatively few Venetian-born Saints by far the most popular is St. Lorenzo Giustiniani, the member of a noble family who was called to the cloister by a miraculous vision and eventually became the first Patriarch of Venice. In the humane modernist, Fra Paolo Sarpi, the Venetians found the perfect exemplar of their religious life.

CHAPTER 16

Markets and Modern Art

Rialto markets—Sant' Giovanni Elemosinario—San Aponal—San Polo—San Giacomo dell' Orio—Palazzo Sanudo—San Stae—Santa Maria Mater Domini—Palazzo Pesaro (Galleria Internazionale d'Arte Moderna)—San Cassiano

The Rialto is the name of a district and not a bridge—the latter is called Ponte di Rialto. Derived from the Latin *Rivoaltus*, a deep channel, Rialto was the original name for the cluster of islands, divided by a deep canal, which we now call Venice. The first settlers lived around this middle bend in the canal which was the main centre of life when the leadership of the lagoon federation passed from Malamocco. Soon the administrative centre was established in the Doges' Palace, and later an ecclesiastical centre grew up around the cathedral at Castello. But the Rialto remained the heart of commercial life in a city where commerce grew ever more important. It is still the main market and those who do their shopping wisely come here.

Towards the end of the twelfth century a bridge of boats was built across the canal at this point. It was succeeded by a series of wooden bridges the last of which, with stalls on its two sides and a drawbridge in the centre, appears in a painting by Carpaccio in the Accademia. Before the mid-sixteenth century this structure was in a very rickety state and the senate determined to build a new stone bridge. Michelangelo, Palladio, Vignola, Sansovino and Scamozzi all produced plans. But those accepted were by a much less distinguished architect, Antonio da Ponte, who eventually built the present bridge between 1588 and 1591. It is hard to see why his design was preferred, save that it combined the function and outline of the old bridge with a modicum of classical

202

decoration. (Shops would have been banished from Palladio's much more grandiose columned design.) As it stands one can hardly consider it a masterpiece of architecture—with buildings far too heavy for the line of the arch, coarse detail and anything but functional decoration. On the side facing " down stream " there are handsome reliefs of the Archangel Gabriel and the Virgin by Agostino Rubini: on the other side there are figures of St. Mark and St. Theodore by Tiziano Aspetti.

The bridge looks at its best as you walk over it. On either side there are shops selling Murano glass, shoes, jewellery, toys and silk. In the centre the high arches frame glittering views of the Grand Canal, down as far as the Palazzo Pisani and up to the Ca' da Mosto. Looking towards the station you can see on the right a series of the most ancient palaces in Venice, with Byzantine style arches and encrustations of carved reliefs. As you descend the bridge you pass, on the right, the white palace of the Camerlenghi —the financial officials of the Republic—built between 1525 and 1528 and enriched with a profusion of finely carved Renaissance ornament.

The bridge leads into the busy **Rialto markets,** as colourful a scene as is to be found anywhere in Venice, and one which makes the most glowing fifteenth-century canvas seem drab. In former times its booths displayed the rich fabrics of Italy and the Levant and intricate work in silver and gold. Now it is devoted to the necessities of daily life—vegetables, fruit, meat and groceries. Every morning it is thronged by housewives and servants who go about their business with all the hauteur of figures in a Titian altarpiece. Most Venetian servants like to buy provisions for no more than a single meal at a time—a bundle of sticks of spaghetti, a sliver or two of meat, a small lettuce, a little rather unripe fruit, a morsel of cheese and an ounce of coffee. This is partly because they enjoy frequent visits to the market, partly because they are shy of tempting Providence—for who knows what may happen between *pranzo* and *cena*?

In a land still mercifully immune from the horrors of deep-frozen, packaged foods, the market stalls record the procession of the seasons. Early in the year they are bright with great piles of Sicilian oranges and tangerines, apples of an unnatural rosiness, giant hands of bananas, long yellow pears, plump white cauliflowers and the richly striped red and yellow Treviso lettuces.

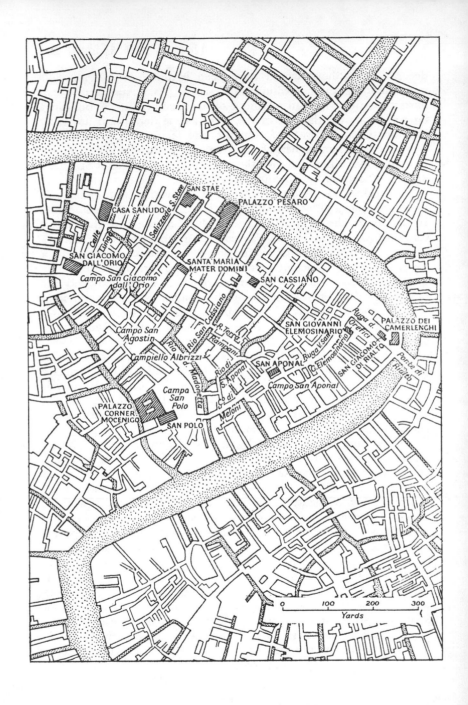

Greeny-purple artichokes and blanched fennel roots of winter and early spring gradually give way to enormous succulent white sticks of Bassano asparagus. Piles of little golden *nespoli*—or Japanese medlars—appear, to be followed after a few weeks by the first gleaming jewel-like cherries. Then come the strawberries, big and small, scenting the air with their peculiar fragrance, golden plums called *gocche d'oro* (drops of gold), the first white-centred peaches, green figs and rough-skinned melons. High summer brings the rather over-large yellow peaches, great green melons red and black inside (better material for the painter than the gourmet), smooth aubergines, stocky green *zucchini* with their yellow flowers, flame-red tomatoes, the myriad varieties of fungus and piles of green and black grapes. The first pears herald the approach of autumn which comes in with piles of walnuts, dusty brown chestnuts and great luminous orange-red persimmons—the apples of the Hesperides. In December strings of hazel-nuts and dried figs festoon the stalls. The first sharp mandarin tangerines arrive from Sicily with green leaves still clinging to them and the procession of the Venetian seasons begins again.

At any season it is a pleasure to walk through the market which flanks the long street—Ruga degli Orefici—from the Rialto bridge. In addition to the greengrocers there are vendors of cheeses— piquant *grana* called Parmesan in England, veined Gorgonzola, packets of creamy white *certosina*, a hard Cheddar-like cheese from Asiago, and snowy mountains of delicious *mascarpone* curd. Some little shops are devoted to the numerous types of *pasta*—spaghetti, tagliatelli, taglierini and so on. There are florists with bunches of gay but sadly scentless carnations. There are also several jewellers displaying fine gold chains, lockets and bracelets.

If you turn to the right you will pass the butchers, stacked high with joints of veal, and the poulterers which, in the season of the *caccia*, are filled with brightly feathered birds—pheasants, partridges, ducks, quails and some pathetic little things I have never had the heart to examine closely. A little farther on you come into the fish market. Stall upon wriggling stall is covered with nacreous creatures—the *branzino*, *palombo*, John Dorys (John the door-keeper called in Italian Sanpiero), boxes of tiny crabs, troughs of grey shrimps and small octopus, neatly arranged rows of surly faced *scampi*, shells smooth and spiky, oysters, mussels and all the little fish classed as *sardini*.

In the Ruga Vecchia San Zuane, at the end of the Ruga degli Orefici (the word Ruga signifies a street lined with shops), stands the church of **San Giovanni Elemosinario,** entered through an unpretentious iron gateway. Here there is one outstandingly fine work of art—Titian's high altarpiece of the patron Saint giving alms, painted in about 1530. St. John the Almsgiver was an Alexandrian who, on the death of his wife and children, gave all his possessions to the poor and became a priest; in answer to the demands of the clergy and laity he was made Patriarch of Alexandria in 610. In the chapel to the right of the high altar there is an altarpiece by Pordenone, dating from the same year, representing St. Catherine, St. Roch, and St. Sebastian with an angel pointing out the straight and narrow path. The rich, dark, velvety colouring of this work shows the influence of Titian. But in every other respect the two paintings differ widely. Whereas Titian's is painted with a sense of classical repose, spaciousness and well-being, Pordenone's crowded canvas, with its vortex-like composition and its strange elongated figures, gives an impression of uneasy nervous intensity. The only other thing of note in the church is a fragment of a Byzantine *Nativity* relief, probably fifth century.

The Ruga Vecchia San Zuane leads on to the **Campo Sant' Aponal** (which malaprops have been heard to call Sant' Apollò). On the church façade there are thirteenth- and fourteenth-century carvings. Inside, to the left of the first altar on the left, there is a little low relief of the Lion of St. Mark, dating from the thirteenth century and one of the earliest carvings of the Venetian symbol. The Calle di Mezzo—with a shop which echoes with the twittering and fluttering of Japanese nightingales and other exotic birds— leads to the Corte Meloni, the Ponte della Madonetta and the **Campo San Polo.** This is the largest of the Venetian *campi*, though its emptiness makes it seem smaller than the busy Campo Santa Margherita or Campo Morosini.

The church is a medieval building much altered in the nineteenth century. The lancet windows are surrounded by delicate panels of moulded terra-cotta. Opposite the main door rises the campanile of 1362 with two thirteenth-century romanesque lions guarding its base. Inside the church there are several notable paintings. To the left of the door hangs a *Last Supper* by Tintoretto —a sacramental rendering of the subject which may be intended as the meditation of the tall pensive figure on the right. The gaily

206

painted ceiling in the chapel to the right of the high altar is by a minor eighteenth-century artist, Gioacchino Pozzoli. The high altar has elegant bronze statues by Vittoria. On the walls of the chancel there are fourteen Stations of the Cross painted by Domenico Tiepolo in 1747, at the age of about twenty, yet remarkably mature works (the seventh and tenth are particularly poignant in their dramatic simplicity). His father, Giovanni Battista, is represented by the fine *Virgin Appearing to St. John Nepomuk* of 1754, over the second altar on the left.

Several large palaces surround the Campo San Polo. Next to the church stands the severe Palazzo Corner-Mocenigo (no. 2128a) which has a much more elaborate façade, designed by Sanmichele, looking on to the canal. Here Baron Corvo stayed while writing his last book, *The Desire and Pursuit of the Whole*. He showed the beautifully inscribed manuscript to his hostess who was so horrified by his descriptions of the members of the English colony in Venice that she promptly turned him out of doors. He was penniless, the weather was icy and he was forced to walk the streets for a night, with the result that he contracted pneumonia. But he recovered, and lived to add a singularly bitter account of his hosts to the book. On the other side of the *campo* there are two fine fifteenth-century Gothic palaces (nos. 2169, 2171) with lacy windows and lion balconies. Next to them stands the eighteenth-century Palazzo Tiepolo (named after the noble family not the painter). If you walk through the *sottoportico* between it and the Gothic palaces you can see from the bridge its much richer water façade. It was, of course, usual for Venetian palaces after the fifteenth century to have their main façades on to the waterway, however unimportant.

Continuing along the narrow *calle* and taking the first turn to the left, you reach a bridge over the Rio Sant' Aponal. At the far end of this *rio*, beyond the next bridge, stands the house where Bianca Cappello lived until 1563 when she fled to Florence with her lover, a banker's clerk who had worked in the opposite building and exchanged sighs and signs with her through the windows. The clerk's uncle was put in prison, where he died, the Capello servants were tortured, and the guilty pair sentenced to death *in absentia*. But when Bianca became, first the mistress, then the wife of Francesco de' Medici, Grand Duke of Tuscany, the Senate chose to forget its death sentence and declared her " the adopted and beloved daughter of our Republic." Nothing succeeded like success in the Renaissance, and nothing failed like failure. When Bianca and her husband died of poison there was no mourning in the Venetian Senate for the Serenissima's daughter and son-in-law.

From the bridge a picturesque *sottoportico* and the appropriately named Calle Stretta—the narrowest street in Venice—leads into the **Campiello Albrizzi.** On one wall an Austrian shell-scar is marked by a marble plaque with an inscription by d'Annunzio, swearing eternal enmity to Austria. The large seventeenth-century building (no. 940) is Palazzo Albrizzi which preserves one of the few complete eighteenth-century interiors in Venice still in the possession of the descendants of those for whom it was built. It is not open to the public. The Ramo Campiello Albrizzi leads to the Calle Rio Terrà Ca' Rampani and (left) the **Ponte delle Tette.**

This strange name—the bridge of the teats—calls for explanation. Tradition states that it records the prostitutes who, in the sixteenth century, were obliged to live in this district. These women used to stand stripped to the waist in the doorways of the brothels into which they beckoned passers-by. Venice was, of course, famous for its whores and most visitors made elaborate notes on them even if they did not purchase their favours. At one time in the sixteenth century the city contained no fewer than 11,654 registered whores each one of whom paid a tax which swelled the revenues of the Republic. The Senate was, however, concerned at the indifference of many Venetian youths to these buxom girls. One writer declares that a pompous summary edict was promulgated, requiring the prostitutes to sit on their window-sills with their legs dangling outside and their bodices unlaced. But the Venetian whores had enough knowledge of psychology to attract reluctant customers in a more effective way—by dressing themselves as boys in doublets and hose.

If you continue along the *calle,* turn left into the Calle Larga and then follow the signs pointing to the Ferrovia you will reach the wide Campo **San Giacomo dell' Orio** (probably called after an *alloro* or bay tree) fringed by low buildings. In the centre stands the rambling church of San Giacomo, founded in the ninth century but frequently altered.

Inside, the floor level has been raised so frequently that the columns of the nave are now standing up to their knees in stone. Overhead there is a very fine fourteenth-century carved wood ceiling. The high altar, arranged for celebration from the eastern side, is

Decoration of the gondola was limited by law from the 16th century. The origin and meaning of the distinctive prow are unknown

A small canal, seen from the Ponte dell'Angelo

set in an apse of Byzantine origin, embellished with inlaid crosses of porphyry and rare marbles in the early sixteenth century. In the centre of the apse there is a richly coloured *Virgin and Child with Saints Andrew, James the Great, Cosmos and Damian* by Lorenzo Lotto (1546)—one of the last works he painted in Venice where, he complained, his labours were inadequately rewarded. The sacristy has some opulent paintings by Paolo Veronese—*Faith* and *The Doctors of the Church* on the ceiling and an altarpiece of *Saints Lawrence, Jerome and Prospero*.

The Calle Lunga leads from the Campo San Giacomo dell' Orio to the Ponte del Megio. The small palace on the left, with pretty Renaissance windows (no. 1757), was the home until his death in 1536 of Marin Sanudo—the John Evelyn of sixteenth-century Venice. Year in, year out, for four decades he attended the sessions of the Great Council and every night recorded its deliberations in a journal which was first published by an Englishman, Rawdon Brown. It is a fascinating book, filled to the brim with gossip and abounding in curious information; a scheme for poisoning the Turkish nation. Wedding festivities in Palazzo Contarini interrupted by a brawl. Nun abducted. Priest condemned to hang in the cage suspended from the campanile. Solemn funeral for ex-courtesan. New Painting by Giovanni Bellini. Cardinals dance in Palazzo Cornaro. Brutal execution in Piazzetta. And so on, and so forth, for fifty-eight volumes.

The *calle* on the right leads to the Salizzada San Stae which goes down to the church of **San Stae** (Venetian for St. Eustace) on the Grand Canal. The elaborate baroque façade, liberally adorned with sculptures, is the masterpiece of Domenico Rossi and was built in 1709. Rossi, a nephew of Giuseppe Sardi, was Swiss by birth. Because he was something of a scapegrace, a roisterer who indulged in frequent banquets during the carnival, he stands out as a more vivid character than his more sober and more expert colleagues. He is said to have been barely literate and to have had no taste in the arts. But although the exuberantly vital façade of San Stae may be wanting in conventional good taste it provides a fitting frontispiece to the last great century of Venetian art.

The interior of the church is of interest mainly for a series of pictures in the chancel, contributed by nearly all the promising young artists of the first decade of the *settecento*. Perhaps the finest painting is Piazzetta's *Martyrdom of St. James the Great* (bottom row left side)—a dramatic scene which owes much to the seventeenth-century tradition yet anticipates the almost abstract colour patterns of his mature work. Balancing it on the right side is a *Martyrdom of St. Bartholomew* by G. B. Tiepolo. Two minor artists seem to be leading the field towards the graceful elegance of the rococo—G. A. Pellegrini whose *Crucifixion of St. Andrew* is next but one to Tiepolo, and Sebastiano Ricci who painted the *Liberation of St. Peter* next to Piazzetta, and the ceiling above the altar.

If you retrace your steps from San Stae, up the Salizzada, and turn left along the Ramo della Riorda you will reach the little church of **Santa Maria Mater Domini.** The interior has all the spruce elegance of the early Renaissance, with circles and semicircles of grey stone cutting the white marble of the vault. There are two attractive marble altarpieces, one on the right as you enter, the other to the left of the high altar—both with delicate statuettes carved by Lorenzo Bregno in the early sixteenth century. In the left transept there is an exceptionally fine mid-thirteenth-century Veneto-Byzantine relief of the Virgin Orans. The second altarpiece on the right is the masterpiece of that rare painter Vincenzo Catena (1520). It represents a scene from the life of St. Christina who was cast into the lake of Bolsena with a mill-stone tied to her neck but rescued by angels. Painted in rich, clear colours, the picture is notable for the vitality of the figures—especially the angels—the magical dreaming landscape, and above all the spirit of calm, pensive adoration which it radiates. Catena was a man of means, probably an importer of drugs and spices, and may perhaps be regarded as the first and greatest amateur in the history of art.

The *campo* Santa Maria Mater Domini, with a fourteenth-century well-head in the centre, is surrounded by a picturesque group of houses. Next to the church stands the fourteenth-century Gothic Palazzo Viaro-Zane (No. 2123). The Casa Barbaro (No. 2179) has rather more luxuriant Gothic windows dating from the next century. The smaller Case Zane (Nos. 2172–4) have thirteenth-century windows and are encrusted with Byzantine style carvings. On the corner by the bridge the eighteenth-century Palazzo Gozzi (No. 2269) was the home of the brothers Carlo and Gaspare Gozzi, the former the playwright, the latter a belles-lettrist who modelled himself on Addison.

A sign in the Campo points the way to Palazzo Pesaro which

now houses a collection of oriental art and the **Galleria Internazionale d'Arte Moderna,** of interest almost as much for its richly decorated eighteenth-century rooms as for the collection of nineteenth- and twentieth-century art shown in them. The entrance is through an imposing *cortile* designed by Baldassare Longhena but not completed until after his death.

Originally founded to display the works of art bought by the city of Venice at the Biennale exhibitions, the Galleria Internazionale includes a fair number of twentieth-century paintings and sculptures (open 9.30–4 except on holidays when 9.30–12.30). Among those by Italians the most interesting are: one of Manzù's several statues of seated bishops, a few paintings and some exquisitely refined etchings of still-life subjects (mostly bottles) by Giorgio Morandi—whom many consider the greatest of recent Italian artists—some shimmering townscapes and landscapes by Filippo de Pisis, a Venetian by adoption and the last painter to reveal new aspects of Venice's beauty. There are many abstract works —which are now much favoured at the Biennale—including paintings by the two leading Venetian artists of to-day: the decorative Santommaso and the ebullient Emilio Vedova. There are also a number of works by foreigners, notably Bonnard, Matisse, Rouault and Chagall.

The strength of the collection lies, however, in its numerous works by nineteenth-century Italian masters. These are now as little regarded by visitors to Italy as paintings and drawings of the *settecento* were a hundred years ago. Although it is true that Italy produced no Manet, Cezanne or Rodin—as she had previously produced no Watteau, Chardin or Houdon—many of her nineteenth-century artists had great merit. Among the sculptors one of the most notable was the Milanese, Medardo Rosso, to whom an entire room is devoted. Seven wax heads reveal the range of his abilities, from the realism of a portrait of Yvette Guilbert to the impressionism of the fascinating *Bambino alla Cucina Economica.* Among the painters, several of the more notable were born in the Veneto. Two were natives of Belluno: Placidio Fabris, author of a striking portrait of the *maître d'hotel* Signor Danieli, and Ippolito Caffi, who is represented by several clearly lit views reminiscent of Corot (whom he knew personally). Francesco Hayez, who became the most fashionable portrait painter in the Milan of Stendhal, was a Venetian: he is represented here by a grave self-portrait.

Later in the century two Venetians, Giacomo Favretto—painter of the beguiling portrait of a lady with her hair piled up on top of her head—and Guglielmo Ciardi—author of numerous misty views of the lagoon—established a school of painting in the city. The works of all these masters, and others of less note, repay the attention of anyone who sets out to discover the charms of the *ottocento*.

The **Museo Orientale,** on the top floor of the palace, is devoted mainly to Chinese and Japanese objects (at the moment unfortunately closed for much-needed renovations). It contains a number of good Japanese screens, lacquer boxes, sword guards, kimonos and a great deal of armour. There is some eighteenth-century and later Chinese porcelain. Good and bad stand cheek by jowl in a manner that will please only the most inveterate museum crawlers. This collection was given to Venice by the Austrians as an indemnity for the damage their shells had caused in the First World War —a poor exchange for a Tiepolo ceiling!

Palazzo Pesaro is two minutes' walk from the *vaporetto* stop in front of San Stae. You may alternatively return to the Rialto by way of the Fondamenta Pesaro (where the Palazzo Agnusdio has a façade decorated with reliefs of the Evangelists), the Calle Tiossi, the Campo Santa Maria Mater Domini, the Ramo Calle della Regina and the Campo San Cassiano. Behind a forbidding, heavily restored exterior the church of **San Cassiano** contains a few fine works of art—a *Crucifixion* and *Descent into Limbo* by Tintoretto (1568) in the chancel, some attractive paintings by Schiavone on the organ balcony, and a pretty eighteenth-century Sacristy with a ceiling by Pittoni. The Calle della Campanile and the second turning to the right lead you back to the Rialto markets.

CHAPTER 17

In a Gondola: The Grand Canal

How light we move, how softly! Ah,
Were life but as the gondola.

Rocked in the wake of motor-boats and half-poisoned by their
fumes, deafened by the gondolier's stentorian flood of information
and anticipating an unpleasant tussle with him over the fare, the
modern visitor to Venice seldom finds himself repeating Clough's
poem, except in irony. Nevertheless, the gondola still holds much
of its charm and all its picturesqueness. And you can still spend
a very happy hour or so gliding round the small canals for a price
that is not too outrageously excessive. But since the gondola
ceased to provide the normal method of transport for Venetians it
has become almost exclusively a pleasure craft for the tourist.
You must hire a gondola by the hour and whether you are in it
for five or fifty-five minutes, whether alone or in a party of five,
the price is the same and no amount of argument, however fluent
and vociferous, will diminish it. The current rate is 12000 lire an
hour for five people, 800 lire for each extra passenger, 5000 lire
for each extra half-hour. (From the station to the main hotels
the rates are slightly lower—5-6000 lire for two people and four suitcases, 8000 lire for five people and eight suitcases.) All the rates
are increased by 30% after 10 o'clock at night (9 o'clock in winter).

The origins of the gondola are very dim and mysterious. The
word, for which Greek and Latin derivations have been offered,
first appeared in a document of 1094 but was then applied to all
types of flat-bottomed boats rowed on the lagoon. Paintings by
Carpaccio reveal that the gondola had taken on an individual
form by the late fifteenth century—a long narrow boat with
decorated prow and stern rowed in much the same way as a modern
gondola. Such vessels often had their cabins covered with richly
coloured and embroidered materials. A sumptuary edict of 1562

213

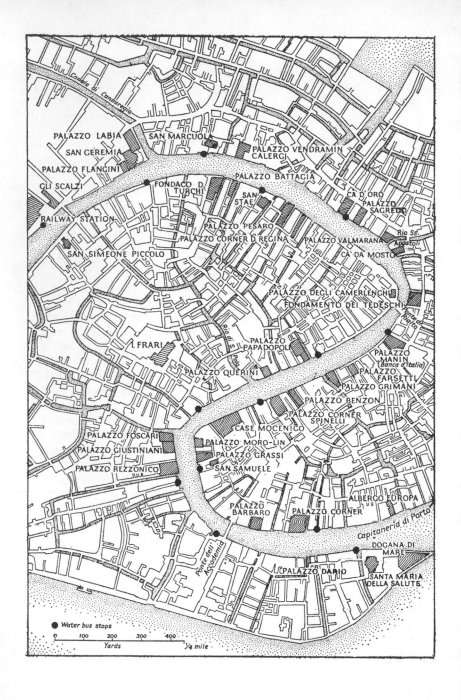

PALAZZO LABIA
SAN MARCUOLA
PALAZZO VENDRAMIN CALERGI
SAN GEREMIA
PALAZZO FLANGINI
PALAZZO BATTAGIA
GLI SCALZI
FONDACO D. TURCHI
CA D'ORO
PALAZZO SAGREDO
SAN STAE
RAILWAY STATION
PALAZZO PESARO
PALAZZO CORNER D. REGINA
PALAZZO VALMARANA
Rio Ss. Apostoli
SAN SIMEONE PICCOLO
CA' DA MOSTO
PALAZZO DEGLI CAMERLENGHI
FONDAMENTO DEI TEDESCHI
Ponte di Rialto
I. FRARI
Rio di S. Polo
PALAZZO PAPADOPOL
PALAZZO MANIN (Banca d'Italia)
PALAZZO FARSETTI
PALAZZO QUERINI
PALAZZO GRIMANI
PALAZZO BENZON
PALAZZO CORNER SPINELLI
CASE MOCENIGO
PALAZZO FOSCARI
PALAZZO MORO-LIN
PALAZZO GIUSTINIANI
PALAZZO GRASSI
PALAZZO REZZONICO
SAN SAMUELE
ALBERGO EUROPA
PALAZZO BARBARO
PALAZZO CORNER
Ponte dell' Accademia
Capitaneria di Porto
DOGANA DI MARE
PALAZZO DARIO
SANTA MARIA DELLA SALUTE

Canale di Cannaregio

● Water bus stops
0   100   200   300   400
Yards   ¼ mile

decreed that henceforth the cabins (*felzi*) were to be plain, that there was to be no gilding on the metal work at the bows and stern (*ferri* or *delfini*), and that all the woodwork was to be painted black. These rules applied to the 10,000 gondolas then in Venice and have been observed fairly faithfully ever since, except for vessels used in regattas.

As paintings by Canaletto and Guardi show, the gondola had taken on its modern aspect by the mid-eighteenth century, with a stylised metal beak and much simpler decoration at the other end. At this time the Venetian architectural theorist, Father Lodoli, used the gondola as an illustration of the beauty of functional design. Surprisingly enough, a further development in the gondola took place at the end of the nineteenth century when Domenico Tramontin at his *squero* near San Sebastiano—still owned by his sons and grandson—began to build gondolas of the type now to be seen on the canals. To increase speed, to enable the vessel to turn on its axis and to allow one, two or four gondoliers to row together, he built vessels which are assymetrical from every point of view. In plan his gondola is not regularly elliptical, as it may appear, but distinctly lop-sided, with one side curving out much more fully than the other, rather like an elm leaf.

The gondola is without ornaments apart from the two little brass sea-horses on either side of the seats, the *ferro* at the stern and the rather more elaborate metal blade at the prow—the significance of the six or seven metal bars on this beak is unknown though popularly supposed to refer to the six *sestieri* of Venice. All its fittings are attractive—the chairs, each with one arm, the fringed black cushions, and, most of all, the *forcola* carved out of a solid block of walnut as a rest for the oar. Indeed, *forcole*, which vary slightly in design, have the qualities of abstract sculpture and a group of them was recently exhibited as such in America.

Several other types of small craft are to be found on the canals and the lagoon. Most prominent are the *sandali*—elegant little skiffs rowed by a single man facing forwards with two oars crosswise. But none has the grace of the gondola—a grace derived as much from the shape of the vessel as the swing of the gondolier rowing it. In an ecstatic passage, Baron Corvo declared that this movement " which includes balance with force thrust forwards and incessant adaptation to fluid circumstances " accounted for the physique of the gondoliers " the noble firm necks, the opulent

215

shoulders, the stalwart arms, the utterly magnificent breasts, the lithely muscular bodies inserted in (and springing from) the well-compacted hips, the long, slim, sinewy-rounded legs, the large, agile, sensible feet of that immortal youth to which Hellas once gave diadems." With rather more characteristic qualifications, Henry James sought to describe the gondolier. " This figure inclines, as may be, more to the graceful or to the grotesque— standing in the ' second position ' of the dancing master, but indulging from the waist upward in a freedom of movement which that functionary would deprecate. One may say as a general thing that there is something rather awkward in the movement even of the most graceful gondolier, and graceful in the movement of the most awkward. In the graceful men, of course, the grace predominates, and nothing can be finer than the large, firm way in which, from their point of vantage, they throw themselves over the tremendous oar. It has the boldness of a plunging bird and the regularity of a pendulum." But as you are propelled forward you are, naturally, unaware of all this—for the gondolier is at your back.

The gondola is an ideal vessel for two passengers and nowhere is one more conscious of three being a crowd. An old Venetian dialect poem relates that it originated when a crescent moon dropped out of the sky to shelter a pair of young lovers. Its very name has the ring of amorous poetry. According to de Musset, you cannot say that you have explored all the mysteries of love if you have never been in a gondola on a moonlit night, between the Giudecca and San Giorgio Maggiore. Others in a morbidly romantic mood have likened the gondola to a coffin and remind one of the poetical equation between love and death which found poignant expression in Robert Browning's *In a Gondola*.

Despite the patronage of summer visitors, the gondola is dying. The number of privately owned ones—proudly rowed down the Grand Canal by pairs of gondoliers in spruce livery—declines every year. Even the richest find the costs of maintenance prohibitive and prefer the quicker and more practical motor-boat. Charges are so high that few tourists hire a gondola except on arrival or departure, between the station and hotel, or for an occasional ride to be indulged in as a luxury. To get from one place to another, most visitors—like the Venetians—either walk or use the public boat services.

Apart from the cheap and convenient *traghetti* which ferry one across the Grand Canal, there are two types of **public transport** in Venice—*motoscafi* and *vaporetti*. The former are the small " express " craft which bustle up and down the Grand Canal stopping only at San Marco, the Accademia, San Samuele, the Piazzale Roma, the railway station and the Rialto. If you buy a ticket for one of these you must ask for the *diretto*. The larger *vaporetti* with their sheltered fore decks chug up and down the Grand Canal at a leisurely pace—officially described as *accelerato* —allowing more time for the inspection of the architectural pageant on either side. Those who can manage no more than one gondola ride will be well advised to reserve it for a trip round the small canals and see the Grand Canal from the *vaporetto*.

Leaving the gondola or *vaporetto* station near the Piazza San Marco, you enter the **Grand Canal** proper as you pass the *Dogana* —the customs-house on the tongue of land in front of Longhena's Santa Maria della Salute (see p. 143). The Albergo Europa on the right was the hotel where Giuseppe Verdi stayed in 1851 while the singers at the Fenice were rehearsing for the first performance of *Rigoletto* (he had to keep back from them until the very last moment the catchy song "*La donna è mobile*" for he realised that once it was out, it would be on the lips of every gondolier and errand boy in the city). Another, later, visitor was A. E. Housman who stayed here for many summers—one may well imagine him in his tweed suit and cap and elastic-sided jemimas setting forth to be rowed out on the lagoon by his favourite gondolier. The house next door, now the Hotel Regina, was once famed as the home of Mrs. Bronson, an American lady of generous hospitality. In the 1880s you might often have found Robert Browning or Henry James enjoying a cigarette on her balcony. The little red house with lacy Gothic windows and balconies—Palazzo Contarini-Fasan —dates from the fifteenth century and has acquired the romantic name of the Casa di Desdemona.

On the other side, after the church of the Salute, stands the former Abbey of San Gregorio with a fourteenth-century relief of St. Gregory over the Gothic doorway. After a few buildings of slight interest comes **Palazzo Dario,** built in the 1470s, possibly to the design of Pietro Lombardo, with a marble encrusted façade and great Venetian chimneys rising from its roof. From 1838 to 1842 it was the home of Rawdon Brown who came to Venice to find the tomb of the " banish'd Norfolk " of *Richard II* and stayed for the rest of his life, transcribing documents in the Archivio. He was a close friend of John Ruskin and of the unfortunate Effie. The next house but one—a white marble bungalow—was begun in 1749 but only the first floor was built. Inside the gate stands a bronze horse and rider by Marino Marini, one of the many works of contemporary sculpture in the collection of the present owner, Mrs. Peggy Guggenheim. Rosalba Carriera, the pastel portrait painter, lived in the next house.

On the right side of the canal the very large classical building with reliefs of Roman breastplates in the spandrels of its arches is Palazzo Corner—now the police headquarters—built in the mid-sixteenth century to the design of Jacopo Sansovino. The little red house with a garden next door was Canova's studio in the 1770s. In the first war it housed that brilliant poet and exceptionally tedious individual, Gabriele d'Annunzio. A little farther on, just before the ugly nineteenth-century palace by the **Accademia bridge,** stands Palazzo Barbaro which Henry James described as the house rented by Milly Theale in *The Wings of the Dove.*

The Grand Canal was spanned only at the Rialto until 1854 when an iron bridge was built by the Accademia, less as a public service than to enable the Austrian military governor to move troops quickly to quell disorders. The present wooden bridge, which replaced it in 1932, was intended to be no more than a temporary structure. But it has become so familiar that one would grieve to see its maritime timbers give way to stone or concrete.

After the bridge, on the right-hand side, there is a very curious building with the shafts of columns and two pieces of rusticated wall—all that remains of a palace begun by the Cornaro family, bought from them by Francesco Sforza, Duke of Milan, in 1461 but never completed. Titian had a studio here for a while. A little farther on, after the San Samuele stop, stands the severe Palazzo Grassi by Giorgio Massari and, facing it across the water, Longhena's vast **Palazzo Rezzonico** (see p. 154). After three simpler buildings on the left come the two Gothic palaces constructed for the Giustiniani family in the mid-fifteenth century. Wagner spent the winter of 1858–9 in the second one where he adapted an apartment to his taste by muffling the frescoed walls, the doors, the chairs and tables in dark red cloth. Here he wrote

part of *Tristan und Isolde* deriving inspiration for the plaintive horn
prelude to the third act from the melancholy cry of gondoliers up
at the Rialto. Another tenant of Palazzo Giustiniani was the
American writer W. D. Howells who worked here as consul from
1862 to 1865. During the summer he used to begin his leisurely
days by taking a swim in the Grand Canal. Next door stands
Palazzo Foscari where Henry III of France was entertained in
silken and gilded state in 1574. It is now a department of the
University.

On the other side, just before the bend in the canal, stands
Palazzo Moro-Lin, sometimes called the house of thirteen windows,
built for the financially—though not artistically—successful seventeenth-century painter Pietro Liberi, to the design of that strange
surrealist artist and poet Sebastiano Mazzoni. The early sixteenth-
century Palazzo Contarini next door was the home of Jacopo
Contarini, a friend of Palladio who was often entertained here.

Then come the several **Case dei Mocenigo,** built as independent
houses but covered by a unifying façade decorated with neo-
classical reliefs of lion heads. Of all the buildings on the Grand
Canal they are the richest in historical associations. Giordano
Bruno, the free-thinking and free-living monk who was burnt as
a heretic in Rome, stayed here in 1579. In 1621 Lady Arundel
took rooms here when she came to Venice to clear the reputation
of Antonio Foscarini who had been executed for plotting against
the state in her house while her husband was English ambassador
in Venice. (It was against the rules for a patrician to meet an
ambassador privately lest he be tempted to treason.) She blithely
revealed that adultery, not treason, had been the motive of his
visits and secured vindication for his shade. The story was no
doubt relished by Byron who had the palace from 1816 to 1819
and indulged in a series of intrigues with dark-eyed mistresses—one
of whom threw herself out of the window—before settling down to
his final attachment to Teresa Guiccoli.

On the left-hand side, the dark red building on the far corner
of the wide **Rio di San Polo** was the home of Sir Austen Layard,
the archaeologist and connoisseur whose collection of paintings is
now in the National Gallery, London. Next to it rise the noble
sixteenth-century Palazzo Civran-Grimani, Palazzo Bernardo, one
of the best Gothic buildings on the canal, and Palazzo Donà with
Byzantine windows and a Donatellesque relief of the Virgin and

Child. A little farther on stands Palazzo Papadopoli, a fine mid-sixteenth-century building with obelisks on the roof.

On the right side of the canal, facing the Layard palace, is **Palazzo Corner-Spinelli,** probably by Coducci, a building on which Renaissance motifs are used in abundance to obtain that effect of richness so much beloved by Venetians. Farther on, after the second *rio,* you pass Palazzo Querini-Benzon, the home of Contessa Marina Querini-Benzon, a great " character " of the Byronic period. When Byron knew her and enjoyed her favours, she was already a plump lady of sixty. She had an inordinate fondness for *polenta* and when she went out in her gondola she tucked a hot slice of this strange delicacy between her abundant breasts, so that she could nibble at it from time to time. The wisp of steam emerging from her *felze* earned her the name of *el fumeto*— the little smoke. In slenderer, less greedy days she had inspired one of the most charmingly lilting of Venetian love songs—*La Biondina in gondoleta,* which still echoes along the canals of the city.

After a few more houses you pass the flowery Gothic Palazzo Corner-Contarini, with low reliefs of horses on the façade, then the towering Palazzo Grimani, one of the finest high Renaissance palaces, designed by Michele Sanmichele. The orange-coloured house, next door but one, was once a popular hotel. Sir Thomas Lawrence and J. M. W. Turner stayed here in 1819. Another guest, in 1838, was the American novelist Fenimore Cooper—a far cry indeed from the Mohicans.

Directly after the Palazzo Papadopoli, on the left side, stand two houses with fine Byzantine relief carvings much admired by Ruskin. From this point there is a *fondamenta* leading to the Rialto bridge on either side of the canal. A succession of handsome palaces stand on the right: first Palazzo Farsetti, heavily restored to what is supposedly its Veneto-Byzantine appearance. Palazzo Loredan, next door, is also of twelfth- or thirteenth-century origin. Peter of Lusignan, King of Cyprus, stayed here in 1363 and in return for financial aid allowed the Loredans to use the rampant lion of Lusignan on their arms— it appears among the decorations of the frieze. The little house, no. 4172, was the birthplace of Doge Enrico Dandolo who, though blind, led the Venetian forces to the fourth Crusade and sack of Constantinople in 1204. A few doors down, a small house with Gothic windows (no. 4168) was the home of Pietro Aretino from 1551 to 1556 when he died of an apoplexy brought on—so the moral story runs—by immoderate laughter at a smutty joke. The very large sixteenth-century palace, now the Banca d'Italia, was designed by Sansovino.

As you chug or glide under the **Rialto bridge** you have a good view to the left of the sparkling white Palazzo dei Camerlenghi (see p. 203). On the other side stands the large grim block of the Fondaco dei Tedeschi (see p. 175) once enlivened by Giorgione's frescoes. Beyond the little *rio* there is an early nineteenth-century palace built on the site of the Persian *fondaco* which must once have glittered with the fabrics of the Orient. Just beyond, the picturesque little Campiello del Remer (named after the oar-makers) opens on to the canal—it is well worth visiting on foot. Farther on stands the **Ca' da Mosto,** an outstanding example of the Veneto-Byzantine style, built in the thirteenth century. At present the façade is picturesquely assymetrical but you can still see quite clearly where windows and arches of the original design have been blocked up. This building was an hotel in the eighteenth century when its visitors included a future Czar of Russia and an Emperor of Austria. It was also patronised by William Beckford, in 1780. On his first evening there he sat at his window " to enjoy the cool, and observe, as well as the dusk would permit, the variety of figures shooting by in their gondolas. As night approached, innumerable tapers glimmered through the awnings before the windows. Every boat had its lantern, and the gondolas moving rapidly along were followed by tracks of light, which gleamed and played upon the waters. I was gazing at these dancing fires when the sounds of music were wafted along the canals, and as they grew louder and louder, an illuminated barge, filled with musicians, issued from the Rialto, and stopping under one of the palaces, began a serenade which stilled every clamour and suspended all conversation in the galleries and porticos; till, rowing slowly away, it was heard no more. The gondoliers catching the air, imitated its cadences, and were answered by others at a distance, whose voices, echoed by the arch of the bridge, acquired a plaintive and interesting tone. I retired to rest full of the sound; and long after I was asleep the melody seemed to vibrate in my ear."

Farther up, just beyond the Rio dei Santi Apostoli, stands the mid-eighteenth-century Palazzo Mangilli-Valmarana built for the English Consul, Joseph Smith, a patron of Venetian artists, especially Canaletto and Piazzetta, whose vast collection was sold to George

III and is now at Windsor. After a few buildings of less note you pass the Campo Santa Sofia, flanked by Palazzo Sagredo, with its muddle of Gothic windows and blazing display of geraniums, and then the **Ca' d'oro** (see p. 166).

Next door but one to the Ca' d'Oro there is the simple Renaissance Palazzo Fontana, the birth place in 1693 of Carlo Rezzonico who became Pope Clement XIII. Opposite, on the left side, stands the early eighteenth-century Palazzo Corner della Regina, a handsome baroque building with grotesque heads peering out of the façade just above the water-level. After a short while you pass **Palazzo Pesaro** begun by Longhena in the 1660s but not completed until 1710. In magnificence it rivals the Palazzo Rezzonico, seeming to have been designed to catch in the deep recesses of its façade the flickering reflections of the canal.

The richly sculptured white façade of San Stae (see p. 209) now comes into view. After the next *rio* there is another Longhena palace—Belloni-Battaglia—with elegantly attenuated obelisks on the roof and delicate grilles to the lower windows. Opposite, on the right side, stands the Palazzo Erizzo, owned in the seventeenth century by a diehard conservative who disinherited his son for wearing red socks and a periwig. It is separated by a square garden from the noble **Palazzo Vendramin-Calergi,** with a roof disfigured by a confusion of television masts (in the winter it houses the municipal casino). It was begun by Mauro Coducci in the first decade of the sixteenth century but finished by an architect of the Lombardo circle. With its large, round-headed windows, crisply carved classical ornaments and discs of inset porphyry, it is one of the finest examples of early Renaissance architecture in Venice. From 1844 the Duchesse de Berry, sister of Ferdinand II of Naples and daughter-in-law of Charles X of France, lived here at the centre of a group of legitimist exiles who maintained to the last gasp the etiquette of the courts. Another inhabitant of the palace was Wagner who died here in 1883.

The large fortress-like building opposite was the Venetian granary. Beside it stands the **Fondaco dei Turchi,** built as a private house in the mid-thirteenth century and converted into the headquarters of the Turkish merchants in 1621. With the decline in the Turkish trade it fell into sorry dilapidation. Ruskin described it as " a ghastly ruin . . . whatever is venerable or sad in its wreck being disguised by attempts to put it to present uses of the basest kinds " though he discerned exquisite Byzantine style carvings among the soft grass and leafage rooted in its crumbling walls. In 1869 it was restored, or rather rebuilt with some of the old materials which you can distinguish if you look closely at the hard, rigid, singularly unmedieval façade. Now it is the museum of natural history, filled with stuffed birds and fishes, shells and stones. Among some carvings under the portico there is a sarcophagus which once contained the decapitated remains of Doge Marino Faliero.

On the other side of the canal the wide **Canale di Cannaregio** opens in front of Palazzo Labia (see p. 199). After the church of Santa Geremia, with an inscription recording the presence of the relics of St. Lucy of Syracuse, you pass the strange narrow Palazzo Flangini. The building was designed in the seventeenth century by Giuseppe Sardi but only two bays were completed before the money ran out. The story that it was inherited by two brothers one of whom demolished his half to spite the other is untrue. But it illustrates the family squabbles that nearly always follow a death in Venice where, as in the rest of Italy, estates must be divided equally between the children.

The boat now approaches the railway station on one side and the church of San Simeone Piccolo on the other, two buildings which appropriately mark the end of the " high street " of Venice. The church, built by Giovanni Antonio Scalfarotto between 1718 and 1738, is a medley of historical motifs. The circular ground plan and portico are based on the Pantheon and Palladio's chapel at Maser; the balloon-like dome is of Veneto-Byzantine inspiration. Inside a circular nave echoes the design of the Pantheon while the domed chancel and apses come from Palladio's Redentore by way of Longhena's Santa Maria della Salute. **San Simeone Piccolo** is indeed an anthology of Venetian architecture, a *capriccio* like those painted by Canaletto soon after it was built. Whereas the church looks back on Venetian history the railway station looks forward to the shape of things to come should Venice ever be developed as a modern city. It is not without a certain beauty which it owes, like so many works of architecture in Venice, to fine materials, the play of Venetian light on their surfaces and the proximity of water.

"There is nothing elusive or reluctant about the gondolier," Henry

223

James once remarked; and you will have no difficulty in persuading one to row you around the smaller canals for an hour or more. It is, however, best to leave him to choose the route which will depend on the time at your disposal and—as many canals are one-way streets—the point from which you set off. In the narrow waterways you need no cicerone—the beauty of the larger palaces and the picturesque qualities of others, the sudden contrasts of opulence and poverty speak for themselves. No one has ever described the sensation of floating along them better than Marcel Proust: " My gondola followed the course of the small canals; like the mysterious hands of a Genie leading me through the maze of this oriental city, they seemed as I advanced, to be carving a road for me through the heart of a crowded quarter which they clove asunder, barely dividing with a slender fissure, arbitrarily carved, the tall houses with their tiny Moorish windows; and, as though the magic guide had been holding a candle in his hand and were lighting the way for me, they kept casting ahead of them a ray of sunlight for which they carved a path."

Nor is it possible to predict what you may see from your comfortable chair—a little girl in her white first Communion dress silhouetted like the child Virgin in Tintoretto's *Presentation* (and yet, how much more touching and beautiful); an old crone watering her geraniums on an upper window-sill or pulling up on a much-knotted cord a basket of provisions; a line tagged with scarlet and blue clothes hung out to dry against a crumbling dove-grey plaster wall; a young couple vanishing arm in arm through some dark, mysterious *sottoportico*; a cat devouring a meal of stale fish thoughtfully left on a pavement; a group of urchins ragging and fighting with more natural grace and abandon than even the most beautifully painted or carved Renaissance *putti*. These and innumerable other fleeting glimpses lead you back to the immemorial Venice—the city which has had the power to inspire so many of its sons and to console so many of its visitors.

The islands of the lagoon. *Above*, a canal on Burano. *Below*, the ambo in the cathedral of Torcello

CHAPTER 18

A Journey on the Lagoon

San Michele—Murano—Burano—San Francesco del Deserto—Torcello—
San Lazzaro degli Armeni—Chioggia

In times when nearly every Venetian owned a boat or could easily
borrow one, the lagoon provided Venice with its main place of
recreation. An old and popular barcarolle contrasts the melancholy of the city with the joys of a boating party on the water:

> Coi pensieri malinconici,
> Non te star a tormentar.
> Vien co mi, montemo in gondola,
> Andaremo fora in mar.

"Don't stay and torment yourself with melancholy thoughts,
come with me, we shall get into the gondola and go forth on the
sea." Nowadays it is the lagoon which seems so melancholy with
its still waters and deserted islands. To explore it thoroughly you
must still take a private boat. But the modern visitor can reach
all the more interesting islands by the public *vaporetti* or *motoscafi*.
San Michele, Murano, Burano and Torcello are easily reached.
San Lazzaro degli Armeni and San Francesco del Deserto are also
accessible though the services are less frequent. And, of course,
the Lido with its smart beaches and smarter hotels (the Hotel des
Bains provides the background for Thomas Mann's enthralling
and horrifying story, *Death in Venice*) may be reached very easily
indeed. Of all these journeys, that to Torcello is by far the most
rewarding.

There are several ways of reaching Torcello. You can take the
motor-boat from Harry's Bar at midday—an inclusive if large fare
covers the journey and luncheon at Cipriani's Locanda on Torcello.
Less expensively, you can take the public boat from the Fondamenta
Nuove. If you have the whole day to spare it is well worth making

the journey slowly and getting off at each of the stops on the route, either in the order suggested below or in any other which may be more convenient. *Motoscafi* (the *Circolare*) leave every fifteen minutes for San Michele and Murano from the Capitaneria del Porto near the Piazza San Marco, the Zattere, the station, and the Fondamenta Nuove. *Vaporetti* leave for San Michele, Murano, Burano and Torcello from the Fondamenta Nuove every hour or so. There are simple but attractive *trattorie* on Murano and Burano (where Da Romano provides an excellent mixed fry of lagoon fish and dry white wine) as well as the rather more expensive restaurant on Torcello.

The boats from the Fondamenta Nuove make their first stop at the cemetery island of **San Michele,** just outside the church. "Come hither," wrote the Venetian humanist Paolo Delfin, " that you may see something great and singular . . . a temple which not only evokes antiquity but actually surpasses it." Begun by Mauro Coducci in 1469, it was the first Venetian Renaissance church, with an austerely classical façade, derived from Alberti's Tempio Malatestiano at Rimini, capped by a semi-circular pediment. Later, in 1530, the very elegant hexagonal Cappella Emiliana by Guglielmo Bergamasco was tacked on to the side.

The entrance to the church is through the cloister where, every morning, sandalled Fransciscans with a quiet businesslike air are engaged in marshalling mourners and coffins to their places in the church and cemetery. With a nave rather too high for its width and uncomfortably narrow side-aisles, the interior represents the lanky, adolescent phase in the development of Venetian Renaissance architecture. By far the best part is the massive screen running across the west end of the nave, and embellished with carvings, some fine and others harshly restored. In the north-east corner a gate opens into the Capella Emiliana, encrusted with green marble which gives it a subaqueous appearance. Pale light filters down from the lantern to illuminate three altarpieces carved in high relief by a minor sixteenth-century sculptor, G. A. da Carona.

A simple stone in front of the main door in the atrium records the last resting place of Fra Paolo Sarpi whose bones were brought here when the Servite monastery was suppressed. On the wall above the door there is a large monument to Cardinal G. Dolfin who died in 1622. The allegories of Faith and Hope are by Pietro Bernini while the very cross-faced bust is the work of his much greater and more famous son, Gian Lorenzo—though it displays little of his genius.

The **cemetery** has a strange fascination, with its mountains of gleaming white Carrara marble, its legion of carved angels, busts and photographs of the dead, its tall dark cypresses and its tribe of cats who slink among the tombs with the expressions of people caught red-handed in particularly discreditable enterprises. It was laid out in the mid-nineteenth century but soon proved to be too small for its purpose. So, apart from those rich enough to buy a plot of ground in perpetuity—some families bought enough to build mausoleums for themselves and their descendants—most Venetians are allowed to rest here in strange little marble drawers for no more than twelve years, after which their bones are removed and dumped on a remote island in the lagoon. Hardly a single Venetian of note lies buried here: the shades we jostle are those of our fellow visitors to Venice. There is the unfortunate Léopold Robert who specialised in the painting of brigands and committed suicide in 1835 on the tenth anniversary of his brother's death: his monument bears an epitaph by Lamartine. In another corner you may find the simple tomb of Frederick Rolfe, alias Baron Corvo. And in the Orthodox section of the cemetery lies Serge Diaghilev at whose burial Lifar caused such an emotional scene by leaping into the open grave.

From San Michele, the boat takes no more than a few minutes to reach **Murano.** Ever since the Venetian glass factories were transferred here, as a safety measure in 1291, the name of Murano has been associated with glass making. One of the very few commodities produced by the Venetians, glass was regarded as an important item in the export trade, and the secrets of its making were jealously guarded. Any glass maker who left the Venetian state was condemned to death *in absentia* as a traitor. But many privileges compensated for this restriction. Boasting their own *Libro d'Oro*, the Muranese enjoyed a much more democratic government than the Venetians. A Venetian nobleman who married the daughter of a glass worker was allowed to retain his seat in the Great Council. Sometimes, indeed, the State seemed insane in its protection of these craftsmen. When a glass-blower murdered a man and fled to Mantua in 1524 he was granted a free pardon on condition that he returned to his work on Murano.

But the fame of Murano is not limited to its glass factories. In the sixteenth century it became a favourite resort of learned humanists, several of whom built houses and laid out gardens on the island. Here there was much talk of the nature of love and kindred subjects, such men as Pietro Bembo and Aldus Manutius swapped Greek and Latin tags, poems were read and *canzoni* sung among the regiments of potted lemon trees, the fountains, the pleached alleys, the quincunxes and arbours. It is all very difficult to imagine to-day. The palace of Daniele Barbaro, Aristotelean philosopher, architectural theorist and patron of Palladio, survives, but is now in a sorry state, transformed into a glass warehouse. Most of the others have vanished entirely.

It is best to get off the boat at the third stop, in Murano's Canal Grande. Signs point the way to the **Museo Vetrario** which occupies the handsome Palazzo Giustiniani, built for the Bishops of Torcello in the late seventeenth century. Inside there is one of the largest collections of Venetian glass in the world—looking a little dusty as old glass always does in vitrines (9.30–4, holidays 9.30–12.30).

Although it is known that glass was made in Venice in the tenth century, no surviving examples may be dated earlier than the fifteenth. The earliest in the museum is a late fifteenth-century marriage cup of dark blue glass decorated with portraits of the young bride and groom and various allegorical devices in brightly coloured enamel (room X). Tradition connects it with the factory of Angelo Barovier who was mentioned in Filarete's treatise on architecture. The golden age of Venetian glass, both artistically and commercially, began in the early sixteenth century when the art of making clear " crystal " glass was perfected. The Murano factories lost no time in exploiting the new process and were soon exporting cups, bowls and dishes, of a clarity rivalled only by rock crystal, to all parts of Europe. Several pieces of this type are included in the collection (room II, vitrine 2)—notably some goblets of exquisite lightness and elegance similar to those from which the Disciples drink in Veronese's *Supper in the House of Levi*. Before the end of the sixteenth century the Venetian taste for the bizarre was answered by the production of more extravagant objects: lamps in the shape of horses, covered cups supported by dragons, preposterously tall goblets. The secret of crystal glass had leaked out before the beginning of the seventeenth century, Venice lost her monopoly and the Murano industry set

228

into a decline. Blown glass mirrors made at Murano since the sixteenth century remained popular throughout the seventeenth and were exported to all parts of Europe, but were superseded by the French ground glass mirrors. J. G. de Keysler, who visited Venice in the 1730s, remarked that those of " any considerable size are extremely dear when other looking-glasses at present are so cheap." The same writer commented that " Venetian glass is very pure and ductile when it is in fusion; on which account it is more easily melted, and answers much better than any other for works of fantasy." In the eighteenth century the Murano factories took full advantage of this quality to produce quantities of plates and bowls decorated with interlacing patterns of gold or white ribbons, elaborate ornaments and vast chandeliers of which there are several good examples in the museum.

If you wish to watch the blowing and moulding processes still employed for the making of glass on Murano you can easily do so. The whole island seems alive with touts enticing visitors into the factories. There is no entrance charge, but it is considered rather impolite for a visitor to leave a factory without making at least one purchase from the showroom where the objects vary in quality of design from the handsome by way of the just endurable to the horrific.

The most important monument on Murano is the twelfth-century church of **Santa Maria e Donato** a few steps from the glass museum. It was once among the most beautiful churches of the lagoon. Ruskin, who praised it highly, deplored its dilapidated state, but between 1858 and 1873 it was subjected to an insensitive restoration which did more harm than the neglect of centuries. For whereas it is easy in the mind's eye to reconstruct a building in disrepair—and ruins have a beauty of their own—no feat of imagination can bring a heavily restored one back to life. Here the modern brickwork screams at the fragments of weather-beaten carving, the old nacreous triangles of marble, the few untouched capitals. The church appears a bastard of the twelfth and nineteenth centuries, resembling neither the building in its pristine state nor one that has been buffetted and caressed by nine centuries. Fortunately the sturdy campanile (late twelfth or early thirteenth century) suffered less from the restorer's hand.

Although many writers have complained about it, the interior of the church is more sympathetic than the outside—a pleasant patchwork of the centuries, a monument to the persistent piety of the local population, which is what a church ought, above all, to be. Each age has added its mite to this interior, expressing its devotion in its own individual language. On entering, one is confronted by the mosaic above the apse—a lovely elongated figure of the Virgin standing in prayer, solitary against the gold of a Byzantine heaven. On the wall beneath this twelfth-century mosaic there is an eighteenth-century relief of the *Annunciation* and the high altar bears baroque statues of St. Lorenzo Giustiniani and St. Theodore. The floor, a great undulating mosaic carpet on which peacocks daintily peck at golden grain and proud cockerels carry a wolf slung on a pole, brings us back to the twelfth century. The columns of Greek marble have Veneto-Byzantine capitals. Over the first altar on the left there is a relief of St. Donato with two tiny donors painted kneeling at his feet, dated 1310 and one of the liveliest examples of Venetian painting of that period. (The relics of St. Donato are in the church, also the bones of a dragon he killed, which may be seen behind the high altar). Above the door to the Baptistery there is a lunette of *The Virgin and Child with Saints and a Donor*, one of the best works of Lazzaro Bastiani who painted it in 1484. The neo-classical Baptistery contains a sarcophagus from Altinum, inscribed with good clear Roman lettering. In the Sacristy, portraits of a succession of dimly painted parish priests look down from the walls. But here the most arresting object is a large machine which would appear to have strayed from the control room of an atomic research station were it not for the maker's legend which reads: *American Carillon—Basilican Bells*. Shortly before noon each day a harassed man is to be found standing by this contraption, watch in hand, waiting to press the button which with a whirring of cogs sets the carillon in motion and, from the loudspeaker in the ancient campanile, sprinkles Disneyland chimes over the midday town.

The *fondamenta* leads from the church, past the glass museum to the Fondamenta Cavour and Ponte Vivarini. From this bridge you have a good view, on the left of the canal, of **Palazzo da Mula,** one of the few *villeggiatura* houses that survive on Murano. It was built in the fifteenth century, decorated with fragments of Byzantine carvings and ogee windows, and altered in the sixteenth century. Both the house and the walled garden around it are now in a sorry state of disrepair.

A Journey on the Lagoon

Farther away, on the other side of the canal, stands the church of **Santa Maria degli Angeli.** The convent beside it was the scene of one of Casanova's more colourful adventures. The story, which has all the complications in plot of a Goldoni comedy, cannot be told in full here. Its main figures are the young and still handsome Casanova, a Venetian girl banished to the convent by her family, and a beautiful nun with a talent for intrigue, the mistress of the French ambassador, Monsieur (later Cardinal) de Bernis who encouraged her to philander with Casanova that he might enjoy the pleasures of a *voyeur*. The décor is attractive: the church with the nuns' choir shut off by a grille through which they can see but not be seen; the nuns' parlour; a casino elegantly furnished in the French taste; a gondola. And the dress—the ambassador in an abbé's black suit; Casanova attired in the *dernier cri* of Venetian fashion, then masked with domino and *bautta*, then in a pierrot's costume; the nun in her habit, then in a " bewitching robe of black velvet," then in a man's coat of rose-pink velvet embroidered with gold, a brocade waistcoat, black silk breeches and diamond buckles, finally. . . . But perhaps detail should be avoided lest you are taken aback by the notices posted on every church door, asking you to respect the traditional standards of high morality in Venice.

From the Ponte Vivarini the *fondamenta* leads past an attractive eighteenth-century pharmacy (no. 139) to the church of **San Pietro Martire,** a dark and not very interesting building which houses two great altarpieces by Giovanni Bellini. The earlier, dated 1488, depicts the Virgin and Child enthroned between St. Augustine and St. Mark who presents the kneeling Doge Agostino Barbaro. The figures are backed by a purple velvet curtain which shuts them off from the wide, airy, Venetian land-scape stretching up to the blue Dolomites. A peacock is perched on the marble balustrade which might have been carved by the Lombardi, and beneath it strut a partridge and a crane. The painting hangs in poor light at the west end of the south aisle. On the opposite side of the church there is an *Assumption* by Bellini, with a semi-circle of Saints in richly contrasting draperies (Saints Peter, John the Evangelist, Mark, Francis, Louis of Toulouse, Anthony the Abbot, Augustine and John the Baptist). The back-ground landscape is reminiscent of that above Vicenza, with castles set on a tumble of little hills, elegant horsemen and a

231

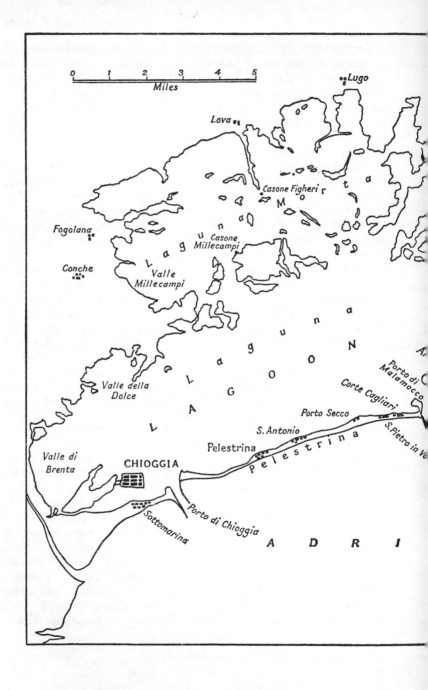

shepherd sleeping beneath the stump of a tree. It is a fairly late work, painted between 1505 and 1515. Next to the *Assumption* there are two paintings by Paolo Veronese with a good deal of studio assistance.

If you cross the bridge opposite the south door of the church, turn right along the Fondamenta Manin, then left along the Viale Garibaldi (passing the Ospizio Briati founded in 1752 for the widows of glass workers) you will reach the lighthouse (*faro*) where the boats stop on their way from Venice to Burano and Torcello.

The boat chugs north-east through an avenue of piles which mark the navigable canal between the treacherous sandbanks. After passing the islands of San Giacomo in Paluo and the Madonna del Monte you catch a glimpse, to the right, of the cypresses on San Francesco del Deserto. The channel then winds its way through the two islands of **Mazzorbo** (originally *major urbs*), a place of some importance in the early history of the lagoon. Now it is no more than a group of market gardens with a few cottages and a simple fourteenth-century Gothic church. The boat pauses here before going on to Burano. If you wish you can get off and walk through the fields and across the bridge to this island.

Burano is a fairly populous island. Most of the inhabitants are fishermen and some of their wives and daughters still make lace of the type for which the place used to be famed. With its gaily painted houses, it has a more southern appearance than anywhere else on the lagoon, and all the charm that nets and tackle, sail cloth, a multitude of small boats, and the smells of fish and tar give to any port. It is a delightful place in which to wander aimlessly.

If you have enough time you can hire a *sandalo* and be rowed across to **San Francesco del Deserto,** the island on which St. Francis is said to have been shipwrecked. Since 1228 it has been owned by Franciscan Friars who have made it a haven of peace and other-worldliness for themselves and the numerous birds that nest here unmolested. The buildings consist of a little church, the conventual house and two cloisters one of which dates from the fourteenth century. But this is no place for the recitation of architectural terms and dates. Here, in sight of the distant Dolomites, surrounded by trees and flowers which make the most exquisite works of art look brash and clumsy, you are enfolded in Eternity. The island echoes with St. Francis's *Cantico delle creature:*

Thank you, my God, for the moon and the stars.
You have formed them in the sky clear, precious and beautiful.
Thank you, my Lord, for brother wind
And for the air, cloudy and serene, and all weather,
By which means you give your children sustenance.
Thank you, my God, for sister water,
Which is very useful and soothing and precious and pure. . . .
Here indeed is a place to " worship the Lord in the beauty of holiness."

On Burano the main street is named after the eighteenth-century composer Baldassare Galuppi, who was born here and nick-named Il Buranello. The subject of one of Browning's greatest poems, he has recently returned to fame in his own right as one of the best Italian composers of his time. At the end of the street stands the church of San Martino, a large austere building mainly of the sixteenth century. It contains one notable work of art—in the oratory of St. Barbara—G. B. Tiepolo's *Crucifixion* painted when he was still quite young. More sombre in colour, more sober in feeling than most of his works, it has an emotional intensity which stems from Tintoretto.

The boat takes no more than a few minutes to reach **Torcello** from Burano. From the landing-stage there is a brief walk along a canal crossed by brick bridges without balustrades and flanked by vine-fenced fields of artichokes, beans and lettuces. (Should you miss the *vaporetto* you can easily find someone to row you over in a *sandalo*.)

In one of the finest passages of *The Stones of Venice*, one of the most beautiful pieces of English prose, Ruskin advises the visitor to Torcello to climb the campanile towards sundown and survey the view that stretches beyond the " waste of wild sea moor." To the north-east, the mountains fringe the horizon; to the east lies the Adriatic.

" Then look farther to the south. Beyond the widening branches of the lagoon, and rising out of the dark lake into which they gather, there are a multitude of towers, dark and scattered among square-set shapes of clustered palaces, a long irregular line fretting the Southern sky.

" Mother and daughter, you behold them both in their widow-hood—Torcello and Venice.

" Thirteen hundred years ago, the grey moorland looked as it

235

does this day, and the purple mountains stood as radiantly in the deep distances of evening; but on the line of the horizon there were strange fires mixed with the light of sunset, and the lament of many human voices mixed with the fretting of the waves on their ridges of sand. The flames rose from the ruins of Altinum; the lament from the multitudes of its people, seeking, like Israel of old, a refuge from the sword in the paths of the sea.

" The cattle are feeding and resting on the site of the city that they left; the mower's scythe swept this day at dawn over the chief street of the city that they built, and the swathes of soft grass are now sending up their scent into the night air, the only incense that fills the temple of their ancient worship. Let us go down into that little space of meadowland."

To be more prosaic. Between the fifth and seventh centuries, the inhabitants of Altinum and other places on the coast, fleeing from the barbarian invaders, established a colony on Torcello. In 638 this exodus was made official and permanent by the Bishop's transfer of the relics and his cathedral from Altinum. The colony prospered and became one of the wealthiest on the lagoon. But as Venice grew, so Torcello shrank. A serious decline in the fortunes of the island set in before the end of the fourteenth century, and by the eighteenth nothing was left but the memory of its former glory, the bishopric, the cathedral and its campanile, the ruins of the seventh-century Baptistery, the little church of Santa Fosca, and a few insignificant secular buildings.

The **Cathedral** was founded in 639, rebuilt in 864 and much altered in 1008. As it appears to-day, the fabric dates mainly from the eleventh century with the exception of the two minor apses and the central portico, of the ninth century, and the galleries on either side of the portico, of the fourteen or fifteenth century (the shutters on the south side of the nave, made of single slabs of stone, are eleventh century). The interior—one of the most poignantly beautiful in the world—has a strangely marine appearance. The grey moiré silk of the marble columns and panelling of the main apse seem to have been patterned by the wash of waves, while the white capitals and other carvings appear to have been fashioned and blanched by the pounding of breakers; there is even a touch of seaweed green about the bases of the columns—as if they had been standing for centuries in an ocean cave.

The mosaic floor dates from the eleventh century, so also do the

236

capitals of the Greek marble columns (except the second and third on the left which are sixth century). The ambo was made up in the thirteenth century from pieces of earlier carved marble. The iconostasis consists of four large panels of marble and columns, dating from the eleventh century, supporting a series of fifteenth-century panel paintings of the Virgin and Apostles. One of the marble panels is carved with two peacocks raising themselves on vines to drink from a tall chalice—a favourite Byzantine symbol in which the tendrils represent the true vine on to which the Christian is grafted through participating in Christ, and the peacocks signify human flesh grown incorruptible by participation in the Eucharist. But it is no mere symbol left to stand on its own. The mathematical nicety of the composition, the symmetrical rhythm of the figures, the exquisite precision of the carving and the fine quality of the material make as strong an appeal to the senses as the symbolism does to the mind. It was almost certainly carved in Constantinople.

In the chancel the seventh-century altar rests on a second- or third-century Roman sarcophagus carved with reliefs of very pagan *amorini* (it is said to have contained the relics of St. Heliodorus, first bishop of Altinum). Behind the altar a semi-circle of stone benches for the clergy rises around the bishop's throne. The apse is crowned by mosaics of the Virgin and Child standing above a frieze of the Apostles. (I sometimes wonder whether Bellini had this apse in mind when he painted his *Assumption* in San Pietro, Murano.) The mosaic of the Apostles seems to have been executed in the early eleventh century. But the Virgin is somewhat later, possibly as much as a hundred years, and appears to have replaced a representation of Christ Pantocrator (such a figure would be more usual and better suit the inscription which reads: " I am God and the flesh of the Mother and the image of the Father; not slow to punish a fault, but at hand to aid those who waver." However, the Virgin is one of the great achievements of Byzantine art, an etherial figure in whom dignity and an almost intimate gentleness are combined. She is probably the work of craftsmen from Constantinople.

These mosaics reveal the way in which Byzantine artists attempted to correct optical illusions. In order to make the two Apostles at the ends of the semi-circle appear the same height as the others, the mosaicist made them much more thick-set. To compensate for the curve of the shell, he elongated the figure of the Virgin. Nowadays these optical corrections do not entirely succeed, partly because we insensibly adjust our eyes to shapes we recognise, partly because the mosaics are lit by a stronger light than that which would have filtered through the alabaster or smoky glass windows originally in the church.

In the chapel to the right of the high altar there is a ninth-century mosaic of Christ between the Archangels Michael and Gabriel with Saints Nicholas, Ambrose, Augustine and Martin on the wall below. Here the green, gold, blue and white colour scheme is particularly beautiful though the workmanship is rather coarse. The west wall of the church is covered by a vast mosaic of the Last Judgement, executed in the late twelfth or early thirteenth century but drastically restored in the nineteenth when many areas were removed and replaced by copies (the original pieces have found their way into museums and private collections). Even so, it is a very impressive work which emanates the same spirit as the early thirteenth-century Franciscan hymn *Dies Irae*. The top tier is occupied by the Crucifixion, on the second Christ descends into Hell flanked by Archangels of an almost Aztec brilliance and fearsomeness, on the third He sits in judgement surrounded by Apostles and Saints, on the next Angels sound the trumpets of doom. On either side of the door, the blessed and the damned are gathered to their destinies.

The adjoining church of **Santa Fosca,** built between the eleventh and twelfth centuries, is of considerable architectural interest as a centrally planned Byzantine church. It is harmoniously proportioned and has great elegance of line. But somehow it has lost its soul—rather like those buildings taken over to America and re-erected in museums.

Other Journeys on the Lagoon

San Lazzaro degli Armeni stands a little off the north-west shore of the Lido and may be reached by *motoscafo* either from there or from the Monumento on the Riva degli Schiavoni. This island, formerly a colony for poor lepers, was given in 1717 to an Armenian monk, Manug di Pietro called Mechitar (the consoler) who had fled from the Turkish conquest of the Morea and founded a monastery for his compatriots. This Order, which still owns the island, is in communion with Rome, though its members use an Orthodox rite. The singing in their church is particularly fine on high days. The large conventual buildings include a printing press (whose productions range from learned books and the only newspaper in Armenian to bottle labels and garish picture postcards) and a school for Armenian boys. There is a vast library which contains some important manuscripts, relics of Byron—who spent much time here—and a visitor's book which includes the signatures of Browning, Longfellow and Marcel Proust. Everywhere there are pictures, but with the exception of *Justice and Peace* by G. B. Tiepolo on the ceiling of the ante-library, they are all by minor masters. You may visit the island any day from 10 to 12 and 3 to 5.

Chioggia may also be reached by boat from the Monumento —but a whole day is needed for the visit. The boat pauses at several small islands—La Grazia, now a hospital for infectious diseases; San Clemente with a seventeenth-century church dominating a group of buildings which house a lunatic asylum; Santo Spirito, a military base; and Poveglia with its slender campanile. Finally it reaches Malamocco on the Lido, the main town in the lagoon confederation until it was captured by Charlemagne's son, Pepin, in 809, and Rialto was deemed a safer capital. In the twelfth century Malamocco was entirely destroyed by an earthquake and never recovered its former size. In the church there is one painting of interest—a huge picture commissioned from Girolamo Forabosco to record a miraculous rescue from shipwreck. The next stop is at Alberoni on the southern tip of the Lido near the Porto di Malamocco where most merchantmen now enter the lagoon. Pellestrina, the narrow island which continues the line of the Lido, is interesting mainly for the Murazzi, the great sea wall built between 1744 and 1751 to control the force of the Adriatic.

Chioggia, a thickly populated island, is connected with the mainland by two causeways. One of the most important Italian fishing ports, its fleets range over the whole Adriatic. But it has a run-down appearance, and the poverty of its streets is emphasised by the rigid grid plan which conceals nothing. There are several churches containing a multitude of paintings and statues by minor Venetian masters, mostly of the eighteenth century. There is a good hotel and restaurant, the Grande Italia, famous for its sea food which brings many visitors to Chioggia.

CHAPTER 19

Terra Firma

The Brenta Canal—Fusina—Malcontenta—Mira—Dolo—Stra—Padua—List of other places on the Venetian mainland

Between Fusina and Noventa Padovana, the banks of the Brenta canal are fringed with villas. Travelling by road or water along this ancient pleasure route you catch glimpse after tantalising glimpse of their façades. Some sit four-square in *cinquecento* solemnity behind their columned porticos; others raise fantastic baroque heads from copses of gesticulating statuary. Some frown from behind the grilles of their iron gates or peep over a protection of low trees. Every so often there is a locked, disused chapel, plaster flaking from its walls, mysterious signs chalked on its rotting door. But usually a bell still hangs precariously in its little belfry as if waiting patiently for the shade of an eighteenth-century abbé—all black silk and silver buckles and dimpled smiles—to trot across the flagstones and call the house-party away from the arbours and frescoed halls where they have been gaming and philandering these past two hundred years. A melancholy poetry hangs about these great gate-posts, these columns, statues and empty flower-pots, about these unkempt gardens and houses tottering to decay. They mark the scenes of so many joys and woes, flirtations, palpitations, seductions, abductions—where the dance of death was tripped to the music of a *gigue*.

In the sixteenth century it became usual for all Venetian families of a certain competence—*borghesia* as well as patricians—to own a house on terra firma as a retreat from the summer heats. Every year on the 4th of June, the vigil of the feast of St. Anthony, all who could afford to go away left Venice for the country with the punctuality of the Madonna lilies (*gigli di Sant' Antonio* in Italian) which always flower on that day. The courts and, except in times

240

of emergency, the Senate went into recess. According to a seventeenth-century poet, the Piazza San Marco became like San Francesco del Deserto. The holiday lasted until the end of July. There was a second period of *villeggiatura* from 4th October until the middle of November or later, according to the duration of that most beautiful of all seasons in Venetia, St. Martin's summer. It is interesting to note that they returned to Venice for the blazing months of August and September when the country is no cooler than the city and you can escape the heat only in an open boat on the water.

As the villas built for the *villeggiatura* were intended for use mainly, if not solely, during the warm months, they differed in many ways from the English country houses which were later to emulate their designs. Venetian villas were very rarely the headquarters of large estates or attached to farms of any size. The farms were small and seem to have been run less as commercial ventures than as conveniences for their owners, to provide wine, grain, vegetables, milk, butter and eggs. This, and the sociability, not to say gregariousness, of the Italian character accounts for the suburban layout of the villas which were often separated from one another by no more than small gardens. Indeed, so thickly were they built on the Brenta that it was likened to an extension of the Grand Canal.

Venetians regarded their villas as resorts of pleasure. With the exception of a very few men in the sixteenth century—like Alvise Cornaro and Lorenzo Emo who discovered the peculiar fascination of watching the procession of the seasons on a farm—their view of the country was a distinctly urban one. Life in the villa, though it might differ from that in the palace, could never be termed rustic. The diversions of the gaming room, the ballroom and the casino were transferred to the villa and its garden. And the countryside provided no more than a beautiful background—like a landscape in an altarpiece by Bellini. The aristocracy tended to wear slightly simpler clothes on terra firma. They left their official togas in Venice. But shopkeepers and their wives donned the most elaborate garments to indicate that they had adopted genteel status on holiday. For both sorts, life on terra firma seems to have revolved around a succession of parties. The expenses of the *villeggiatura* are, indeed, said to have ruined many a Venetian family.

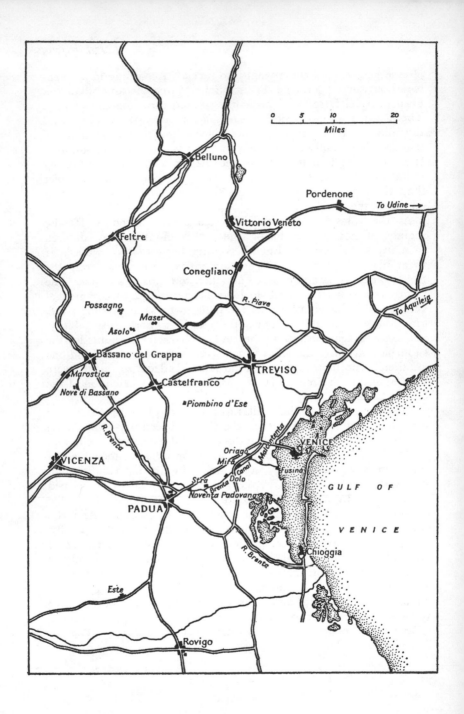

Accessibility made the banks of the Brenta the most popular place for villas. Those who had no private conveyance for themselves, their families, retainers and furniture—most villas were stripped of all but the larger pieces of furniture when not occupied —were able to travel by the *burchiello*, a large barge which plied daily between Venice and Padua. This craft was much admired by foreign visitors. Early in the seventeenth century Fynes Moryson commented on its convenience and said that he found pleasant company aboard, quoting the proverb which declared that it would sink on the day it bore neither a friar, a student nor a courtesan. The President de Brosses was lyrical in its praise, calling it " *un fort petit enfant du vrai Bucentaure, mais aussi le plus joli enfant du monde* " and describing the cabin hung with Venetian damask and furnished with leather-covered chairs and tables. Goethe also recorded how he enjoyed his voyage on it, " gliding through a fresh and animated world."

Recently the **burchiello** has been revived in motorised form— provided with arm-chairs and a bar and a hostess who recites a multilingual commentary on the journey. Those who wish to see the villas of the Brenta in comfort will be well advised to travel on it. The fare includes a tolerably good luncheon at Orlago and the return journey from Padua by bus. It leaves the Pontile Giardinetto near the Piazza San Marco at ten each morning. (15th May to 30th September).

After chugging down the wide Giudecca canal, the *burchiello* crosses that part of the lagoon called the Mare Morto, passing by the island of San Giorgio in Alga (St. George in seaweed), to **Fusina** on terra firma. Looking back from here you can see the view which greeted Thomas Coryate after his 952-mile walk from Odcombe in Somerset in 1608: " I saw Venice . . . which yeeldeth the most glorious and heavenly shew upon the water that ever any mortal eye beheld, such a shew as did even ravish me both with delight and admiration." Some two centuries later Shelley described the same prospect in a rather more imaginative manner:

> Underneath day's azure eyes,
> Ocean's nursling, Venice lies. . . .
> As within a furnace bright,
> Column, tower, and dome, and spire,
> Shine like obelisks of fire,

Pointing with inconstant motion
From the altar of dark ocean
To the sapphire-tinted skies;
'As the flames of sacrifice
From the marbled shrine did rise
As to pierce the dome of gold
Where Apollo spake of old. . . .

Shortly after entering the mouth of the Brenta you pass the Villa Foscari, usually known as the **Villa della Malcontenta** to record the imprisonment of one of the Foscari ladies in the house (other less romantic explanations of the name have been offered). It was designed by Andrea Palladio and built in about 1560. Rising square and solid above the flat land, with its handsome columned portico reflected in the water, it stands as the ideal Venetian villa. Indeed, one tends to take it for granted, almost as if it were a natural outcrop of the plain, without considering the originality of its design or asking why it takes a form that was to be copied by later architects throughout Europe. Basically, the house consists of an oblong block with a portico jutting out from the centre of the main façade. The shape of the block and its relations to the portico are controlled by those mystic laws of harmonic proportions which were supposed, by Palladio and his patrons, to reflect the harmony of the universe and to provide the key to the grandeur of Roman architecture. (See pp. 110 and 116). More obviously the ionic portico stresses the classical design of the villa.

Palladio was the first architect to make frequent use of such temple fronts on domestic buildings. In his book on architecture he was at pains to show that they were not only beautiful but useful. For, he wrote, they " show the entrance to the house, and add very much to the grandeur and magnificence of the work, the front being thus made more eminent than the rest; besides they are very commodious for placing the ensigns or arms of the owners, which are commonly put in the middle of the front." But the historical precedent which he then goes on to quote was his main reason for adopting the portico: " The ancients also made use of them in their buildings as is seen in the remains of the temples and other public edifices, and . . . they very probably took the invention and principles of them from private . . . houses." We now know that this is a fallacy and that Roman houses were not adorned with temple porticos. But in the sixteenth century very few examples of Roman domestic architecture were to be seen. Later architects adapted and wove variations on Palladio's designs and the temple portico came to be accepted as an essential element of the country house—even after the historical fallacy had been exploded—in England, Holland, Germany, Russia and America no less than in Venetia.

Inside, the house provides a perfect example of Palladio's symmetrical planning—derived also from Roman ruins—and his use of harmonic proportions. The area of the portico is in the ratio of 12 : 32 which serves as an overture to the general scheme in which the smallest rooms measure 12 by 16, the square ones 16 by 16, the largest 16 by 24 and the hall is 32 units wide, thus producing the arithmetical progression: 12 : 16 : 24 : 32. Before the present owner, Mr. Landsberg, restored the house in the 1930s the frescoes had been half-stripped from the walls, leaving only ghosts to remind one of the decorations which Battista Franco and Zelotti had painted.

La Malcontenta has received many famous visitors. Henry III of France, Ferdinand II Grand Duke of Tuscany, Augustus II Elector of Saxony, Frederick IV of Norway and Augustus IV of Poland are among the most illustrious. But none of them is more important for the history of architecture than certain English tourists who glimpsed the house between the trees as they passed down the Brenta in the seventeenth and eighteenth centuries. They included the Earl of Arundel and Inigo Jones in 1613 and Thomas Coke (later Earl of Leicester) and William Kent who followed just over a century later.

After Malcontenta, the banks of the Brenta become gradually more closely packed with villas large and small, dating from various periods between the fifteenth and eighteenth centuries. At **Oriago** the *burchiello* stops for luncheon. The next small town you pass is **Mira** which William Beckford described in 1781 as a " village of palaces, whose courts and gardens, as magnificent as statues, terraces, and vases can make them, compose a grand, though far from rural, prospect." He preferred the lower courses of the Brenta where, he thought, " the tranquil streams and cultivated banks, in short the whole landscape, had a sort of Chinese cast which led me into Quang-si and Quang-Tong "—not, of course, that he had seen any Chinese landscapes other than those on Coromandel screens.

245

The next town is **Dolo** where, among several handsome villas, the most impressive is the Villa Ferretti-Angeli, a long low building with an engaged portico and obelisks rising from the wings on either side, designed by Vincenzo Scamozzi in 1596. Dolo is the setting of Aldous Huxley's short story, *Little Mexican*, one of the most penetrating and witty accounts of Italian life written in this century.

Soon the *burchiello* reaches **Stra,** a small town dominated by the vast white façade of **Palazzo Pisani,** one of the several country houses owned by the rich Pisani family (9–12.30 and except holidays 3–6). It was begun in 1735 to the design of Girolamo Frigimelica and completed by Francesco Maria Preti. By far the largest and most imposing of the houses on the Brenta, it always reminds me of the villa of Senator Pococurante, the prototype of the dissatisfied millionaire, visited by Candide.

Inside, room after cool empty room lead out of one another in a seemingly endless sequence. Some are frescoed by minor masters, some are hung with indifferent eighteenth-century canvases. A few are furnished sparsely with flounced beds, pot-bellied commodes, or roughly laquered chairs and tables; others with prim, upright Empire pieces of French or Italian make. The sparseness is, of course, historically correct; houses contained far less furniture in the eighteenth century than they do to-day. And the whole place gives a good impression of the grandeur with which a ducal family wished to surround itself. It is a very tinselly grandeur, with *trompe l'oeil* paintings of columns and marble panelling instead of the real thing, which makes the villa seem like a series of stage sets for a comedy by Goldoni, rather than the palace of the richest family in Venice.

One room is outstanding, the ballroom—and it would be worth going to Stra to see that alone. The ceiling is the most grandiose that G. B. Tiepolo painted in any Italian house: it is also the last work that he executed in Italy, finishing it early in 1762 just before he set off on his journey to Spain where disillusion and death awaited him. Painted with a palette of jewel-like brilliance, the ceiling represents the glory of the Pisani family. Their fame is trumpeted to the four corners of the earth by an angel while the Pisani themselves, dressed in their richest silks and satins, sit listening appreciatively, like a row of good children waiting to receive their prizes on Speech Day. Sitting beneath them, and quite uninterested in all this show of magnificence, a musician serenades a girl under a group of stone pines—the annals of the house of Pisani " will cloud into night, ere their story die." On the walls behind the richly wrought balcony there are grisaille paintings—allegories of the arts, sciences, commerce, agriculture, peace and war, by Domenico Tiepolo.

The garden at the back of the villa is the best preserved of the many that once adorned the banks of the Brenta. The circuit of the wall is broken by elaborate gateways; there are gazebos and other " delights "; there is a maze; there are balustrades and vases and statues delicately patinated with lichen. At the end of the canal stretching back from the villa stands an impressive stable block with a portico and curving wings and statues on the roof. Inside the stalls are separated by Tuscan columns each of which bears a statuette of a horse. This building provides an example of successful *trompe l'oeil* architecture, for when seen from the villa it appears to be roughly double its real size and twice as far away. The planting of trees cunningly suggests that the park stretches far beyond the stable block which, in fact, marks the boundary. The whole lay-out is as artful a piece of deception as any *trompe l'oeil* painted by Tiepolo's ingenious assistants.

Many famous people have stayed in the Villa Pisani—Napoleon, Eugène Beauharnais (while Viceroy of Italy), a Czar of Russia and an Emperor of Austria. In 1866 it passed to the King of United Italy who promptly removed from it nearly all the best paintings and *objets d'art* and sent them to Turin. Unfortunately, in 1934, it also witnessed one event of tragic consequence—the first meeting between Mussolini and Hitler.

Shortly after leaving Stra, the *burchiello* passes **Noventa Padovana** where you can see, to the right, the late seventeenth-century Villa Giovanelli, easily recognised by its curious concave-sided portico, which was admired by William Kent who drew a little plan of it when he stopped here in 1714. At that date Kent was interested mainly in painting—it was not until some years later, under the influence of that arch-devotee of Palladio, Lord Burlington, that he began to work as an architect, deriving much inspiration from sixteenth-century Venetian villas.

The *burchiello* reaches **Padua** at five o'clock. This gives you time for a very brief look at the city before returning to Venice by bus. The most important monuments in Padua are the Scrovegni

247

Chapel, the churches of the Eremitani and the Santo, and the Prato della Valle.

The **Cappella Scrovegni,** standing in the ruins of the Roman amphitheatre, contains one of the most beautiful cycles of frescoes in all Italy, painted by Giotto between 1305 and 1310 (open 9.30–12.30 and, except holidays, 2.30–5.30). It was built by one Enrico Scrovegni as an act of atonement for his father's illgotten gains from moneylending and as a plea for the Virgin's intercession on his behalf. Giotto's paintings of scenes from the life of the Virgin were thus intended to illustrate a sermon on the Redemption with special reference to the sin of usury. The theme is stated on the entrance wall where Scrovegni offers up the chapel to the Virgin and his Patron Saints while usurers are bound to sacks of money in a Dantesque *Inferno.* Opposite, the paintings above the chancel arch depict the appointment of the Virgin as the Instrument of the Incarnation and the Intercessor for mankind. The scenes on the walls are arranged in such a way that they lead up to those on the archway—the Visitation, the Annunciation, and Judas receiving the bribe. The relationship between the scenes on the two registers is also carefully planned so that, for instance, the Scourging of Christ is placed beneath the Massacre of the Innocents and the Resurrection under the Raising of Lazarus.

From an artistic point of view this series of frescoes is revolutionary, for it is the first work which displays the range, the vitality and humanity of Giotto's genius. Each scene is composed with a vivid appreciation of its dramatic qualities. Every figure is a human being, every gesture is pregnant with meaning, every face registers some human passion, be it grief, joy, resignation, brutality or cunning. What is still more extraordinary, considering the date, is that both the figures and the buildings behind them exist in three dimensional space. Indeed, Giotto included two paintings of nothing but space in the *trompe l'oeil* views of two little chapels on either side of the chancel arch. One has only to think of the Veneto-Byzantine icons or mosaics in Venice to see how decisively Giotto broke away from their outworn tradition; one has only to record that the Scrovegni chapel was painted in the first decade of the fourteenth century to realise that it took Venetian artists one hundred and fifty years to catch up with his discoveries. In the Scrovegni chapel one is, indeed, present at the birth of modern painting in Europe. And, as in Dante, it is possible to discern through the medieval twilight the first glow of Renaissance dawn on the hills.

On the altar there are statues of the Virgin and Child with two angels by Giovanni Pisano, dating from the same period as the frescoes and similarly showing a break with the hieratic Byzantine relief tradition. The central figure reveals that the sculptor had derived some inspiration from France—evident in the elegance of the figure and the tender relationship between Mother and Child —and that he had also looked back beyond Byzantium to Rome. These figures have the nobility and repose of classical statues.

Near the Capella Scrovegni stands the large church of the **Eremitani.** Here, in the chapel to the right of the high altar, you may see the sad remains of Mantegna's great frescoes. Painted in 1448, they were the first outspokenly Renaissance paintings executed in Venetia. They proclaimed a debt to antiquity in their statuesque figures no less than their architectural details. They also showed the influence of Donatello who was working for the Santo in Padua while they were being painted. Unfortunately the church was hit by a bomb in the Second World War and only the two scenes of the martyrdom of St. Christopher escaped even partially intact.

Signposts in practically every street point the way to the **Santo** at the other end of Padua. With its many domes and minaret-like towers it has a still more oriental look than San Marco in Venice. Though the largest church in the city it is not the Cathedral. Begun in 1232 to enshrine the relics of St. Anthony of Padua—a disciple of St. Francis of Assisi—it soon became a very popular pilgrimage centre and assumed its present vast form before the middle of the fourteenth century.

Outside the church stands one of the finest of all Renaissance statues—that by Donatello to Erasmo of Narni called Gattamelata, Captain-General of the Venetian armies. Executed between 1443 and 1453, it is the first of the series of Renaissance equestrian monuments which sought to revive the splendours of antiquity in the streets of Italian towns. It is significant that, like Mantegna's frescoes in the Eremitani, it should have been executed not in Venice but in the subject city of Padua where the humanist tradition inspired by the University was so much stronger.

Donatello is also represented inside the church by the Crucifix statues of the Virgin and six Saints and a series of low reliefs, all in bronze, on the high altar (though not, alas, in their original disposition). This great work, executed between 1446 and 1449, established the Renaissance style of sculpture in Venetia and provided models for the succeeding generation of artists in Padua and Venice. In front of the high altar stands the paschal candle-stick, the masterpiece of Il Riccio. The chapel of St. Anthony is surrounded by relief carvings by Tullio and Antonio Lombardo, Sansovino and others. In a chapel on the opposite side of the nave there are frescoes by Altichiero (dated 1377), the first of the north Italian artists to follow Giotto's lead. In striking contrast, the *tesoro* at the east end of the church is a seventeenth-century addi-tion, rich in exuberant sensual and even slightly sinister sculpture by Filippo Parodi.

From the Santo the Via L. Belludi leads to the **Prato della Valle.** A miniature park of oval plan, ringed round by a canal, guarded by statues of the real and legendary *alumni* of Padua, and decorated with obelisks of a daring elegance, it is a masterpiece of late eighteenth-century urban development.

There are many other things worth seeing in Padua. The Museo Civico contains a good collection of Venetian paintings. Next door to it in the Scuola di Sant' Antonio a room is surrounded with paintings by Titian and others. In the Oratorio di San Giorgio, between the *scuola* and the Santo, there is a cycle of frescoes by Altichiero (as the scenes are larger the general impression is more striking than that of Giotto's chapel). Those particularly interested in Gothic painting will find a visit to the Baptistery, next to the *duomo*, worth while—it contains a fine series of frescoes painted by Giusto de' Menabuoi in the 1370s. Those interested in sixteenth-century architecture should visit the Palazzo Municipale and also the airy church of Santa Giustina (at the end of the Prato della Valle). Garden fanciers will be interested in the Orto Botanico, the oldest botanic garden in Europe. Doctors of medicine and those interested in the English in Italy should pause at the university where William Harvey studied. And no one should leave Padua without drinking at least a cup of espresso coffee at the Café Pedrocchi—the most palatial café in Europe.

Many other expeditions may be made from Venice. One of the most attractive takes in Piombino d'Ese, Castelfranco, Asolo, Maser and Treviso but can be made only by motor-car. However, all these towns and villages—and many others—may be visited individually by bus or train from Venice. The following brief list may be of help to those who wish to explore Venetia.

Aquileia, a village built among the ruins of the important Roman city. The Basilica, begun in the early fourth century, has a mosaic pavement of that date and numerous eleventh-century and later paintings. The museum (open 9.30–12 and 3–6) contains a well-displayed collection of objects found at Aquileia, sculpture, gems, pottery and a very fine array of Roman glass.

Asolo, an attractive hill-town with spectacular views of Monte Grappa and the Venetian plain. Crowned by a castle (*rocca*) of Roman origin, it also preserves a few remains of the castle in which Caterina Cornaro lived after she had been given this feud in return for Cyprus. One of her chief courtiers was Pietro Bembo who invented the word *asolare*, to sit in the sun and do nothing, revived after four centuries by another visitor to Asolo, Robert Browning who entitled his last book of poems *Asolando*. In the Colleggiata or main church there is one great work of art, Lorenzo Lotto's *Assumption* with a strange landscape predella, possibly by another hand. Many of the houses in the arcaded streets have frescoed façades.

Bassano del Grappa, a small and picturesque town with a covered bridge crossing the Brenta. Several houses in the centre have attractively frescoed façades. The Museo Civico (open 10–12 and 3–6 except on Mondays) includes an outstanding collection of paintings by Jacopo Bassano and his kinsmen besides many other works of art—painted cross by Guariento, bust by Danese Cattaneo, two handsome Magnascos, drawings and plaster models by Canova. The town is popularly famous for the production of *Grappa*, a fiery spirit similar to the French *Marc*.

Belluno, a fairly large town of almost Tyrolean appearance in a wonderful mountainous setting. The best works of art are the carved altarpieces by Andrea Brustolon in the church of San Pietro. The campanile (1732–43) beside the Cathedral was designed by the great baroque architect Filippo Juvarra who worked mainlv in Piedmont. In the Cathedral there are paintings by Andrea Schiavone, Jacopo Bassano and Palma Giovane.

Castelfranco, a busy little market town, the central part of which is enclosed by crumbling red walls and a moat. Famed mainly as the birthplace of Giorgione who is represented in the *duomo* by one of his finest paintings *The Virgin and Child with St. Francis and St. Liberale* set in a magically beautiful landscape. The church itself, by F. M. Preti, is a notable example of eighteenth-century Palladianism. Preti also designed the nearby theatre (now Università Popolare) *c.* 1770, a very pretty building redecorated in the early nineteenth century. Just outside the town, on the road to Treviso stands the Villa Bolasco which has an interesting garden (open Tuesday and Friday afternoons)—partly a romantic *giardino inglese* with lakes and shrubberies, partly the remnant of a grandiose formal lay-out which includes an amphitheatre surrounded by eighteenth-century statues.

Conegliano, the birthplace of G. B. Cima who painted in 1493 an exceptionally fine altarpiece for the *duomo* (fourth altar on left) representing *The Virgin and Child with Saints John the Baptist, Catherine of Alexandria, Apollonia, Francis and Peter.* It is a lively small town with a picturesque old zone, dominated by the ruins of a medieval castle on the hill above, and a modern industrial area on the plain. Conegliano is locally famous for wine, notably the fairly dry, sparkling white Prosecco.

Este, a town of Roman origin, now a minor centre of the ceramic industry. In the *duomo* there is a vast and glittering painting by G. B. Tiepolo (1759) representing St. Tecla praying for the liberation of the city from the plague. In the fourth chapel on the right there is an elegant marble group of *The Triumph of the Eucharist* by Antonio Corradini (1725).

Feltre, a picturesque little town commanding wonderful mountainous views. The churches and museums are rich in paintings by Pietro Mariscalchi, a minor sixteenth-century painter strongly influenced by Jacopo Bassano.

Marostica, a large sleepy village dominated by a very picturesque fourteenth-century castle with battlemented walls running down the sides of a hill. There is now an excellent restaurant in the castle. The *piazza* is used once a summer for a game of living chess.

Maser. The Villa Barbaro, now Volpi, is the most impressive of Palladio's domestic buildings (open June to September, Tuesday, Friday and first Sunday in every month, 3–6; 300 lire). The main rooms are among the masterpieces of Paolo Veronese, frescoed with landscapes, mythological and *genre* scenes, in his unique combination of coolness and splendour. The same qualities mark the statue-guarded nymphaeum, behind the house, which realises a Renaissance dream of classical tranquillity. The circular chapel is another outstanding work by Palladio, with a white interior of crystalline perfection. The stucco statues here and on the house are attributed to Vittoria.

Nove di Bassano, a straggling village which is a Mecca for fanciers of modern pottery. The place contains some fifty potteries each of which has a showroom where objects may be bought. Several of the factories continue to use eighteenth-century models for table wares—tureens in the form of cauliflowers, turnips, cabbages, etc.

Piombino d'Ese, of interest only for Palladio's impressive Villa Cornaro with a two-story portico. It is now an infant school run by nuns who are usually ready to admit visitors. The interior is richly decorated with frescoes of Old Testament scenes (1717) by Mattia Bortoloni, an interesting minor eighteenth-century painter with a taste for fantasy.

Pordenone, a rather heavily modernised small town of interest mainly as the birthplace of the painter Giovanni Antonio Sacchiense, known as Pordenone. There are notable works by him in the *duomo* and *municipio*. It was also the birthplace of the Blessed Odoric, one of the first missionaries to go to China, who died in 1331 and is buried in the *duomo*.

Possagno, the birthplace of Antonio Canova, who is buried in the Doric Pantheon he built as a parish church for the village. The *Gipsoteca* (open 9.30–12 and 3–6) contains either the models for or a cast of nearly every one of his works. There are also many personal relics and a good portrait of him by Sir Thomas Lawrence.

Rovigo, notable mainly for the Accademia dei Concordi museum (open 9.30–4; holidays 9.30–12.30) which contains many minor sixteenth-century paintings, a fascinating *Death of Cleopatra* by S. Mazzoni, and fine portraits by Piazzetta and Tiepolo. The late sixteenth-century octagonal church of Santa Maria del Soccorso is decorated with vast seventeenth-century canvases, several by Maffei. About 10 km. from the town in the direction of Lendinara, there is the village of Fratta Polesine with Palladio's Villa La Badoera (1568–70) built on a plan which was to be copied extensively in eighteenth-century England—a square central block with engaged portico and colonnaded quadrant wings.

Treviso, a busy market town with a great deal to offer—a good

253

museum rich in Venetian paintings, several interesting churches, and numerous picturesque streets. The *duomo,* with a pedimented neo-classical façade (1836) contains a very beautiful *Annunciation* by Titian (chapel to right of high altar) and a handsome crisply cut monument to Giovanni Zanetti by Pietro Lombardo (left wall of chancel). San Nicolò, a large Gothic church, has a Lombardo monument to Agostino Onigo with pompous page-boys painted in the surround by Lotto (left wall of chancel), numerous seventeenth-century paintings and an important cycle of frescoes by Tommasa da Modena (1352) in the Sala del Capitolo. A few miles outside Treviso at Istriana on the road to Castelfranco, stands the Villa Lattes now owned by the Treviso city corporation (ring for custodian). It is an excellent example of a small eighteenth-century villa. On the top floor there is a bewildering collection of musical-boxes which the custodian is only too ready to set a-twittering.

Udine, rather far away from Venice (138 km.) but worth the journey if only to see the frescoes painted by G. B. Tiepolo in the Palazzo Arcivescovile between 1725 and 1728—the first works which show the characteristics of his mature style. There are further paintings by Tiepolo in the Cathedral and also in the very large and interesting museum.

Vicenza, the home of Palladio and one of the most beautiful cities in Italy. Buildings by Palladio are numerous: among the most outstanding are the Basilica (or town hall), the very richly decorated Loggia del Capitano opposite, Palazzo Valmarana (Corso A. Fogazzaro 16), Palazzo Thiene (Contrada Zanella, now Banca Popolare), the fascinating Teatro Olimpico with its elaborate permanent stage set built to Palladio's designs in 1584, and the Palazzo Chiericati, now the Museo Civico which as well as much else contains a notable collection of paintings by Vicentine artists, Bartolomeo Montagna, Francesco Maffei and Giulio Carpioni). In the church of Santa Corona there is Giovanni Bellini's *Baptism,* one of his finest works (fifth altar on left, switch for electric light by collecting box). In the outskirts of the city there are numerous villas of interest; signposts point the way to them as to the most important monuments in the city. Palladio's famous Villa Valmarana, usually called La Rotonda, can be seen from the road but is not open to the public. Up above the city stands the eighteenth-century Villa Valmarana ai Nani (10–12 and 3–6; tip), the main house frescoed by G. B. Tiepolo and the *foresteria* or guest-house decorated by Domenico Tiepolo—two of the finest, gayest and most elegant groups of eighteenth-century paintings to be seen anywhere. The hill above the city is crowned by the late seventeenth-century pilgrimage church of Monte Berico, richly adorned with sculpture. In the refectory of the monastery there is a large painting of *The Supper of St. Gregory the Great* by Paolo Veronese (1572).

Vittorio Veneto, two small towns, Ceneda and Serravalle, united in 1866 and named after Vittorio Emanuele II to mark the entry of the Venetian states into united Italy. In the Cathedral, rebuilt in the eighteenth century, there is an altarpiece by Titian, *The Virgin and Child with St. Peter and St. Andrew* painted in 1547 with a fair amount of studio assistance.

CHAPTER 20

Epilogue: The Way to the Station

The bags are packed, the bill is paid, and one sits in the hall of the hotel or *pensione* waiting for the gondola or motor-boat, or for the *facchino* to carry the luggage to the *motoscafo*. Disconsolately, sentimentally, the lines of an old barcarolle come to mind— as hackneyed as anything else that is beautiful in this city:

La campagna me consola,
Ma Venezia zè la sola
Che me posa contentar,
O Venezia benedetta
Non le vogio più lasar.

" The countryside consoles me, but Venice is the only place that can content me; O blessed Venice I don't want to leave you again." One sits paralysed like Proust in *Albertine Disparue*, unable to make the fatal move towards the mainland.

An English friend of mine, among the most erudite lovers of Venice, said to me at the end of one of his annual visits: " I shall never come back. The pain of parting is too great, and it is worse every time." On going away from Venice I have myself felt a greater sadness than on leaving any other city. On the way to the Piazzale Roma I seem to hear a voice saying, " look hard, for it will never be the same again." Why should one have this sensation so much more strongly in Venice than in other beautiful cities, Florence, Rome, Vienna, Copenhagen or Paris? There are several reasons.

The beauty of Venice is so delicately fragile that the least thing can shatter it. A neon sign, a garish shop-front, a pent-house built on the roof of an old *palazzo*, can alter the look of an entire *campo*. A modern building, well designed and faced with good materials, which might pass unnoticed in any other city, becomes a horrific monster in Venice, simply because it is not, like all its neighbours,

Venetian born and bred. Some new buildings are successful, like
the S.A.D.E. office block which you pass on the *motoscafo* " short-
cut " through the Rio Nuovo to the Piazzale Roma and railway
station. With the aid of modern engineering techniques, their
architects have achieved that elegant lightness of form, that dis-
solution of the façade in a pattern of light and shade, for which
earlier Venetian architects strove. They are, however, rareties
and few other recent buildings respect the Venetian *genius loci* as
sensitively.

Town planning problems have recently divided Venice by a
feud more bitter than that between the Castellani and the Nicolotti
in the Middle Ages. One party, represented by the members of
Italia Nostra, is in favour of preservation and has evolved an admirable, if costly, scheme for making the city into an intellectual
capital, for converting slum tenements into pleasant flats and so
on. The other party, led by an association called *Venezia Viva*, is
in favour of ruthless modernisation and has produced a disquieting
plan for building more and taller office blocks, for converting the
Zattere and Fondamenta Nuove into car parks, for throwing roads
across the lagoon and for further developing the port of Venice.
They say that Venice is not a museum and could be made more
prosperous if industrialised and freed from dependence on tourists.
Some extremists have even suggested that the Grand Canal might
be drained and turned into a road. Why they do not apply their
energies to Mestre which could hardly look worse than it does
to-day and which could easily be developed as a modern city, is
a mystery. However, they prefer to scheme for the destruction of
Venice. Although I find it difficult to take their proposals seriously
I never leave Venice without the uneasy feeling that they may one
day have their way.

The city has for long been faced by a far more serious danger
than that of the town-planners—water. Venice is slowly sinking
and, to make matters worse, the level of the Adriatic seems to be
rising. The islands of Venice consist of mud for about one hundred
feet down, then a stratum of heavy clay about ten feet thick,
floating on levels of peat and watery sand. All the buildings of
Venice rest on wooden piles driven through the mud to the clay
substratum which is firmer in some places (Dorsoduro) than others.
But it is not so much the clay that bears the city as the quicksand
beneath it. By the laws of hydraulic resistance, the heavier the

weight on the quicksand the stronger the counter upthrust. Gradually, however, the pressure on the clay from above and below has compressed it, with the result that it is losing its elasticity which compensated for any movement in the quicksand. There have in the past been occasional subsidences which have caused buildings to lean (there are few perpendicular campaniles in the city) and sometimes to topple over. Other areas have subsided more evenly, as in the Piazza and Piazzetta where successive layers of pavement have had to be built to keep the level above the water. In many places columns and doorways once at ground level are now well below it. At the same time the wooden piles are slowly rotting away, their condition being aggravated by the increase in motor-boat traffic on the canals.

As the city sinks, so floods become more frequent. They are caused by a combination of circumstances. A scirocco wind blowing up the Adriatic stirs up the sea on the Lido shore and blocks the mouths by which the tidal waters escape from the lagoon into the open. These tidal waters are thus driven back on Venice and, when high, gradually overflow from the canals to cover all the more low-lying streets in the city. In the eighteenth century such floods were rare enough for characters in Goldoni's plays to refer to " the year of the *acqua alta* " much as their contemporaries on the English stage might mention the winter when the Thames was frozen over. Even in the late nineteenth century a flood was still uncommon enough to cause a stir. Horatio Brown describes how the streets would fill with people " most of them bound for the Piazza to see the fun. There is laughter and jesting everywhere and the impression of a capital joke in bare legs and top-boots; the people get their amusement out of it all, though the basements of their houses are soaking and their winter firewood slowly taking in the water." But the *acqua alta* is no longer a laughing matter. Several times each winter the Piazza becomes a lake and little causeways of planks on trestles are built for people to cross it. In some parts of the city, the Campiello Albrizzi and the area between the Gesuiti and the Santi Apostoli, for example, the water frequently rises two or three feet above the pavement. It rises slowly, but the unwary may find themselves marooned on a bridge and forced to wade through ice cold water to regain dry pavement. Estimates of the rate at which Venice is sinking vary widely. The gloomiest puts it at one inch in every five years.

In 1851 Ruskin described Venice as " a ghost upon the sands of the sea, so weak—so quiet—so bereft of all but her loveliness, that we might well doubt, as we watched her faint reflection in the mirage of the lagoon, which was the City and which the Shadow. I would endeavour to trace the lines of this image before it be for ever lost, and to record, as far as I may, the warning which seems to me to be uttered by every one of the fast-gaining waves, that beat, like passing bells, against the Stones of Venice." He clearly thought that he was only just in time.

The knowledge that Venice is sinking into the water, however slowly, cannot but colour our view of her churches and palaces. Their peril makes us the more keenly aware of their beauty, and we tend to gaze on San Marco, the Ca' d'Oro or Santa Maria della Salute with the same clinging intensity with which we watch a morning glory flower that will fade before noon, a rose whose petals will fall at evening, an autumn glade which will be swept bare of its leaves by the next storm. It is this melancholy beauty that has so held the sensitive lovers of Venice.

But the beauty of Venice does not lie solely, or even mainly, in the architectural merits of her buildings, great though they may be. The more one tries to write about Venetian architecture, the more one finds that it is impossible to consider it in purely objective, intellectual terms. The Rialto bridge might look as Gibbon described it—" a fine bridge spoilt by two rows of houses on it "—were it not for the coruscations of light reflected from the water on the underside of the arch. Everywhere in Venice you are constantly distracted from architectural motifs by those flickering, undulating patterns of light and shade which the buildings were designed to catch and reflect. There are also other distractions. As you look at the façade of San Giorgio Maggiore, your eye wanders up and beyond to the soaring domes of cumulus cloud gathering in the sky above; as you study the intellectual precision of the Redentore you are diverted by a *sandalo* swooping along the Giudecca canal. So much that is beautiful in Venice derives from its setting.

Similarly, Venetian paintings appeal partly because they are Venetian, because they depict the mood or the light if not the actual buildings of the city as we know it to-day. Hence the perennial attraction of Carpaccio's paintings. Even in the works of the greatest masters, Bellini, Titian, Tintoretto and Veronese, the purely local Venetian touches give an added charm—a distant view of the mountains like that from the campanile at Torcello, the stance of a velvet-clad lady looking for all the world like Contessa Z surveying the foyer of the Fenice, a muscular figure so like a gondolier caught in the swing of his rowing, a sunset sky so similar to that we admired last evening above the Giudecca. Venice and her works of art complement one another: the more we love the former the more irresistibly are we drawn to the latter. Venetian literature too acquires a similar fascination from the mere fact that it is a product of this unique place. (Who would bother about Goldoni's comedy of manners if the minor characters spoke in the dialect of Bologna or Milan?). It is Venice itself, so much greater than the sum of its paintings, sculpture and architecture, its fantastic furniture, radiant silks, its gold and glass; it is the thought of Venice slowly sinking into the water that brings a lump to the throat when the singer reaches the tremulous climax of his song:

Oh Blessed Venice,
I do not wish to leave you any more.

When the moment for departure comes, the impressions which are strongest in the memory are more likely to be of the city and the lagoon than of its artistic treasures. No cicerone can indicate, no guide-book can predict, what these will be. It may be no more than a glimpse through an escutcheoned gateway to a *cortile* hung with washing, or the elation on emerging from a long dank *calle* on to a smiling *fondamenta*. A wedding party in a train of gondolas, a greengrocer and a porter abusing each other in the sibilant dialect of Goldoni's pantaloons, a gondolier polishing the brasswork on his boat, an old woman crouched in devotion in some quiet cool church where a Bellini Madonna stares down in compassion, the flicker of candles before a shrine illuminating the carved marble flowers of a Tullio Lombardo, or perhaps some sight as simple as a cat sunning itself on an old well-head, or a pair of pigeons silhouetted against the sky on one of those arches which thrust the palaces apart across some narrow *calle*. Though they may be sinking, the buildings of Venice will see out our time; but such scenes as these, which form an essential part of the memory of every lover of Venice, neither will nor can be quite the same again.

Appendix

I   Places of interest not mentioned in the text   *page* 263
II   Hotels   265
III Some restaurants   271
IV   Some books about Venice   272
     Shops   274
     Index   276

Places of interest not mentioned in the text

Esposizione Internazionale d'Arte Moderna, a group of permanent exhibition buildings erected in a small park near the Giardini Pubblici, may be reached either by *motoscafo* from the Monumento or by walking along the Riva degli Schiavoni. The buildings are of slight architectural merit, most of them rather 1920ish in style and contrast strangely with the paintings and sculpture shown in them during the biennial exhibitions (held in even years, 1962, 1964, etc.).

San Biagio, a small church on the Riva di San Biagio (continuation of the Riva degli Schiavoni) near the Arsenal (see p. 76). Its only interesting work of art is a very life-like statue of Admiral Angelo Emo by Giovanni Ferrari (1792).

San Francesco della Vigna, a church in a remote and quiet quarter of the city, though rather too close to the gas works. It may be reached from Santi Giovanni e Paolo along the Barbaria delle Tole, Calle del Caffetier, Calle Zon and Campo Santa Giustina. Sansovino designed the church to which Palladio added the façade (see p. 116). It contains numerous fine works of art: a fine large Virgin and Child by Antonio da Negroponte, c. 1450 (right transept), some pretty eighteenth-century paintings by F. Fontebasso (chapel to right of high altar), Giustiniani chapel decorated with fifteenth-century marble carvings (left of high altar), very beautiful fifteenth-century cloister (reached through Sacristy) with chapel which contains a *Virgin and Child* by Giovanni Bellini, magnificent altarpiece by Vittoria with statues of St. Anthony the Abbot, St. Sebastian and St. Roch (fourth chapel on left of nave).

San Giovanni Decollato or San Zan Degolà, between San Giacomo dell' Orio and the Fondaco dei Turchi. An eleventh-century church recently restored to its original simplicity, it contains some of its original eleventh-century mural paintings.

San Nicolò da Tolentino, usually known as I Tolentini, near the Piazzale Roma (see map on p. 54). Handsome late sixteenth-century church by V. Scamozzi with an early eighteenth-century portico façade by Andrea Tirali. It contains a large number of seventeenth-century works of art among which the most important are the monument to Francesco Morosini by Francesco Parodi—the best baroque monument in Venice—(left wall of chancel), *The Charity of St. Lawrence* by Bernardo

Places of interest not mentioned in the text

Strozzi (outside third nave chapel on left) and the very freely painted *St. Jerome* by Giovanni Liss (left wall of chancel).

San Pantaleone, between Campo Santa Margherita and the Frari (see map on page 156). A seventeenth-century church notable mainly for a very handsome vast ceiling painting by G. A. Fumiani (1680–1704), an elaborate baroque high altar designed by Giuseppe Sardi, and a fine *Coronation of the Virgin* by Giovanni d'Alemagna and Antonio Vivarini, dated 1444 (Cappelina del Sacro Chiodo, on left of chancel).

San Pietro in Castello, the cathedral church of Venice until 1807. May be reached along the Via Garibaldi from the Riva di San Biagio (a continuation of the Riva degli Schiavoni). The fabric dates mainly from the late sixteenth and early seventeenth centuries. Numerous works of art include *St. Peter Enthroned with four Saints* by Marco Basaiti (third altar on right), and a bust of St. Lorenzo Giustiniani by a follower of A. Rizzo (at west end of nave on right).

Museo Storico Navale, (Riva degli Schiavoni, 2148). This contains a large collection of models of gondolas, galleys, the Bucintoro, etc. as well as an important collection of manuscripts.

San Giobbe, near Palazzo Labia (see map on page 192). A handsome fifteenth century church unfortunately despoiled of its best altarpieces which are now in the Accademia (see page 120). The statues of St. Anthony of Padua, St. Bernardino, St. Louis of Toulouse and the lunette of St. Job and St. Francis of Assisi on the façade above the main door are by Pietro Lombardo who also designed the Tuscan-style chancel and carved the exquisite reliefs of *putti* supporting the cupola. Evangelists in the spandrels and reliefs on the chancel arch (*c.* 1475). The second chapel on the left, which belonged to the Lucchese silk weavers in Venice, contains painted and glazed terra-cotta reliefs from the Florentine Della Robbia studio. In the Cappella Contarini (after fourth altar on right) there is a Nativity by Girolamo Savoldo.

San Simeone Grande, near the Scalzi bridge (see map on page 57). Notable mainly for a recumbent statue of St. Simeon the prophet carved in 1317 by the otherwise unknown Marco Romano (chapel to left of high altar).

Hotels

Listed according to category

DE LUXE

Bauer-Grünwald, Canal Grande—San Moisè 1440
Cipriani, Fondamenta San Giovanni, Giudecca, 10
Danieli Royal Hotel, Riva degli Schiavoni, 4196
Europa & Britannia, Canal Grande—Via XXII Marzo, 2159
Royal Excelsior, Riva degli Schiavoni, 4196
Gritti Palace Hotel, Canal Grande—Santa Maria del Giglio, 2467

FIRST CLASS

Gabrielli Sandwirth, Riva degli Schiavoni, 4110
Londres et Beau Rivage, Riva degli Schiavoni, 4171
Luna, San Marco-Ascensione, 1243
Monaco & Gran Canale, Canal Grande—Calle Vallaresso, 1325
Park Hotel, S. Croce, Fondamenta Condulmer, 246
Regina & Di Roma, San Marco, 2205
Saturnia & International, Via XXII Marzo—San Marco, 2398

SECOND CLASS

Ala, San Marco, 2494
Bonvecchiati, Calle Goldoni, 4488
Boston, San Marco, 848
Carpaccio, Canal Grande—S. Polo, 2765
Cavaletto & Doge Orseolo, San Marco—Calle Cavaletto, 1107
Concordia, Calle Larga San Marco, 367
Corso—Continental, Canal Grande—Lista di Spagna, 166
De La Gare & Germania, S. Croce—S. Simeone Piccolo, 578
Patria e Tre Rose, Calle dei Fabbri, 905
Principe Grand Hotel, Ferrovia—Lista di Spagna, 146

265

Hotels

Savoia & Jolanda, Riva degli Schiavoni, 4187
Taverna La Fenice, Campiello della Fenice, 1937 a
Terminus, Ferrovia—Lista di Spagna, 116
Union, Ferrovia—Lista di Spagna, 127
Universo & Nord, Ferrovia—Lista di Spagna, 121

THIRD CLASS

Adriatico, Lista di Spagna, 224
All' Angelo, San Marco, 403
Antico Panada, San Marco, 646
Astoria, Calle Fiubera, San Marco, 951
Ateneo, San Marco—San Fantin, 1876
Atlantide, Calle Misericordia, 375 a
Basilea, Rio Marin, 817
Bel Sito, Santa Maria del Giglio, 2517
Caprera, Lista di Spagna, 219 a
Castello, Castello—Calle Sagrestia, 4365
Diana, Calle Specchieri, 449
Florida, Cannaregio, 106
Gallini, S. Angelo—Calle della Verona, 3673
Gardena, S. Croce, 239
Gorizia, Calle dei Fabbri, 4696
Graspo de Ua, San Marco, 5093
Leonardo, San Leonardo, 1385
Lux, Calle delle Rasse, 4541
Malibran, Cannaregio, 5846
Marconi & Milano, Canal Grande—Rialto, 729
Mignon, SS. Apostoli, 4535
Nazionale, Ferrovia—Lista di Spagna, 158
Noremi, San Marco—Calle dei Fabbri, 909
Olimpia, Fondamenta Burchielle, 395
Pausania, San Barnabà—Fondamenta Gerardi, 2824
Pellegrino, Calle delle Rasse, 4551 a
Piazzale Roma, Santa Croce—Tre Ponti, 390
Rialto, San Marco, 5147
San Marco, Calle dei Fabbri, 877
Santa Chiara, Piazzale Roma, 548
Scandinavia, Santa Maria Formosa, 5240
Serenissima, San Marco, 4486
Stella Alpina-Edelweiss, Calle Priuli, 99 d
Teson, Castello, 3980
Trovatore, Calle delle Rasse, 4534
Zecchini, Lista di Spagna, 152

266

FOURTH CLASS

Adua, Lista di Spagna, 233 a
Alex, Rio Terrà dei Frari, 2606
Gobbo, S. Geremia, 312
Guerrini, Lista di Spagna, 265
Hesperia, Cannaregio, 459
Marte, Cannaregio, 338
Mercurio, San Marco, 1848
Minerva e Nettuno, Ferrovia—Lista di Spagna, 228
Santa Lucia, Cannaregio—Calle della Misericordia, 358

Pensioni

FIRST CLASS

Locanda Cipriani, Isola di Torcello, 29

SECOND CLASS

Accademia, San Trovaso—Fondamenta Bollani, 1058
Ca' d'Oro, SS. Apostoli, 4391
Calcina, Zattere, 780
Dinesen, San Vio, 628
Seguso, Zattere, 779

THIRD CLASS

Alboretti, Accademia, 882
Al Gazzettino, San Marco 4971
Alla Salute, Dorsoduro, 222
Bucintoro, Riva San Biagio, 2135
Campiello, Castello—Campiello del Vin, 4647
Casa de Stefani, San Barnabà, 2786
Casa Fontana (German Nuns), Campo San Provolo, 4701
Doni, San Zaccaria, 4656
Firenze, San Moisè, 1490
Kette, Piscina San Moisè, 2053
Wildner, Riva degli Schiavoni, 4161

267

Hotels

Hotels on the Lido

(the majority close in winter)

DE LUXE

Excelsior Palace Hotel, Lungomare Marconi, 41

FIRST CLASS

Grand Hotel des Bains, Lungomare Marconi, 17

SECOND CLASS

Ada Villa Nora—Biasutti, Viale Dandolo, 27
Adria Urania—Biasutti, Viale Dandolo, 29
Bortoli, Lungomare G. d'Annunzio, 2
Cappelli Wagner—Villa Paradiso, Grand Viale, 41
Centrale, Via M. Bragadin, 30
Helvetia, Gran Viale, 6
Hungaria Palace, Gran Viale, 28
Quattro Fontane, Via Quattro Fontane, 16
Riviera, Gran Viale, 1
Villa Eva e Quisisana, Gran Viale, 49
Villa Otello, Via Lepanto, 12

THIRD CLASS

Atlanta Augustus, Via Lepanto, 15
Belvedere, Piazzale S. M. Elisabetta, 4
Cristallo, Gran Viale, 51
Reiter, Gran Viale, 57
Rivamare, Lungomare Marconi, 44
Vianello, Alberoni—Via Ca' Rossa, 10
Villa Pannonia, Via Michiel, 48

FOURTH CLASS

Giardinetto, Piazza S. M. Elisabetta, 3

Pensioni on the Lido

SECOND CLASS

Kopp-Belloli, Riviera San Nicolò, 8
Meridiana, Via L. Marcello, 31
Panorama, Piazza S. M. Elisabetta, 1
Villa Albertina, Via Valaresso, 1
Villa Cipro, Via Zara, 2
Villa Laguna, Via Sandro Gallo, 6

THIRD CLASS

Edera, Via Negroponte, 13
Stella, Via Sandro Gallo, 111
Villa Aurora, Riviera S. Nicolò, 11 a
Villa Mirella, Via Dardanelli, 29
Villa Parco, Via Rodi, 1
Villa Tiziana, Via Gritti, 3

Some Restaurants

Arranged according to category: *** *expensive,* ** *moderate,* * *inexpensive*

*** Antico Martini, San Marco, 1980 (near the Fenice theatre)
*** La Colomba, San Marco—Frezzeria, 1665
*** Al Graspo de Ua, San Bartolomeo, 5094 (behind San Bartolomeo)
*** Harry's Bar, Calle Valaresso, 1323 (by the San Marco motor-boat station)
*** Quadri, Piazza San Marco, 120
*** Taverna La Fenice, San Marco, 1938 (by the Fenice theatre)

** All' Angelo, Calle Larga San Marco, 408
** Antica Carbonera, San Luca, 4648 (in Calle del Carbon, leading down to the Grand Canal from Campo San Luca)
** Da Nane Mora-Malibran, San Giovanni Grisostomo, 5864 (behind the church of San Giovanni Grisostomo)

* Al Campanile, San Polo 2088
* Al Gambero, San Marco, 4685 (in Calle dei Fabbri)
* Città di Milano, San Marco—San Zulian, 599 (near the church of San Zulian)
* Letizia, Rialto, 695 (in Rio Terrà San Silvestro near the Riva del Vin)
* Madonna, Calle della Madonna, 595 (just off the Riva del Vin)
* Malamocco, San Zaccaria, 4650 (just off the Riva degli Schiavoni)
* Montin, near Campo San Barnabà
* Noemi, San Marco, 912 (at the San Marco end of the Calle dei Fabbri)
* Ridotto, Calle Valaresso

271

Some books about Venice

The following is not a bibliography but a reading list for those who may wish to pursue various aspects of Venice more profoundly. I should, however, like to take the opportunity of expressing my indebtedness to the works of O. Demus, M. Levey, G. Lorenzetti, P. G. Molmenti and R. Wittkower which I have plundered for ideas as well as facts.

GENERAL

HORATIO BROWN: *Life on the Lagoons* (revised edition, 1894), *In and Around Venice* (1905), *Studies in Venetian History* (2 vols. 1907). The fruit of many years love and study of Venice, these works have great " period " charm in addition to being informative.

WILLIAM BECKFORD: *Dreams, Waking Thoughts and Incidents* (1783, best modern edition 1928).

JACQUES CASANOVA DE SEINGALT: *Histoire de ma vie* (complete edition, 1960).

THOMAS CORYATE: *Coryate's Crudities* (1611). Contains a vivid account of Venice; see also M. Strachan: *The Life and Adventures of Thomas Coryate* (1960).

CARLO GOZZI: *Memorie Inutili* (1798, good English translation 1962).

W. D. HOWELLS: *Venetian Life* (1867 revised ed. 1907). A charming account of life in nineteenth-century Venice.

HENRY JAMES: *Italian Hours* (1909). Includes one of the best evocations of the atmosphere of Venice.

G. LORENZETTI: *Venezia e il suo estuario* (1956). Invaluable: by far the fullest guide, also available in a not very good English translation.

P. G. MOLMENTI: *Storia di Venezia nella vita privata* (1907). There is a six-volume English translation (by H. Brown) of this great repository of Venetian social history.

PHILIPPE MONIER: *Venise au XVIIIe siècle* (1908).

JAMES MORRIS: *Venice* (1960). Brilliant account of contemporary Venice.

A. J. A. SYMONS: *The Quest for Corvo* (1934).

G. TASSINI: *Curiosità Veneziane* (1913, augmented edition 1933). A vast compendium of information about Venice listed under the names of streets, canals and *campi*.

272

Some books about Venice

WORKS OF ART

BERNARD BERENSON: *The Venetian Painters of the Renaissance* (1894), *Lorenzo Lotto* (1895), *Italian Pictures of the Renaissance Venetian School* (1957).
OTTO DEMUS: *The Church of San Marco in Venice* (1960).
FRANCIS HASKELL: *Patrons and Painters* (1963). The latter half of this work is devoted to eighteenth-century Venice.
JAN LAUTS: *Carpaccio* (1962).
MICHAEL LEVEY: *Painting in XVIII Century Venice* (1959).
ROBERTO LONGHI: *Viatico per cinque secoli della pittura veneziana* (1946).
A. MORASSI: *G. B. Tiepolo* (1955).
R. PANE: *Palladio* (1948). Well illustrated.
JOHN POPE-HENNESSY: *Italian Gothic Sculpture* (1955), *Italian Renaissance Sculpture* (1958), *Italian High Renaissance and Baroque Sculpture* (1963). These volumes contain the best account of Venetian sculpture.
JOHN RUSKIN: *The Stones of Venice* (1851–3).
ADRIAN STOKES: *Venice* (1944).
HANS TIETZE: *Tintoretto* (1948); *Titian* (1950).
R. WITTKOWER: *Architectural Principles in the Age of Humanism* (1952) by far the best account of Palladio; *Art and Architecture in Italy 1600-1750* (1958) in the Pelican History of Art.

TERRA FIRMA

G. MAZZOTTI: *Le Ville Venete* (1953). A complete catalogue of all eighteenth-century and earlier villas on the Venetian mainland.

FICTION

L. P. HARTLEY: *Eustace and Hilda* (1947).
ALDOUS HUXLEY: *Little Mexican* (1924).
HENRY JAMES: *The Aspern Papers* (1888), *The Wings of the Dove* (1902).
THOMAS MANN: *Der Tod in Venedig* (1912).
MARCEL PROUST: *À la Recherche du Temps Perdu: Albertine Disparue* (1925).
HENRI DE RÉGNIER: *La Peur de l'Amour* (1907).
: *L'Entrevue* (1925).

Shops

Antique dealers: Barozzi, San Marco—S. Maria del Giglio, 2500.
Cesana, Calle Larga San Marco, 4392.
Dominici, Calle Larga San Marco, 659.
Trois, Calle Larga XXII Marzo, 2251.
Books: (new) Libreria Serenissima, San Marco—San Zulian, 739;
(old and prints) Cassini, Calle Larga XXII Marzo, 2424.
Buttons, trimmings, etc.: Bucintoro, Merceria del Capitello, 4924.
Cameras: Ditta Sambin, San Marco, 593.
Chemists: Farmacia Internazionale, San Marco—San Moisè, 1473.
Farmacia Mantovani, Calle Larga San Marco, 412.
Clocks and watches: Rocca, Merceria dell' Orologio, 215.
Clothes: (ladies) Ma Boutique, Calle Larga San Marco, 282.
Roberta, Castello, 6123;
(men) Ortolani, Piazza San Marco, 89.
Embroidery: Jesurum, Piazza San Marco, 60.
Flowers: San Marco, San Marco della Mandola, 3741.
Glass: Barovier, Fondamenta Vetrai, 28, Murano.
Venini, San Marco—Piazzetta dei Leoncini, 314 (the best).
Gramophone Records: Barera, Merceria del Capitello, 4948.
Groceries, wines, etc.: Venturini, San Marco—Ponte degli Ostreghi, 2355.
Hairdresser (ladies): Carol's, Calle Larga XXII Marzo, 2423.
Jewellery: Missiaglia, Piazza San Marco, 125.
Leather goods, umbrellas, etc.: Voghini, San Marco—Ascensione, 1292.
Righini, Merceria dell' Orologio, 193.
Photographs of works of art: Böhm, San Marco—San Moisè, 1349.
Rubber articles (galoshes, water wings, etc.): Brighenti, San Marco—
Frezzeria, 1584.
Shoes: (ready made) Zecchi, Merceria dell' Orologio, 299;
(made to measure—ladies) Franz, San Marco—San Stefano, 2770.
Silks and other textiles: Bevilacqua, San Marco—Ponte di Rialto, 5337.
Rubelli, San Marco, 1089.
Vandelli, Merceria San Zulian, 725.
Stationery: Testolini, San Marco—Bacinorseolo, 1744.

274

Toys: Linetti, Merceria del Capitello, 4855.

Various (charming printed papers applied to note-books, pen stands, etc.):
Piazzesi, San Marco—Campiello della Feltrina, 2511.

Index

Calli, campi, case, churches, Doges, fondamenti, palazzi, ponti, rii, salizzade, scuole and villas are listed under those headings. Dates in brackets refer to the lives of artists and the reigns of Doges. Where there are several references those in bold type indicate the most important.

Abbondi, Antonio (1505-49), 62
Accademia, Galleria dell', 56, 84, **119-30**
Acqua alta (flood), 257-8
Adam, James, 19
Albergo (hotel) del Cavaletto, 189
 Danieli, 80
 Europa, 217
 Gabrielli, 78
Alberoni (Lido), 239
Aldine Press, 98-9, 188
Alexander III, Pope, 34, 135
Alexios I Comnenos, Emperor, 34
Altichiero, Altichieri (1320-95), 250
Altinum (mainland), 236
Amigoni, Jacopo (1675-1752), 141
Antico, Pier Jacopo Alari Bonaccolsi called L' (c.1460-1528), 171
Antonello da Messina (c.1430-79), 102
Antonio da Negroponte (fl.c.1450), 263
Aquileia (mainland), 29, 251
Archivio di Stato (State Archive), 56
Aretino, Pietro, 19, 20, 39, 61, 96, **187,** 220
Armenians in Venice, 238-9
Arsenale (arsenal), 76
Arundel, Lady, 219
Ascension, Feast of the, 26, 104
Asolo (mainland), 251
Aspetti, Tiziano (1565-1607), 47, 101, 203
Ateneo Veneto, 181
Augustus IV, King of Poland, 245

Bacino (harbour or basin) Orseolo, 188

Baldassare Estense (c.1443-1504), 102
Balzac, Honoré de, 52
Bambini, Nicolò (1651-1736), 184
Banca (bank) d'Italia, 221
Baratta, Pietro (c. 1668-1733), 172
Barbari, Jacopo de' (c.1440-c.1515), 101
Barbaro, Antonio, 182
Barbaro, Daniele (1514-70), 228
Barbarossa, Frederick, Emperor, 34
Barovier, Angelo (1424-61), 228
Barthel, Melchiorre (1625-72), 58
Basaiti, Marco (fl.1496-1530), 119, 264
Bassano del Grappa (mainland), 251
Bassano, Jacopo da Ponte called (c.1510-92), 45, 112, **125,** 251
Bastiani, Lazzaro (c.1449-1512), 127, 230
Beauharnais, Eugène, 247
Beccafumi, Domenico (c.1485-1551), 148
Beckford, William, 221, 245
Bello, Gabriele (fl.1760), 93
Bellano, Bartolomeo (c.1434-c.1496), 171
Bellini, Gentile (1429-1507), 70, 127-8, 148
 Giovanni (c.1430-1516), 48, 59, **70-1,** 81, 84, 89, 93, 102-3, 119, **120-1,** 138, 169, 174, 195, 231, 254, 263
 Jacopo (c.1400-1470), 70, 102
Bellini, Vincenzo, 182
Belluno (mainland), 251
Beltrame, Marco (fl.c.1650), 179

Bembo, Pietro, 88, 97, 251
Bennato, Jacopo di Marco (*fl.c.*1375), 36
Berenson, Bernard, 59, 122, 148
Bernardi, Giuseppe (*c.*1694-1774), 140
Bernini, Giovanni Lorenzo (1598-1680), 149, 171, 226
Pietro (1562-1629), 226
Bernis, François Joachim de, 200, 231
Berry, Duchesse de, 222
Bessarione, Cardinal, 98
Biblioteca (library) Marciana, 97-9
Querini-Stampalia, 92
Biennale exhibition, 77, 211, 263
Bombelli, Sebastiano (1635-*c.*1716), 93
Bon (or Buon), Bartolomeo (*fl.*1422-64), 43, 167
Bartolomeo (z.1492-1508), 62
Giovanni (*fl.*1382-1442), 43
Bonazza, Antonio (*fl.c.*1750), 89
Giovanni (*fl.* 1695-1730), 89
Bonnard, Pierre (1867-1947), 211
Bordone, Paris (1500-71), 122
Borro, Luigi (1826-86), 188
Borsato, Giuseppe (1771-1849), 105
Bortoloni, Mattia (1696-1750), 253
Bosch, Hieronymus (1450-1516), 44
Boschini, Marco, 24, 107
Boswell, James, 19
Brancusi, Costantin (1876-1957), 149
Bregno, Lorenzo (*fl.*1500-23), 58, 89, 210
Brenta, river and canal, 25, 240-47, 251
Briosco, Andrea, see: Riccio
Broglio, 43
Bronson, Katherine de Kay, 217
Brosses, Charles de, 79, 243
Brown, Horatio, 150
Brown, Rawdon, 209, 217
Browning, Robert, 93, 159-60, 216, 217, 235, 239, 251
Brulle, Albert van der (*fl.*1595), 112
Bruno, Giordano, 219
Brustolon, Andrea (1662-1732), 57, 155, 251
Bucintoro (Venetian state barge), 104, 264
Buon, Bartolomeo and Giovanni, see: Bon

Buora, Giovanni di Antonio (*fl.*1450-1513), 109, 114
Burano (island), 234-5
Burchiello (vessel plying between Venice and Padua), 243
Byron, Lord, 18, 219, 220, 239
Byzantine Empire, Venetian relations with, 25, 29-32

Ca' (abbreviation of *casa*—house)
d'Oro, 166-71, 222
Da Mosto, 203, 221
Cafés, Florian, 18, 27
Quadri, 18, 27
Caffi, Ippolito (1809-66), 211
Calle (street) dell' Angelo, 95
degli Avvocati, 186
della Bissa, 139-40
del Ca' D'Oro, 167, 171
del Caffetier, 55, 56
Canonica, 95
del Capitello, 197
Castelli, 84
Contarini Corfu, 153
delle Erbe, 84
della Fava, 140
dei Fuseri, 188
Goldoni, 188
della Guerra, 141
Lunga (SS. Giovanni e Paolo) 90, (Frari) 55, (Fondamenta Nuove), 171
della Malvasia, 197
di Mezzo, 206
delle Muneghe, 187
dei Nomboli, 66
del Ospedaletto, 90
Pesaro, 186
del Pestrin, 76
della Racchetta, 171
del Remedio, 95
Rio Terrà Ca' Rampani, 208
dei Specchieri, 141
Stretta, 208
del Traghetto, 155
del Teatro S. Moisè, 180
Valaresso, 177
Vendramin, 191
delle Veste, 181

Index

Calle (street)
della Vida, 188
Zancani, 194
Calle Larga (wide *calle*) Prima, 66
S. Marco, 141-2
XXII Marzo, 180
Camelio, Vittore Gambello called
(*c*.1460-1537), 169
Campagna, Girolamo (1549-1626), 89,
111, 134
Campanile, the (S. Marco), 26, 97
Campiello (small *campo*) Albrizzi, 208,
258
Querini-Stampalia, 95
del Remer, 221
Testori, 171
Campo (a square) Bandiera e Moro, 75
dei Carmini, 162
dei Gesuiti, 173
del Ghetto Nuovo, 198
della Maddalena, 191
Manin, 188
dei Miracoli, 84
dei Mori, 195
Morosini, 183
Pisani, 184
S. Alvise, 197
S. Antonin, 75
S. Anzolo, 186
S. Aponal, 206
dei SS. Apostoli, 173
S. Barnabà, 155
S. Bartolomeo, 139
S. Beneto (or Benedetto), 186
S. Cassiano, 212
S. Fantin, 181
S. Fosca, 191
S. Geremia, 199
S. Giacomo dell' Orio, 208
S. Lio, 140
S. Margherita, 160
S. Maria Formosa, 90, 92
S. Maria del Giglio, 182
S. Maria Mater Domini, 212
S. Maria Nuova, 83
S. Maria Zobenigo, 182
S. Marziale, 194
S. Maurizio, 183
S. Polo, 206-7

S. Samuele, 154
S. Sofia, 222
S. Tomà, 66
S. Vio, 149
S. Zaccaria, 72
Canaletto, Antonio Canale called
(1697-1768), 126
Canal Grande (Grand Canal), 217-23
Canale di Cannaregio, 223
Candi, Giovanni (*fl*.1475-1506), 188
Canova, Antonio (1757-1822), 59, 93,
106, 127, 149, 185, 218, 251, 253
Cappello, Bianca, 207
Carissimi, Giacomo, 79
Carlevaris, Luca (1665-1731), 162
Carmagnola, Francesco Bussone called,
85
Carona, Giovanni Antonio da (*fl*.1477-
1534), 226
Carpaccio, Benedetto (*fl*. 1477-1534),
73
Vittore (*c*.1465-*c*.1525), 48, **73-6,**
103, 113, 119, 127-9, 167, 183, 184
Carpioni, Giulio (1611-74), 254
Carriera, Rosalba (1675-1757), 126,
218
Casanova, Jacques de Seingalt, 52, 231
Casa (house) Barbaro, 210
dei Mocenigo, 219
Zane, 210
Casino (small pleasure house) degli
Spiriti, 171
Venier, 135
Casinò Municipale (gaming rooms),
222
Castagno, Andrea (1423-57), 67, **69,** 71
Castelfranco (mainland), 251
Castellani, 141, 152
Catena, Vincenzo (*c*.1470-1531), 94,
120, 210
Cattanco, Danese (*c*.1509-73), 89, 251
Ceccarini, Sebastiano (1703-83), 148
Cellini, Benvenuto (1500-71), 96
Cemetery, 227
Chagall, Marc (b.1887), 211
Chiari, Pietro, 22
Chioggia, 239
Churches: general information, 10
Angelo Raffaele, 163

Frari, 56-61
Gesuati, 150
Gesuiti, 172-3
Madonna dell' Orto, 195
Ospedaletto, 90
Redentore, 116-18
S. Alvise, 197
S. Antonin, 75
S. Aponal, 206
SS. Apostoli, 173
S. Barnabà, 160
S. Bartolomeo, 139
S. Beneto or Benedetto, 186
S. Biagio, 263
S. Cassiano, 212
S. Fantin, 181
S. Fosca (Torcello), 238
S. Francesco della Vigna, 96, 116, 263
S. Geremia, 199, 223
SS. Gervasius e Protasius, 152
S. Giacomo dell' Orio, 208
S. Giobbe, 81, 120, 264
S. Giorgio dei Greci, 72
S. Giorgio Maggiore, 107-13
S. Giovanni in Bragora, 75
S. Giovanni Decollato, 263
S. Giovanni Elemosinario, 206
S. Giovanni Grisostomo, 135, 174-5
SS. Giovanni e Paolo, 86-90, 123
S. Giuliano, 96, 133
S. Gregorio, 149, 217
S. Lio, 140
S. Luca, 187
S. Lucia, 199
S. Marco, 25, 28-40; atrium 34, baptistery 38, bronze horses 32, 40, façade 28, 32-4, iconostasis 36, mosaics 35-8, Pala d'oro 38, museum 40, treasury 39
S. Marcuola, 190
S. Maria degli Angeli (Murano), 231
S. Maria Assunta, 172-3
S. Maria del Carmelo, 161-2
SS. Maria e Donato (Murano), 229
S. Maria della Fava, 140
S. Maria Formosa, 91, 105
S. Maria dei Frari, 56-61
S. Maria del Giglio, 182

S. Maria Maddalena, 191
S. Maria Mater Domini, 210
S. Maria dei Miracoli, 83-4
S. Maria di Nazareth, 200-1
S. Maria della Pietà, 78
S. Maria della Presentazione, 115
S. Maria del Rosario, 150
S. Maria della Salute, 143-8, 217
S. Maria Zobenigo, 182
S. Martino, 76
S. Martino (Burano), 235
S. Marziale, 194
S. Maurizio, 183
S. Michele, 226
S. Moisè, 179-80
S. Nicolò dei Mendicoli, 163
S. Nicolò da Tolentino, 263
S. Pantaleone, 262
S. Pietro di Castello, (formerly cathedral) 29, 264
S. Pietro Martire (Murano), 231
S. Polo, 206
S. Rocco, 65
S. Salvatore, 135-9
S. Sebastiano, 164-5
S. Simeone Grande, 264
S. Simeone Piccolo, 223
S. Stae, 209, 222
S. Stefano, 184
S. Trovaso, 152
S. Vitale, 184
S. Zaccaria, 67-71, 105
SS. Zanipolo, 86-90
S. Zulian, 96, 133
Gli Scalzi, 200-1
Le Zitelle, 115
Church (Anglican) of St. George, 149
Ciardi, Guglielmo, (1842-1917), 212
Cima, Giovanni Battista (c.1459-1518), **76**, 119, 148, 169, 195, 252
Cimarosa, Domenico, 186
Cini, Vittorio, 113
Clement XIII, Pope, 222
Clough, Arthur Hugh, 213
Coducci, Mauro (c.1440-1504), 55, 69, 85, 91, 173, 220, 226
Coins, Venetian, 104
Colleoni, Bartolomeo, 85-6
Coli, Giovanni (1636-1681), 115

279

Index

Cominelli, Andrea (*fl.c.*1720), 199
Commynes, Philippe de, 166
Conegliano, (mainland), 76, 252
Contarini, Jacopo, 219
Contino, Bernardo (*fl.*1568-90), 137
Convents, Venetian, 71
Cooper, J. Fennimore, 220
Cornaro, Alvise, 241
Cornaro, Caterina, Queen of Cyprus, 128, 139, 251
Corradini, Antonio (1668-1752), 155, 162, 179, 252
Corte (courtyard) Contarini del Bovolo, 188
  Meloni, 206
  del Milion (prima and seconda), 175
Corvo, Baron (alias Frederick Rolfe), 18, 84, 115, 149-50, 207, 215, 227
Coryate, Thomas, 44, 45, 243
Council of Ten, 46
Courtesans, Venetian, 162-3, 208
Cozzi, Marco (*fl.*1455-85), 119, 185
Crosato, Giovanni Battista (1697-1756), 157, 183

D'Annunzio, Gabriele, 208, 218
Dante Alighieri, 18, 76
Delfin, Paolo, 226
De Pisis, Filippo (1896-1956), 164, 211
Diaghilev, Serge, 227
Diana, Benedetto Rusconi called il (*c.*1460-1525), 127
Dickens, Charles, 52, 80
Diziani, Gaspare (1689-1767), 161, 183, 185
Dogana (customs house), 145
Doges, general: 20, 29, 44-5, 52
  Cornaro (or Corner), Marco (1365-8), 86
  Dandolo, Andrea (1343-54), 37, 38
  Enrico (1192-1205), 45, 51, 220
  Da Ponte, Niccolò (1578-85), 149
  Falier, Marino (1354-5), 45, 48
  Ordelaffo (1102-18), 31
  Foscari, Francesco (1423-57), 45
  Gradenigo, Pietro (1289-1311), 48
  Loredan, Leonardo (1501-21), 89
  Malipiero, Pasquale (1457-62), 88
  Manin, Lodovico (1789-97), 50

Mocenigo, Giovanni (1478-85), 88
  Pietro (1474-6), 88
  Tommaso (1414-23), 88
  Morosini, Francesco (1688-94), 47, 51, 77, 104, 185
  Pesaro, Giovanni (1658-9), 58
  Priuli, Girolamo (1559-67), 137
  Lorenzo (1556-9), 137
  Tron, Niccolò (1471-3), 58
  Vendramin, Andrea (1476-8), 88
  Venier, Antonio (1382-1400), 88
  Francesco (1554-6), 137
  Ziani, Sebastiano (1172-8), 104
Doges' Palace, 25, 41-52; Anti-Collegio 45, armoury 47, Collegio 45, Consiglio dei Dieci 46, Ducal apartments 44, façade 41, Maggior Consiglio 47, Porta della Carta 43, Prisons 52, Sala della Bussola 46, Sala dello Scrutinio 50, Scala d'Oro 44, Senate 46
Dolo (mainland), 246
Donatello (1382-1466), 58, 67, 86, 88, 249
Dorigny, Louis (1654-1742), 162
Dorsoduro, 143, 257
Dyck, Anthony van (1599-1641), 125, 169

Eliot, George (Mary Ann Cross), 91
Emo, Lorenzo, 241
Ernst, Max (b.1891), 149
Erasmus, Desiderius, 188
Este (mainland), 252
Evelyn, John, 131

Fabriano, Gentile da (*c.* 1370-1427), 48
Fabris, Placidio (1802-59), 211
Falcone, Bernardo (*fl.*1659-94), 139, 200
Farmacia (chemist's shop), G. Mantovani, 141
Favretto, Giacomo (1849-87), 212
Feltre (mainland), 252
Ferdinando II de' Medici, 245
Ferrari, Ettore (1849-1929), 79
Ferrari, Giovanni called Torretti (1744-1826), 263

Fetti, Domenico (*c.* 1589-1624), 125
Fondaco (merchants' warehouse) dei
  Tedeschi, 122, 127, **175-6,** 221
  dei Turchi, 222
Fondamenta (street beside a canal)
  del Arsenale, 77
  di Cannaregio, 198
  dei Forlani, 75
  Foscarini, 162
  Nani, 151
  Nuove, 171-2
  degli Ormesini, 197
  Remedio, 95
  S. Sebastiano, 164
  Sanudo, 84
  della Sensa, 197
  del Zattere, 150
Fondazione (foundation) Giorgio Cini,
  113-17
Fontebasso, Francesco (1709-69), 172,
  183, 263
Food, Venetian, 15, 203-5
Forabosco, Girolamo (1605-79), 239
Fortuny silk factory, 115
Fortuny y de Mandrazo, Mariano
  (1871-1950), 186
Foscarini, Antonio, 219
Franca, Veronica, 162
Francesco da Faenza (*fl.*1442-51), 69
Francesco di Giorgio Martini (1439-
  1501), 162
Franchetti, Baron, 167
Francis of Assisi, St., 234
Francis Xavier, St. 150
Franco, Battista (*c.*1498-1561), 44, 245
Franco, Cesare (*fl.*1579-99), 137
Frederick IV, King of Norway, 245
Frigimelica, Girolamo (1653-1732),
  246
Fumiani, Giovanni Antonio (1643-
  1710), 161, 264
Furniture, Venetian, 93-4, 155-7, 167
Fusina (mainland), 243

Gabrielli, Giovanni, 185
Gabrielli, Trifone, 78
Galileo Galilei, 19
Galleria (art gallery) dell' Accademia,
  119-30

Internazionale d'Arte Moderna, 211
  Querini-Stampalia, 92-4
Gallina, Ludovico (1752-87), 105
Galuppi, Baldassare, 234
Gambello, Antonio (*fl.*1458-81), 69
Gattamelata, Erasmo da Narni called,
  47, 249
Gatti, Gasparo (*fl.*1595), 112
Gautier, Théophile, 160
Gherardi, Filippo (1643-1702), 115
Ghetto, 197-8
Giambono, Michele (*fl.*1420-62), 102,
  119, 152, 169
Gibbon, Edward, 19
Giordano, Luca, 125, 147, 148
Giorgi, Francesco, 117
Giorgione (*c.*1478-1510), 64, **121,** 127,
  148, 174, 175, 251
Giotto (1266-1337), 248
Giovanni d'Alemagna (*fl.*1441-50), 70,
  264
Giovanni di Martino (*fl.c.*1410), 88
Giudecca island, 115-18, 197
Glasshouses, 227-9
Goethe, Johann Wolfgang von, 18, 79
Goldoni, Carlo, 22, 66, 139
Gondola, 151, 213
Gondoliers, 215, their cries, 189
Gozzi, Carlo, 22, 66, 210
  Gaspare, 210
Graeme, William, 158
Grand Canal see: Canal Grande
Grapiglia, Girolamo (*fl.*1600), 89
Greeks in Venice, 72
Guardi, Francesco (1712-93), 126, 158,
  163, 169
  Giacomo (1764-1835), 104
  Giovanni Antonio (1698-1760), 158,
  163
Guariento (1338-*c.*1370), 47, 251
Guggenheim, Peggy, 149, 218
Guglielmo Bergamasco (*fl.* 1515-30),
  226
Guiccoli, Teresa, 219
Guylforde, Richard, 128, 166

Hahn, Reynaldo, 18
Harry's Bar, 179
Harvey, William, 250

Index

Hayez, Francesco (1791-1882), 211
Henry III, King of France, 49, 219, 245
Henry IV, King of France, 47
Hitler, Adolf, 247
Hotels, general, 12
Hotel Bauer-Grünwald, 180
Regina, 217
Housman, A. E., 217
Howells, William Dean, 52, 219
Huxley, Aldous, 246

Ignatius Loyola, St., 150
Inquisitors of State, 47

Jacobello del Fiore (*fl.*1394-1439), 197
James, Henry, 18, 20, 79, 107, 190, 216, 217, 218, 223
Jensen, Nicholas, 98
Jesuits in Venice, 150, 172
Jews in Venice, 197-8
Jones, Inigo, 245
Juvarra, Filippo (1678-1736), 251

Kent, William, 243, 247
Keysler, J. G. de, 229

La Grazia, island, 239
Lamartine, Alphonse de, 227
Lamberti, Niccolò (*fl.*1403- 56), 43
Piero di Niccolò (*ff.*1423-34), 88
Law, John, 180
Lawrence, D. H., 19
Lawrence, Sir Thomas (1769-1830), 220, 253
Layard, Sir Austen, 101, 115, 219
Lazzarini, Gregorio (1665-1730), 161
Lear, Edward, 19
Le Corte, Giusto (1627-87), 149
Leopardi, Alessandro de (*fl.*1482-1522), 85, 185
Liberi, Pietro (1605-87), 219
Libraries see: Biblioteca
Libreria Sansoviniana, 26, 96-9
Lido di Venezia, 11, 24, 225, 239
Lippi, Filippino (1457-1504), 148
Liss or Lys, Jan (*c.*1595-*c.*1630), 125, 264
Lista di Spagna, 199

Lodovico da Forli (*fl.*1425-69), 70
Loggietta (small loggia at base o Campanile), 97
Lombardo, Antonio Solari called (*fl.*1506-16), 81, 88
Pietro Solari called (*fl.*1435-1515), 55, 66, **81-5,** 88, 185, 217, 254, 264
Sante Solari called (1504-60), 92
Tullio Solari called (*fl.*1500-32), 81, **88-9,** 135, 140, 148, 169, 174
Longfellow, Henry Wadsworth, 239
Longhena, Baldassare (1598-1682), 90, 109, 114, **143-7,** 211, 222
Longhi, Alessandro (1733-1813), 94
Pietro (1702-85), 94, 126, 158
Loredano, Francesco, 90
Lorenzo di Credi (1459-1537), 93
Lorenzo Veneziano (*fl.*1356-72), 119
Lotto, Lorenzo (*c.*1480-1556), 89, 122, 162, 209, 251, 254
Lusignan, Peter of, King of Cyprus, 220

Maderno, Stefano (1576-1636), 170
Madonna del Monte, Island, 234
Maffei, Francesco (1625-60), 94, 157, 174, 253, 254
Maggior Consiglio (great council), 48
Maggiotto, Domenico (1713-94), 183
Francesco (1750-1805), 56
Magnasco, Alessandro (1667-1749), 251
Maiolica, 103, 165
Malamocco (Lido), 24, 239
Malcontenta (mainland), 244
Malipiero, Gian-Francesci, 184
Manin, Daniele, 27, 104, 180
Mann, Thomas, 20, 225
Mansueti, Giovanni (*fl.*1485-1526), 127
Mantegna, Andrea (1431-1506), 37, 70, 120, 148, 169, 249
Manutius, Aldus, 98-9, 188
Manzoni, Alessandro, 19, 183
Manzù, Giacomo (b.1908), 211
Marchiori, Giovanni (1696-1778), 65, 200
Marco Romano (*fl.c.*1400), 264
Mare Morto, 243
Marini, Marino (b.1901), 218
Mariscalchi, Pietro (*c.*1520-84), 252

Marius Pictor, Mario de Maria called (1852-1924), 115
Mark, St., 29
Marostica (mainland), 252
Marriage with the sea, ceremony of, 104
Masegne, Jacobello and Pierpaolo (*fl.*1383-1403), 36, 88
Maser (mainland), 252
Massari, Giorgio (*fl.c.*1700-50), 55, 79, 150, 218
Matisse, Henri (1869-1954), 211
Mazza, Giuseppe (1652-1740), 89, 118
Mazzoni, Sebastiano (*c.*1615-85), 162, 186, 219, 253
Mazzorbo, island, 234
Medici, Cosimo de', 109
Menabuoi, Giusto de' (*fl.*1375), 250
Merceria (street of shops) Due Aprile, 139
    dell' Orologio, 131-2
    di S. Giuliano (Zulian), 135
    di S. Salvatore, 135
Mesarites, Nicholas, 35
Methodios, 39
Meyring, Heinrich (*fl.*1690-1700), 179, 200
Michelangelo Buonarotti (1475-1564), 115, 202
Michelozzi, Michelozzo (1396-1472), 109
Migliori, Francesco (1684-1734), 180
Mira (mainland), 245
Molo (the quay by Palazzo Ducale), 41
Monckton-Milnes, Richard, 189
Montagna, Bartolomeo (*fl.*1480-1523), 254
Montaigne, Michel Eyquem de, 19, 162
Monteverdi, Claudio, 57, 79, 80, 181
Morandi, Giorgio (1890-1964), 211
Morlaiter or Morleiter, Giammaria (1699-1782), 65, 89, 150, 190
Moro, Giulio del (*fl.*1573-1615), 138, 182
Moryson, Fynes, 243
Mosaics, 34-8, 230, 237-8
Motoscafi (public motor boats) 10, 217, 226

Murano, island, 227-34
Murazzi (sea-wall), 237
Museo (museum) Archeologico, 99-101
    di Ca' d'Oro, 166-71
    Correr, 101-6
    Orientale, 212
    di Palazzo Rezzonico, 154-9
    del Risorgimento, 103-4
    Storico Navale, 264
    Vetrario (Murano), 228-9
Museums, see: Museo and Galleria
Musset, Alfred de, 18, 80, 115, 216
Mussolini, Benito, 247

Napoleon Buonaparte, 27, 55, 198, 247
Negri, Pietro (*fl.*1675), 65
Newspapers, 177
Nicolotti, 141, 152
Nietzsche, Friedrich Wilhelm, 18, 79
Nievo, Ippolito, 50
Nove di Bassano (mainland), 253
Noventa Padovana (mainland), 247

Odoric, the Blessed of Pordenone, 253
Oriago (mainland), 245
Oselle (type of medal), 105
Ospizio Briati (Murano), 234
Othello, 162
Otway, Thomas, 19

Padua (mainland), 248-50
Palazzo (large city house) Agnusdio, 212
    Albrizzi, 208
    Ariani, 163
    Barbarigo, 158
    Barbaro, 218
    Bellavite, 183
    Belloni-Battaglia, 222
    Bernardo, 219
    Bosso, 66
    Brandolin, 153
    dei Camerlenghi, 203, 221
    Centani, 66
    Civran-Grimani, 219
    Contarini (Grand Canal), 219
    Contarini (S. Benedetto), 187
    Contarini del Bovolo, 188
    Contarini-Fasan, 217

Index

Palazzo (large city house)
  Contin, 191
  Corner, 218
  Corner della Regina, 222
  Corner-Contarini, 220
  Corner-Mocenigo, 207
  Corner-Spinelli, 220
  Da Mula (Murano), 230
  Dandolo, 80
  Dandolo (ridotto), 177
  Dario, 217
  Donà, 219
  Donà delle Rose, 191
  Ducale, see: Doges' Palace
  Duodo, 186
  Erizzo, 222
  Falier, 174
  Farsetti, 220
  Flangini, 223
  Fontana, 222
  Foscari, 219
  Giustiniani, 218
  Giustiniani (Murano), 228
  Gozzi, 210
  Grassi, 154, 218
  Grimani, 187, 220
  Gritti-Badoer, 75
  Labia, 199, 222
  Loredan, 184
  Malipiero-Trevisan, 92
  Mangilli-Valmarana, 221
  Manin, 103
  Mastelli, 195
  Moro, 139
  Moro-Lin, 219
  Morosini, 199
  Munster, 115
  Nani, 153
  Navagero, 78
  Papadopoli, 220
  Papafava, 141
  Patriarcale, 29
  Pesaro (S. Benedetto), 186
  Pesaro (Grand Canal), 210, 220
  Pisani, 184
  Pisani (S. Maria dei Miracoli), 84
  Pisani (Stra), 246-7
  Querini, 92
  Querini-Benzon, 220

Rezzonico, 154-60, 218
Sagredo, 222
Sanudo, 84
Savorgnan, 199
Seriman, 173
Surian-Bellotto, 198
Tiepolo, 207
Vendramin-Calergi, 191, 222
Viaro-Zane, 210
Vitturi, 92
Zaguri, 183
Zen, 173
Zenobio, 162
Palladio, Andrea Monaro called (1508-80), 96, 109-18, 199, 202, 219, 244-5, 252-4, 263
Palma Giovane, Jacopo Negretti called (1544-1628), 51, 134, 138, 181, 251
Palma Vecchio, Giacomo Negretti called (c.1480-1528), 91, 93
Paolo da Venezia (fl.1321-58), 119
Parodi, Filippo (c.1630-1708), 47, 250, 263
Pellegrini, Giovanni Antonio (1675-1741), 158, 180, 210
Pellestrina (Lido), 239
Pellipario, Niccolò (fl.1528-42), 103
Pensione (boarding house), 13
Pensione Calcina, 118
Petrarch, Francesco Petrarca called, 19, 38, 78, 98
Pianta, Francesco (fl.1675), 64
Piave, river, 25
Piazza S. Marco, 17-18, 24, 26-7, 128
Piazzetta (small piazza) di S. Marco, 96-7, columns of, 26
Piazzetta, Giovanni Battista (1682-1754), 90, 127, 140, 151, 158, 209, 253
Piero della Francesca (c.1410-92), 120
Pinacoteca (picture gallery) Manfrediana, 148-9
Piombino d'Ese (mainland) 253
Pisanello (c.1395-1455), 48, 170
Pisano, Giovanni (c.1250-c.1314), 249
  Nino (c.1315-68), 86
Pittoni, Francesco (fl.1687-1712), 180
  Giovanni Battista (1687-1767), 212

Pius VII, Pope, 112
Pius X, St., Pope, 38
Polo, Marco, 44, 175
Ponte (bridge) dell' Accademia, 218
  dei Baretteri, 135
  della Feltrina, 183
  dei Greci, 72
  della Guerra, 141
  delle Guglie, 199
  degli Incurabili, 150
  della Madonetta, 206
  del Megio, 209
  Molin, 171
  dei Mori, 194
  delle Ostreghe, 182
  della Paglia, 43
  di Rialto, 128, 202-3, 221
  Rosso, 84
  S. Antonio, 139
  SS. Apostoli, 174
  S. Fosca, 193
  S. Marziale, 194
  S. Stin, 56
  degli Scalzi, 55
  del Teatro Rossini, 187
  delle Tette, 208
  del Vin, 67
Ponte, Antonio da (c. 1512-97), 202
Pordenone (mainland), 253
Pordenone, Giovanni Antonio Sacchiense called (1484-1539), 65, 124, 186, 206, 253
Possagno (mainland), 253
Post Office, central, 176
Poussin, Nicolas (1593-1665), 125
Poveglia, island, 239
Pozzo, Giuseppe del (fl.c.1700), 172
Pozzoli, Gioacchino, 207
Preti, Francesco Maria (1701-84), 246, 252
Printing presses, Venetian, 98-9
Prisons, 52
Procuratie (offices of the Procurators of S. Marco) Nuove, 26-7
  Vecchio, 26-7
Procurators of S. Marco, 26
Proust, Marcel, 18, 80, 224, 239, 256
Puligo, Domenico (1492-1527), 148
Punta della Salute, 145

Querini-Benzon, Marina, 220

Rangone, Tommaso, 133
Regnier, Henri de, 77, 151
Restaurants, 13-14
Rialto, 139, 202
Rialto, Ponte di, 202-3, 221
Ricci, Sebastiano (1659-1734), 94, 151, 184, 194, 210
Riccio, Andrea Briosco called Il (c.1470-1532), 169-70, 250
Ridolfi, C., 59
Ridotto (gambling hell), 177
Righetti, Francesco (1749-1819), 112
Rio (canal) della Madonna dell' Orto, 195
  Marin, 55
  dei Mendicanti, 84
  Nuovo, 257
  S. Aponal, 207
  SS. Apostoli, 221
  S. Barnabà, 160
  S. Polo, 219
  S. Sebastiano, 164
  3. Trovaso, 152-3
  S. Vio, 150
  della Sensà, 194
Rio Terrà (canal filled in to make a street) Canale, 160
  della Maddalena, 191
  S. Tomà, 56
Rioba, Sior Antonio, 194-5
Ristorante All' Angelo, 142
Riva (street flanking the water) degli Schiavoni, 67, 77
Rizzo, Antonio (fl.1465-1500), 44, 58, 264
Robert, Léopold (1794-1835), 227
Roccatagliata, Niccolò (fl.1593-1636), 112, 179
Rolfe, F. see: Corvo, Baron
Romano, Gian Cristoforo (c.1465-1513), 169
Rossi, Domenico (1678-1742), 172, 209
Rossini, Gioacchino Antooni, 181
Rosso, Medardo (1858-1928), 211
Rouault, Georges (1871-1958), 211
Rousseau, Jean-Jacques, 79, 198
Rovigo (mainland), 253

Index

Rubens, Peter Paulus (1577-1640), 125, 183
Rubini, Agostino (*fl.*1583-4), 203
Ruer, Tommaso (d.1696), 118
Ruga (street lined with shops) degli Orefici, 205
Vecchia S. Zuane, 206
Rusconi, Giovanni Antonio (*fl.*1538-77), 134
Ruskin, John, 18, 28, 55, 63, 80, 85, 90, 103, 118, 149, 150, 179, 182, 189, 196, 222, 229, 259

Sacca (bay) della Misericordia, 171
Salizzada (paved street) S. Antonin, 75
S. Canciano, 83
S. Giovanni Grisostomo, 175
S. Lio, 141
S. Moisè, 177
S. Pio X, 139
S. Provolo, 72
S. Stae, 209
Seriman, 173
del Teatro, 187
Salviati, Giuseppe Porta called (1520-75), 63
S. Clemente, island, 239
S. Francesco del Deserto, island, 234-5
S. Giacomo in Paluo, island, 234
S. Giorgio in Alga, island, 243
S. Giorgio Maggiore, island, 107-15
S. Lazzaro degli Armeni, island, 239
S. Michele, island, 226
S. Spirito, island, 239
Sand, Georges, 80
Sandolo, 215
Sanmichele, Michele (1484-1559), 209, 220
Sansovino, Jacopo Tatti called (1486-1570), 26, 37, 38, 39, 43, 46, 58, 96, 133, 135, 137, 139, 147, 149, 165, 172, 181, 202, 218, 221, 263
Santommaso, Giuseppe (b. 1907), 211
Sanudo, Marino, 209
Sardi, Giuseppe (*fl.*1664-99), 135, 139, 182, 200, 209, 223, 264

Sarpi, Pietro called Fra Paolo, 191-4, 226
Sartre, Jean-Paul, 63
Savoldo, Giovanni Girolamo (*c.*1480-1548), 122, 264
Scalfarotto, Giovanni Antonio (*c.*1700-64), 223
Scamozzi, Vincenzo (1552-1616), 26, 96, 202, 246
Schiavone, Andrea Meldolla called (1522-63), 99, 162, 212, 251
Scuola (confraternity), general, 53-5
degli Albanesi, 167, 183
dei Calegheri, 66
della Carità, 173
dei Casselleri, 92
dei Mercanti, 196
di S. Giovanni Evangelista, 55, 127
S. Girolamo, 181
S. Giorgio degli Schiavoni, 55, 73-4
S. Marco, 84-5
S. Maria del Carmine, 160-1
S. Maria della Carità, 119
S. Nicolò, 72
S. Rocco, 55, 61-5
S. Teodoro, 119, 139
dei Varotari, 160
Vecchia della Misericordia, 171
Sebastiano Luciani called Del Piombo (*c.*1485-1547), 139, 174
Selva, Giovanni Antonio (1757-1819), 181, 183
Seminario (seminary), 148
Senate, 46
Shakespeare, William, 117, 162, 175
Shelley, Percy Bysshe, 243
Sile, river, 25
Smith, Joseph, 221
Solimena, Francesco (1657-1747), 125
Sottoportico (street running under a building) S. Zaccaria, 67
Spavento, Giorgio (*fl.*1486-1509), 135
Spira, Johannes de, 98-9
Squero (gondola building yard), 151
Stampa, Gaspara, 60-1, 97
Stra (mainland), 246-7
Strada (street) Nuova, 171
Stravinsky, Igor, 182
Street, George Edmund, 85, 163, 195

Strozzi, Bernardo (1581-1644), 94, 125, 186, 264
Synagogue, 198

Taglioni, 167
Tanguy, Yves (1900-55), 149
Tarsia, Antonio (*c.*1663-1730), 184
Teatro La Fenice, 181
Temanza, Tommaso (1705-89), 191
Terilli, Francesco (*fl.c.*1615), 118
Terra Firma (the mainland), 240-55
Theodore, St., 26, 31
Tiepolo, Bajamonte, 49, 133
Tiepolo, Giovanni Battista (1696-1762), 64, 79, 94, 126, 140, 151, 157-8, **160-1**, 173, 186, 197, 199, 200, 207, 210, 235, 239, 246, 252, 253, 254
  Giovanni Domenico (1727-1804), 56, 140, **158-9**, 207, 255
Tiepolo, Jacopo, 48
Tintoretto, Jacopo Robusti called (1518-94), 45, 47, 48, 51, **61-5**, 67, 99, 100, 112, 114, 124, 125, 152, 153, 182, 184, 191, 194, 195-6, 206, 212
Tirali, Andrea (*c.*1660-1737), 198, 263
Titian, Tiziano Vecellio called (*c.*1488-1576), 20, 39, **59-63**, 64, 67, 89, 96, 99, 124, 129, 138-9, 140, 147, 148, **172-3**, 175, 206, 250, 254, 255
Tito, Ettore (1859-1941), 200
Tommaso Lombardo (*fl.c.*1550), 165
Tommaso da Modena (1325-79), 254
Torcello, island, 235-8
Torretto, Giuseppe (*c.*1660-1743), 172
Traghetti (ferries) 217
Tramontin, Domenico, 215
Transport, public, in Venice, 10, 217
Traversi, Gaspare (d.1769), 127
Tremignon, Alessandro (*fl.c.*1660), 179
Treviso (mainland), 253-4
Trissino, Gian Giorgio, 109
Tura, Cosmè (*c.*1430-95), 102, 120
Turner, Joseph Mallord William (1775-1851), 63, 220
Twain, Mark, 28

Udine (mainland), 254

Vaporetti (public motor boats), 217, 226
Vasari, Giorgio (1511-74), 96
Vecchia, Pietro Muttoni called della (1605-78), 75, 140
Vedova, Emilio (b.1919), 211
Verdi, Giuseppe, 181-2, 217
Verrocchio, Andrea del Cione called (1436-88), 85
Veronese, Paolo Caliari called (1507-73), 45, 46, 48, 63, 90, 99, 114, 118, **123-4**, 134, 148, **164-5**, 187, 209, 234, 252
Vicenza (mainland), 254-5
Vignola, Giacomo Barozzi called (1507-73), 202
Villas (large country houses) general, 240-1
Villa La Badoera, 253
  Barbaro (now Volpi), 252
  Bolasco, 252
  Cornaro, 253
  Ferretti-Angell, 246
  Foscari, 244-5
  Giovanelli, 247
  Lattes, 254
  della Malcontenta, 244-5
  Pisani, 246
  Valmarana ai Nani, 255
  Valmarana (la Rotonda), 254
Vittoria, Alessandro (1524-1608), 44, 58, 71, 111, 134, **138**, 148, 165, 169, 181, 184, 185, 207, 253, 263
Vittorio Veneto (mainland), 255
Vivaldi, Antonio, 78
Vivarini, Alvise (1446-*c.*1505), 76, 118
  Antonio (*c.*1415-84), 70, 100, 119, 264
  Bartolomeo (*c.*1432-*c.*1499), 75, 91

Wagner, Richard, 18, 80, 191, 218, 222
Walpole, Horace, 19
Wines, 15
Wolf-Ferrari, Ermanno, 184
Wordsworth, William, 50

Index

Wotton, Sir Henry, 194

Zanchi, Antonio (1631-1722), 65, 134, 181, 183
Zandomeneghi, Luigi (1778-1850), 89
Zane, Emanuele (1610-90), 73

Zattere, 150
Zecca (mint), 97
Zelotti, Giovanni Battista (c.1526-78), 245
Zotto, Antonio dal (1852-1918), 139
Zuccari, Federico (1540-1609), 63